THE NEW
MATHEMATICS
OF ARCHITECTURE

JANE BURRY + MARK BURRY

THE NEW MATHEMATICS OF ARCHITECTURE

with 628 illustrations, 435 in colour

This book is dedicated to John E. Pallett

First published in the United Kingdom in 2010 by
Thames & Hudson Ltd, 181A High Holborn, London WC1V 7QX

First paperback edition 2012

Copyright © 2010 Jane Burry and Mark Burry

British Library Cataloguing-in-Publication Data
A catalogue record for this book is available from
the British Library

ISBN 978-0-500-29025-5

Printed and bound in China by Toppan Leefung Printing Limited

To find out about all our publications, please visit
www.thamesandhudson.com. There you can subscribe
to our e-newsletter, browse or download our current catalogue,
and buy any titles that are in print.

CONTENTS

WEAPONS OF THE GODS

THE PARADOXICAL MATHEMATICS OF CONTEMPORARY ARCHITECTURE

Brett Steele

The mathematical phenomenon always develops out of simple arithmetic, so useful in everyday life, out of numbers, those weapons of the gods: the gods are there, behind the wall, at play with numbers.

LE CORBUSIER

It has long been said that architecture is a game played with clear objectives, but no guiding set of rules. Mathematics, on the other hand, has forever been described by its believers as a form of knowledge best understood as a game with lots of rules, but no clear objective. For evidence of the enduring beauty of this paradoxical combination of two distinct (intertwined, even if opposing) human endeavours, look no further than this wonderful book, which Jane and Mark Burry have edited as an invaluable contribution to mathematics in the architecture of our time.

Early on in the 20th century, Le Corbusier observed that, however different or new modern architecture was, mathematics was still at its heart. It seemed an obvious point for the Swiss master to make then, and one no more (or less) surprising today, when we remember that architects have needed mathematics since at least the time when one of their kind drew a right angle with a stick in the sand and realized numbers went a long way to help reliably communicate its idea to someone else (and recall, this is what architects most fundamentally do: they communicate ideas – instructions – to others). That mathematics is an important part of architecture is pretty obvious a point to

a field of enquiry whose own origins lie with the publication of Vitruvius' Ten Books some two thousand years ago, made up as it is by a series of (numerically ordered) universal formulae and mathematical equations explaining how architects might best arrange architectural matter in meaningful, lasting ways. In other words, to say that mathematics is integral to architecture is like saying numbers are helpful when trying to count.

So what's the big deal about architecture and mathematics conversing in the ways they do today? Plenty, I'd say, without one having to judge a book by (the title on) its cover. The most surprising feature of a recent and evolutionary leap in Le Corbusier's 'weapons of the gods' is the simultaneity of, on the one hand, a growing power and complexity of mathematical processes in architecture, and, on the other, a marked disappearance of numbers themselves within its own language and discourses. Architects no longer speak the language, as did their ancestors, of whole numbers or predictable geometries, any more than they do of drawings made at fixed dimension or measurable scales. This situation owes itself to another kind of contemporary revolution of course: architects' near-universal assimilation of digital, information-based design platforms in their studios, which have now become the basis for not only architectural practice, but, as well, the very communication media through which their ideas are now conceived, flow and proliferate.

In considering the ubiquity of computing and information

systems within design studios today, the pervasiveness of mathematical processing within this regime is often overlooked, most often owing to the design of programmes whose appearance deliberately seeks to conceal their (higher-order) mathematical and logical composition. Consider, for example, even the most basic or traditional of architectural design activities; say, the simple drawing of a line. Within a digital modelling environment, this activity (itself either a sequence of clicks or keyboard strokes) now invokes an astonishing series of logical and mathematical operations of stunning complexity, undertaken at unimaginable speeds, in order for a programme to do something as simple as displaying that line to an architect for his or her further contemplation.

And this is where things have suddenly gotten very interesting; at least, regarding a contemporary re-animation of the relationship between architecture and mathematics. From the time of ancient Vitruvian geometric ideals to modern Corbusian regulating lines and Miesian modular grids, architecture has always been bound to (if not by) a conscious use of numbers. As a consequence, architects of all stripes have invariably embedded the language of numbers and mathematics into their own language of architecture, something that the past several centuries of architectural treatises readily confirms. A recent and decided disappearance of literal numbering or geometric descriptions (now concealed within software modelling environments that keep this information behind what a user sees on a software interface) has, accordingly, left a very real void in the language of architecture. And this is where the projects that follow offer such a valuable contribution: not only in the accomplishments of their form, beauty or material realization, but also their willingness to take on directly the challenges of reinventing the very language – and numbers – lying hidden behind their surface.

MATHEMATICS AND DESIGN

We have reached the end of a decade and a half in which digital computation has given architects new creative opportunities with which to access the geometrical space opened up by post-17th-century mathematicians. The resulting new wave of interest in the relationship of mathematics to space-making has been aesthetically driven, and yet its expression has transcended the metaphorical. It has found expression from within the process of making as a new species of architecture, and has infiltrated architectural process in ways that have forged radical change. This book is an account of the ways in which this new mathematical focus has manifested in designed and built projects since the mid-1990s. Had it been written ten years earlier, the phenomenon would have been fresh and urgent, but the book itself would have been much more theoretical and speculative. And yet there is still a sense of being at the cusp of a much greater revolution in the representation and production of architecture to which this deep interest in the beauty of the mathematical idea has contributed.

The New Mathematics of Architecture has no pretension to present a comprehensive, or even cursory, history of the complex and multiple relationships between mathematics and architecture. They have always been very closely related; both have their deepest roots embedded in geometry. Architecture has been concerned with the creation of space; mathematics with its description and definition. In mathematics particularly, this has encompassed increasingly diverse and abstract kinds of space. The terms 'mathematics' and 'geometry' are not synonymous. Auguste Comte wrote of mathematics in 1851 that 'the plural form of the name (grammatically used as singular) indicates the want

of unity in its philosophical character, as commonly conceived'.[1] Mathematics is gathered from different activities. Geometry was one of the seven liberal arts, belonging to the Quadrivium, along with arithmetic, astronomy and music (the additional Trivium included grammar, rhetoric and dialectic). The 'liberal' in liberal arts implied the study of subjects that, unlike architecture, were not necessarily directed to a profession. To geometry and arithmetic add algebra, and you have the basis of mathematics as it has developed since the Renaissance. But it is clear that these three disciplines, while closely related, developed in response to different impulses and practical needs.

The mathematically thematic chapters that follow, and into which the architectural projects have been grouped, are concerned in part with geometry in architecture. In particular, they are concerned with the embrace by architecture of geometry's expanded definition to the multiple geometries espoused in Felix Klein's Erlangen programme (1872), not just geometry as defined by the transformations under which Euclidean figures in the plane remain unchanged. But there are also chapters that consider less geometrical topics. The construction of and the search for relationships among things may operate in space more abstracted from perception and conception than even geometry.

'Geometry' is a word of Greek origin meaning 'land measurement'[2] or 'earth measure'.[3] The Greek historian Herodotus (c. 485–425 BC) attributed the origin of geometry to the Egyptians' apportionment of land by equal measure and the relationship of the revenue claimed by the pharaoh according to the land area and any reduction in that area, duly measured by the pharaoh's overseers, during the annual flooding of the Nile. So geometry is considered to be descended from the concrete subdivision and organization of space. In this sense, architecture and geometry are mutually implicated in their conception and development. Both have the power to express and organize space using concepts outside the constraints of a direct mapping to a physical representation. The principal distinction lies in their levels of abstraction and generality. Geometry looks for generalities and, once established (demonstrated or proved), offers them up for use; architecture employs these general relationships constructively to underpin and create specific spatial relationships. It is assumed that practical geometry has been practiced since prehistoric times (in building, for example), but that the Greeks took it further, abstracting and systemizing it and leaving us with Euclid's axioms. Geometrical knowledge developed and crystallized.[4]

'Arithmetic' is also from the Greek, derived from the word αριθμός, meaning number. It is clear that the concept of number is deep in the human psyche; as architectural theorist Sanford Kwinter reminded us, Alfred North Whitehead observed that the day a connection was forged in the human mind between seven fish in a river and seven days, a landmark advance was achieved in the history of thought.[5] Near newborn infants are found to distinguish between one, two and three objects (a process known as subitizing), and we are still quite young when three or more is discretized into more precise denominations. Mathematics calls on conceptual metaphor to locate these numbers on a line, which gives us cognitive access to negative numbers, and numbers in between numbers – the real numbers that, as Kwinter points

out, are anything but.[6] By the time we have engaged addition, subtraction, multiplication and division, the natural numbers that can be equated with fish and days are already found wanting. Zero, negative numbers, fractions, irrationals, and – more recently – real and imaginary numbers gradually, over millennia, find their way into the lexicon as part of the conceptual landscape and, in most (but not all) cases, onto the number line. This continuity of development is there to see in the imprint of the Babylonian sexagesimal system, evident in our measurement of time in groups of 60 seconds and 60 minutes, or angles of rotation with 360° to a full rotation. Notation has been a key innovation in the development of modern algorithms; the adoption of Arabic numerals with their use of decimal place ordering has reduced the weighty tomes needed to describe quite rudimentary mathematical relations, expressed in language in the manner of the Greeks.

What is the relationship of numbers to architecture? Numbers give us dimensions and proportions, fix the geometry as shape, and inscribe sacred meaning in significant buildings. And what of algebra, the third constituent of mathematics? Ingeborg M. Rocker, in her article 'When Code Matters', has this to say: 'Today, when architects calculate and exercise their thoughts, everything turns into algorithms! Computation, the writing and rewriting of code through simple rules, plays an ever-increasing role in architecture.'[7] Algebra is the primary meta-language of mathematics, in which both geometrical objects and numbers are further abstracted and generalized. The formal (logical) languages of computer code are not algebra, but algebra has provided the language in which to couch all the spatial, proximal and numerical relationships the algorithm-writing architect has in play. Its development marked the beginning of a progression to the ever-higher levels of abstraction and generalization that continue to empower mathematicians over new dominions of thought today.

What, therefore, is the philosophical impulse, the aspect of mathematical thought, that has excited the architectural activity of recent years, and to what is it reacting? The empirical experiments in perspective of the Renaissance artist and architect drove subsequent developments in projective geometry. By contrast, the archetypal modern-day architect has been seen as a mathematical reactionary, distant from the revolutions in geometry and newly possible understandings of space of the 19th and 20th centuries. In the late 1920s, architecture, in embracing one idea of industrialized production, sidelined the more expressionist, nationalistic and biologically inspired streams of Modernism to espouse the aesthetic dogma of the International Style, the pre-Renaissance interest in Vitruvius' proportions of the human body, Platonic interpretations of the Cosmos, geometrical ordering of the Euclidean plane, and the certainties of Cartesian space. The size, homogeneity and power of this idea, grounded in the ancient philosophical tradition of the search for absolute truth, has been so robust that the Postmodern vanguard movements in architecture that followed have tended to be just that: critiques of Modernism. Whether ironic, 'effetely Derridean or ponderously Tafurian', the critical practices of the vanguard prospered on the certainties of Modernism – on ideas, theories and concepts given in advance.[8] In relation to mathematics, architect and historian Robin Evans referred to the architectural use of 'dead' geometries.[9]

Outside this critical framework, the imagination of many leading architectural figures was caught by the chaotic systems of Edward Norton Lorenz and the fractal geometries of Benoît Mandelbrot, whose essay 'Fractals: Form, Chance and Dimension' (1975) provided the main conduit from complexity science to architecture. The three destabilizing ideas of discontinuity, recursivity and self-similarity were subsequently taken up by a string of architects as ideas for organizing principles.[10] But by the 1990s, there was already a trend to deny the inspiration of chaos, and to disown a fashion seen as having little tangible connection to the central concerns of architectural production. It was, in effect, an idea before its time. Given very few years and the computational means with which to explore the generative potential of recursive systems, these ideas re-entered architecture as if by stealth at a much more engaged level, and became part of the working design lexicon. Meanwhile, the distributed, networked and overlapping space of the post-20th-century human experience has brought connectivity into the foreground when considering spatial models, and given architects, as space-makers, an entrée into the conceptual spaces first defined by mathematicians and philosophers in the 19th century. Topology in architecture is no longer a critique of the power of the plane and gravitational vector in mainstream Modernism. Instead, it is the reality that we experience. Metrics and vectors have given place to distributed networks. This is a fundamentally different space in which to live.

What is the significance for architecture? Philosophically, Gilles Deleuze gave us the 'body', any corporeal arrangement composed of an infinite number of parts that are held together when they move in unison at the same speed, more or less powerful, more or less able to effect change in their environment, depending on the degree to which they are capable of being affected themselves.[11] Michael Speaks argues that contemporary architectural practise as such a body becomes more powerful 'to the degree that it transforms the chatter of little truths into design intelligence'.[12] 'Intelligence' has become a word much overused in our time. It remains ill-defined, and in its current popular usage smacks of 'artificial intelligence', with the deliberate excision of the unpopular idea of artificial. The rise of the biological sciences has created a new atmosphere of respect for the living; now artificial systems are rated according to the extent to which they ape biological systems, a reversal of the situation that once pertained, whereby logic-based systems were looked to for insight into thought.

Dynamic, variable, spatial models are not new in spatial design, and are certainly not confined to electronic computation. But the power to integrate many variables, make links outside the confines of three geometrical dimensions, and simulate scenarios has given the concept of intelligent models new and more mainstream life. At the most general level, computing itself has had an undeniable influence on the mathematics and collective perception of human organization. At the same time, it promises to immerse architects into the very systems of complexity that had excited them metaphorically. It is bringing chaotic and unpredictable behaviour from the metaphorical to the operational sphere. Virtual models of emergent systems, parametric models that exhibit chaotic, even catastrophic, behaviour through their string of dependencies – in the last ten years there has been an architectural interest in formal systems that has been grounded theoretically only to the extent that modelling itself is grounded theoretically (that is, mathematically). This interest has offered up formal outcomes that were initially novel and are now recognizable, and a timely sense in which design, freed from Modernist doctrine, has been at liberty to explore newer, more diverse mathematical models. The stock-in-trade of mathematics is the useful generality, while design is concerned with the specific problem, whether related to site, programme, social context or technical issues. But currently there is a fierce contextual generality across design: the need for rapid and universal quantum reduction in consumption and environmental degradation. The mathematics–design nexus in its newly pluralist and agile manifestation is ubiquitous in this mission.

This book is about architecture, but not exclusively about architects. In many of the projects on the following pages, the design teamwork between different professions is explicit. There is a historical perspective here. Robin Evans, in his book *The Projective Cast*, gives a fine account of the geometrical baton passing from the architects to the engineers. The two building-design disciplines were hitherto divided along civil and military lines, but after the 18th century, and specifically the work of the French engineer Gaspard Monge, the knowledge of descriptive geometry that had been so vital but subsequently lost in the architecture profession was appropriated by engineers, reappearing in the great ship-building and railway projects of the 19th century.[13] Mathematical knowledge in construction design from this time onwards became more or less the exclusive domain of the engineer.

During the 20th century, built works outside the rectilinear dogma of Modernism are attributable in great number to notable engineering authorship, including Félix Candela, Pier Luigi Nervi, Heinz Isler and Frei Otto, to name a few. What is interesting about these engineers is their use of physical analogue models to find structurally efficient shapes that provide the general principle of the model as a responsive dynamic system. Moreover, in the last century there have been architect-led works that espoused the themes discussed in the chapters that follow, which were designed without the power of digital computation – seminal works that whisper of closer geometrical affinity to natural form. Why is Le Corbusier's chapel of Notre-Dame-du-Haut at Ronchamp absent from the discussion of surfaces? Even more pressingly, how can we discuss datascapes in the absence of the progenitor of all datascapes – the Philips Pavilion for Expo 58 – a parametrically conceived architecture driven by sound and manifest in an assembly of ruled surfaces? Undoubtedly, the partnership of Le Corbusier and Iannis Xenakis lead us by the soul to the essence of the poetics of mathematics in architecture. As with all books, a line has been drawn around the subject, and this one has corralled the widespread zeitgeist that access to electronic computational power, in tandem with accessible graphical interaction with virtual space, has brought to mathematical creativity in architecture.

Have architects regained mathematical literacy? Certainly there are more architects working in more abstract symbol-articulated spaces. Digital computation has been generous in its rewards, and the incentives for addressing the machine in its own powerful languages are significant. The profession is grappling with logic as never before. This has more significance than a mere change of protocol: it is a whole new spatial and temporal context for design that is free from the static Cartesian strictures of the two-dimensional drafting plane. It is a meta-zone of multiple simultaneous possibilities. The magnitude of the change is similar to the way the introduction of analysis and algebra has increased the curves or surfaces represented by a single, economical line of mathematical notation to a large and infinite number.

The subjects of each of the book's six chapters have been architecturally, rather than mathematically, selected, suggested by the works themselves. What all the projects have in common in the first chapter, 'Mathematical Surfaces and Seriality', is that the shape of their curved surfaces is a principal expressive element in the architecture. They are diverse in the nature of that surface and its creation. All use mathematical rules or technique. Here we see mathematics used to offer solutions to the 'problem' of defining and building free-form surfaces, a minimal surface used for its complex configuration and symbolic mathematical identity, hyperbolic surfaces substracted from the building mass, surfaces created through inversion in the sphere, toroid surfaces used for their rational tilable qualities, and surfaces shaped by gravity to solve the problem of structural minimalism.

The second chapter, 'Chaos, Complexity, Emergence', includes projects in which fractals and self-similarity are at the heart of their expression, and where the simple elements of a system result in intriguing emergent results at another scale. Work that is fundamentally digital in production is contrasted with that created using more traditional techniques. 'Packing and Tiling' has some overlap with the previous topic in its inclusion of fractal tilings, but also introduces the phenomenon of aperiodicity: tilings and three-dimensional space-filling packings that do not map to themselves when translated. This contrasts with traditional Islamic tiling, which, while it includes complex multiple symmetries, is generally periodic. The exploration of aperiodicity is a relatively recent area of mathematics that has been given architectural expression.

'Optimization' is perhaps the best example of the use of computation in architecture. It includes projects in which diverse optimization methods find structurally economical form, elegantly resolve the panellization of surfaces, minimize the size of structural members, and resolve the perfect acoustic space. In general, the computer is used in a variety of ways to search a defined solution space, and to sculpt material by responding to strain. 'Topology' is a collection of works that have been driven less by shape and more by relationships of proximity and connection. Some projects explicitly investigate the architectural possibilities of non-orientable surfaces, such as the Möbius band and the Klein bottle – one adopts knots and the other the multiple instances of a single, topological description of a space. The final chapter, 'Datascapes and Multi-dimensionality', is a rare collection of interactive spaces, ranging from installations to urban design, which respond to stimuli from approaching humans to atmospheric change. These are genuinely multi-dimensional spaces by any mathematical definition that test Theo van Doesburg's ninth proposition in his manifesto, 'Towards a Plastic Architecture', published in *De Stijl* in 1924: '. . . with the aid of calculation that is non-Euclidean and takes into account the four dimensions, everything will be very easy.'[14]

Reviewing the projects presented, there is a natural division between those in which the primary mathematical constituent is an idea, and those where mathematics is first and foremost positioned as a problem-solver. In some, the two roles are balanced or combined, and in all, the mathematical idea or problem-solver is also instrumental in the design process and to the form of the architectural outcome. In all this activity, there is no real evidence of convergence between architect and mathematician, but there is a sense in which mathematics and mathematical ideas have contributed to the formation and cohesion of diverse creative teams. In 2002, Lionel March, a pioneer in the study of mathematical applications in architecture using computation, published an essay entitled 'Architecture and Mathematics Since 1960', a review of work in which March himself had been involved and that encompassed a range of research from land use and built-form studies to more qualitative investigations of form based on group theory of symmetries.[15] He cited educationalist Friedrich Fröbel, who observed that relational studies of form were 'forms of life'. In recent years, we have seen a steep uptake curve of the application of mathematical thinking in architecture, as this theoretically grounded work is followed by a period in which the mathematics has indeed come to life in the practice of architecture at every creative level. We wait, breathless, to see how this will play out in the working relationships and built environment in the years to come.

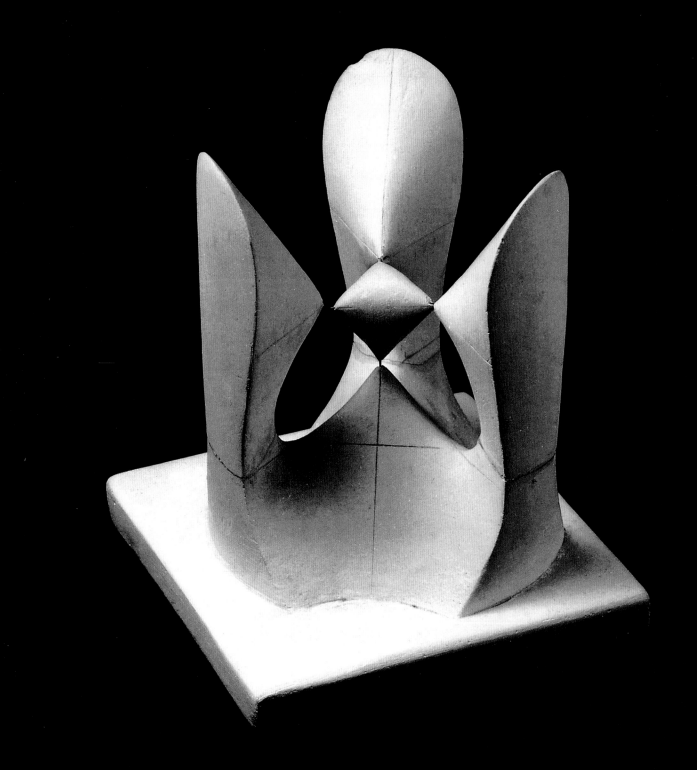

1 MATHEMATICAL SURFACES AND SERIALITY

Surface (a two-dimensional space, less than gossamer-thin) and *series* (a one-dimensional idea of sequential elements that build, within a defining relationship, a changing path) are mathematical concepts that become rich when embedded in three and four dimensions, and represented through the medium of inhabitable space. This chapter explores recent projects in which definitions of intrinsic surface space and series that govern growth or change are at the heart of the space-making process.

At their least abstract, surfaces are the boundaries of matter, the interface between solid or liquid matter and gaseous elements or space. They are generally complex and dynamic at molecular scale. Designers tend to engage with more abstract and idealized surface descriptions; in architecture, surface is predominantly a geometrical *idea*. There is much about the idea of surface to excite the designer, including the notion of impossible thinness (Gauss's disappearing dimension); the qualitative differences between surface as plane, curved in one direction or warped in two; and self-intersection. Some surfaces, when immersed in three dimensions, pass through themselves. The Klein bottle is the most famous topologically non-orientable example, but the Enneper minimal surface is one that is defined by its curvature. This is a spatial paradox that has become quicker and easier to represent, at least virtually, in the digital era.

Thinness The quest to find a form of materiality that dematerializes and leaves the suggestion of a two-dimensional threshold between one space and another without substance or weight. The tensile structures of Frei Otto had the power to do this, as did Anish Kapoor's *Marsyas* installation, which filled the Tate Modern's Turbine Hall with a taut, curved red surface that evoked the satyr's flayed skin after his defeat by Apollo.

The plane A surface rarely experienced in the physical world except when built; a piece of constructed Cartesian idea space that suggests infinite extension in an idealized, three-dimensional, continuous, homogenous space. This belongs in architecture to Mies van der Rohe, but we can trace the preoccupation back to the Renaissance and the development of projective geometry.

Single-curvature Dennis Shelden's 'developable surfaces [that] sneak up on you' refer to architect Frank Gehry's paper-modelling design process and the tacit constraint system of the medium in which one works; in this case, paper and its bending behaviour.[1]

Double-curvature The majority of the examples in this chapter concern surfaces that exhibit double-curvature; in each case, the outcome of a slightly different set of conditions and intentions, and significantly different mathematics. There was a worthy tradition throughout the 19th and 20th centuries in the development of thin shell structures that exploited such shapes for strength; the geometries of tensile fabric structures also come once more to mind. We must acknowledge Antoni Gaudí for developing an architectural language of ruled surfaces, along with Félix Candela, Heinz Isler, Iannis Xenakis and Frei Otto, all of whom found surfaces through a variety of physical analogue modelling techniques, and Gerd Fischer, who published two hundred years of mathematical surface models that were produced in plaster for study.[2] To designers using digital computation, these surfaces are now available as instant graphical representations from their algebraic descriptions. The challenge is only to consider fabrication techniques that embrace the design possibilities presented.

Self-intersection The chapter on topology includes projects where architects have engaged with non-orientable surfaces (those with no clear inside and outside), and have found ways to represent this quality of self-intersection, which is manifest in three dimensions but disappears in the fourth. Surface is an important concept in topology. In this context, a surface is

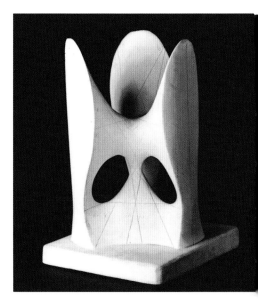

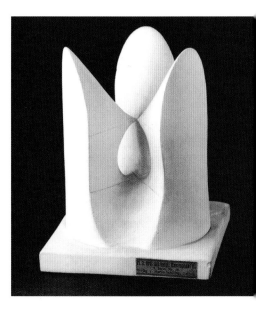

TOP Diagonal surface, seen from the side.

ABOVE Cubic with a D4 double-point.

PRECEDING PAGE Cubic with four A1 double-points.

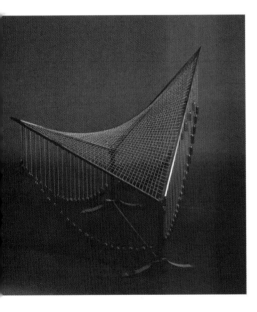

TOP Hyperboloid of one sheet (variable thread model).

ABOVE Hyperbolic paraboloid (variable thread model).

called a two-dimensional manifold ('manifold' being the term in topology and differential geometry for a mathematical space).

Curvature The mathematician Stephen Hyde has described both curvature and non-Euclidean geometry (see below) as fundamental to the modelling of matter at molecular and atomic scales.[3] They are also fundamental space-makers for architectural modellers. Within mathematics, surface is an idea that has grown in significance since curvature – and particularly the ability to quantify it – took centre stage, an idea that goes back to the introduction of calculus in its various guises in the 17th century. 'Curvature' is a slightly fast and loose term, and divides into extrinsic curvature and intrinsic curvature. A straight line has zero curvature, whereas a circle has constant curvature equal to the inverse of its radius. As the radius increases, the curvature of a larger circle (as opposed to a smaller one) reduces. In order to measure the curvature of a one-dimensional curve, it must be embedded in two or three dimensions. For this reason, its curvature is termed 'extrinsic'; it is only known from outside the space of the object. Surfaces, on the other hand, have an extrinsic curvature that is visible when they are embedded in a three-dimensional space, but their curvature is also intrinsic. As we walk across a curved surface in two dimensions, the curvature is still perceptible: the horizon is not a line.

Non-Euclidean geometry Geometries that emerged following the break with Euclid's planar geometry in the 19th century. One of Euclid's postulates has always caused headaches for mathematicians. The fifth, or parallel, postulate implies that for any given infinite line and point off that line, there is one and only one line through the point that is parallel. In 1830 and 1832, Nikolai Lobachevsky and János Bolyai independently published their respective discoveries of hyperbolic geometry, in which there are many parallel (non-intersecting) lines through a given point (P) to a line (L) that does not pass through (P). The hyperbolic plane can be imagined as a saddle-shaped surface in three dimensions. Another form of non-Euclidean geometry is elliptical (or Riemannian) geometry, in which there are no lines through (P) that are parallel to (L), which does not pass through (P). In the simplest case, lines are the great arcs of a sphere. The best-known application of hyperbolic geometry in art is in the work of Escher, who used it to represent spaces that would confront the viewer's intuition.

Minimal surfaces Surfaces that are defined as having a mean curvature of zero. This does not mean that they are planar, but that the sum of their curvature in two principal directions on the surface is zero; the positive and negative curvature might be thought of as cancelling each other out. In this way, they are stable surfaces of low energy. Their most familiar manifestation is in the surfaces that form when a wire is dipped into a soap solution. The classic examples of minimal surfaces are catenoids and helicoids, along with the Enneper surface, which self-intersects in three dimensions. Another is the more recently discovered Costa-Hoffman-Meeks minimal surface, described topologically as a thrice-punctured torus.

Mathematical surfaces Common to all of the 'mathematical' surfaces discussed in this chapter is that they can be described in analytical geometry. While they belong to generic families that vary parametrically, the characteristics of their shape matters. This is different from a topological engagement with surface, in which topologically homologous (equivalent) surfaces may be very different in shape.

Series An idea that engages metrics, rather than merely the more mathematically abstract proximity and connectedness of things as considered in topology. A series is the sum of a sequence of terms, and therefore it is not just the order of the sequence or set of members that matter, but the actual values of each object and their collective value. Gregory Bateson's 'pattern that connects' refers to the genotypical and phenotypical variations within species; while every crab has the same number of legs and each leg has a recognizably characteristic shape, no two crabs are the same size and nor are their legs the same shape.[4] Algorithms that harness the idea of series can introduce this level of repetition with its implicit 'genetic' variation into architecture within a geometric schema that allows an overall meta-level of pattern-making to be read.

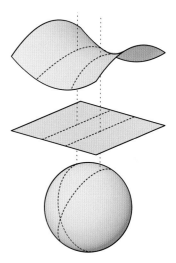

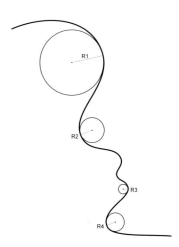

TOP Euclid's fifth postulate translated to hyperbolic geometry (top), in which there are many possible parallels through a single point, and elliptical geometry (bottom), where there are none.

ABOVE Curvature is defined as the inverse of the radius $\frac{1}{R}$, and may differ at every point along the curve. A circle is a curve of constant curvature.

OPPOSITE What scaling algorithm do the successive branches of a fern conform to? There is a pattern of apparently similar shapes and self-similarity between the frond and its parts, but also a pattern governing the progressive diminution towards the tip.

Australian Wildlife Health Centre

MINIFIE NIXON
Healesville Sanctuary, Australia

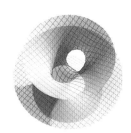

The practice of Minifie Nixon has frequently drawn on abstract mathematical ideas as a source for novel design technique. At this centre for native fauna near Melbourne, the technique chosen engaged a 20th-century discovery with strong links to the natural world: the Costa-Hoffman-Meeks minimal surface. Central and emblematic to the building, its shape is close to that of a heart valve. Also deployed here is the cellular automaton, a method used in the 1950s as a potential model for biological systems.

The building is organized around a public entrance and ring of exhibition spaces that form a glazed ambulatory, which overlooks the operating theatres and treatment rooms that are distributed radially around it. The design turns the traditional paradigm inside out, putting on prominent display procedures and operations that would normally occur out of sight – a unique approach to involving the public in the

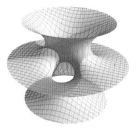

process of rescuing and treating wildlife. The ambulatory encloses the glass walls of a small, covered, semi-external courtyard at the heart of the building, where information videos are screened via back projection. The whole area is united by a single 3-symmetrical golden roof of tensile fabric that follows the form of a Costa surface, continuing the sense of a building turned inside out through its surface gymnastics.

The Costa minimal surface was only discovered in 1984 through, as architect Paul Minifie explains, 'experimental mathematics, whereby computers [were] used to investigate a large number of cases prior to deriving formal proofs'. To find the particular Costa surface that fitted the constraints of the health centre, a 'computational process that iteratively finds a final form from a set of constraints' was required.[5] With such a process, it was possible to marry the programmatic

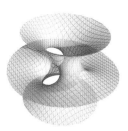

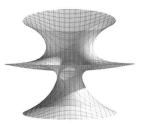

OPPOSITE Detail of the interior of the tensile roof in the shape of a Costa surface, from the ambulatory space.

RIGHT Sections of a Costa minimal surface, described as a thrice-punctured torus – various views showing the singularities.

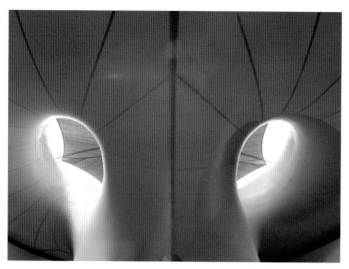

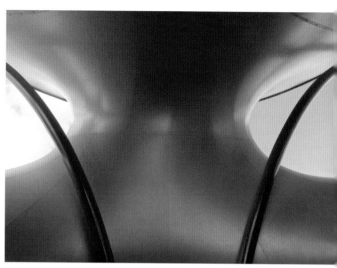

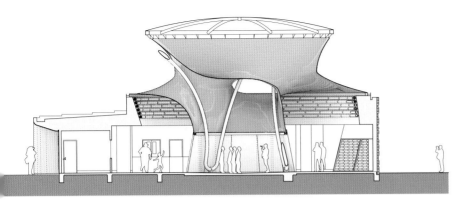

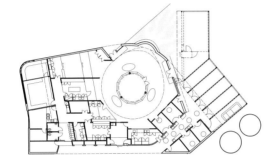

ABOVE Section through the central courtyard and ambulatory.

RIGHT Plan.

BELOW Cellular automaton iterations Parameters: distance: 3 cells; adjacency weight: 0.7; horizontal weight: -0.5; vertical weight: 0.1.

OPPOSITE, TOP LEFT AND RIGHT View of the roof from the ambulatory and from the courtyard.

OPPOSITE, BOTTOM The entrance to the centre.

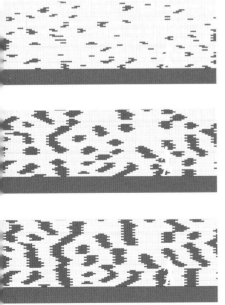

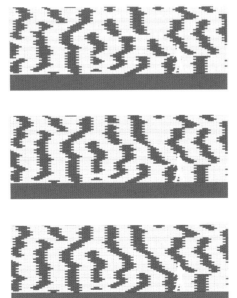

demands of the brief and the formal intentions of the designer through a form-finding exercise that would determine a final form, which itself would meet these constraints within the geometric and topological definition of the surface. The surface is genus 3 (meaning that it has three holes), with three oculi bringing natural light into the courtyard and acting as solar chimneys. It opens on the opposite side of the building fabric to create three skylights that are evenly distributed around the main ambulatory viewing space.

To set out the bicoloured masonry of the façade, a second mathematical idea – the cellular automaton – was appropriated. 'A cellular automaton', explains Minifie, 'is a collection of "coloured" cells on a grid of a specified shape, which evolves through a number of discrete time steps according to a set of rules based on the states of neighbouring cells. Cellular automata were studied in the early 1950s as a possible model for biological systems. The particular rules used at the AWHC are a weighted sum of the regions surrounding a given cell and applied to an initially random seeding. The sequence always converges to a stable pattern, which is expressed as a masonry set-out. The horizontal or vertical components of the rules are weighted according to the proximity of the various building elements, allowing the building skin to respond to both expressive requirements and building programme.'[6]

• Cellular automaton (p. 254)
• Minimal surfaces (p. 261)

Beijing International Airport
FOSTER + PARTNERS
Beijing, China

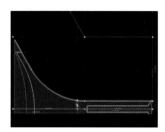

The beauty of this proposal for a new international airport lies in the resolution of what may be the world's largest covered space into a small number of arcs of grand radius. The aim was to create a sense of calm through the use of simple geometry and gradual curves. 'We wanted to simplify the mathematics,' says architect Jonathan Parr. 'The plans for the terminals are based on three curves, for example.'[7] Ultimately, all of the geometry was generated from arcs and straight lines to create a vast, doubly curved, doubly spanning roof that encloses over a million square metres.

The arcs begin in plan, their radii determined by the optimal arrangement of the aircraft stands, based on the wing span of the planes arrayed along the curves. Two Y-shaped terminal buildings are defined by arcs of radius large enough to dock 126 planes; the concave Y-shapes are in effect a circle, reflected in three chords to increase the ratio of perimeter length to volume enclosed. A third slender, H-shaped building links the others in a linear sequence parallel to the runways. Two taxiways separate the three buildings, while an automated people-mover dives beneath as it carries passengers on their long journey between terminals.

The BIA train station roof reuses the geometry first employed by the architects at London's Canary Wharf station: the toroid patch, a shape generated by different arcs running in orthogonal directions.[8] Here, the roof varies in curvature in three dimensions. The slow curvature (the minimum radius of curvature is 250m) allowed the geometry to be found by lifting the regular node grid of the lightweight space-frame vertically from the plan onto the surface. Theoretically, the variable curvature implied that the 18,262 connection points and 76,924 members would all be different, but in practice, some were sufficiently similar to be replicated.

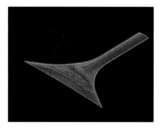

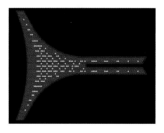

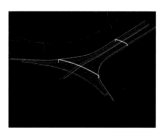

OPPOSITE The inclined external columns at the terminal's periphery.

RIGHT, FROM TOP Automated generation of the node surface area; upper and lower node surface; roof plan with roof lights; principal parametric curves generating the roof shape.

Members were omitted in the bottom layer of the diagonal space-work of tetrahedrons and octahedrons to produce a pattern of equilateral triangles and hexagons. The roof is supported on flexible, tapering steel columns; the heights vary dramatically, but each is at least 750mm in diameter at roof level to accommodate water run-off. This leads to twenty-three different column sizes in one of the terminals, all tapering at $\frac{1}{50}$, including variations to the steel thickness to minimize the variation in diameter. The curved edge is defined by the surface of a cone reflected in the inclination of the external columns, supporting a daring 45m cantilever.[9]

With the terminals almost a kilometre in length and 800m across, the minimum proportion for the ceiling height was judged to be 20 to 30m. Sixteen shades of red and yellow vary in spectral steps across the terminals, reflecting the slow change of the geometry and the arrival and departure sequences (domestic passengers depart from the dramatic upper level of their terminal, while international travellers have a comparable encounter on arrival). Triangular roof lights rise like dragon scales from the grid of the roof to admit light and passive warmth through the bosque of space-work above.

The success of the simple formula was also in its transmissibility. The contractor received from the architect a geometrical method statement; in effect, a recipe for constructing the geometry as a mighty 1:1-scale model of the building.

• Curvature (p. 255)
• Toroid patch (p. 266)

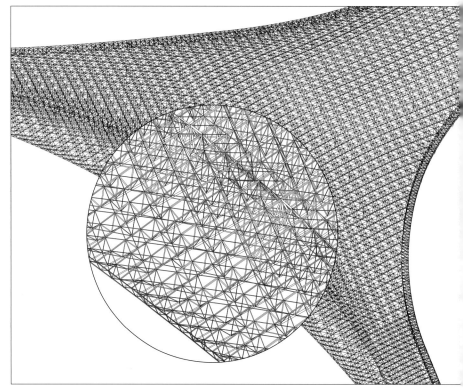

RIGHT Sections through the roof light.

BELOW, LEFT Roof-light detail.

BELOW, RIGHT View of the terminal building towards a tip of the Y, showing the dragon-scale lights across the roof's curving skin.

BOTTOM A view east–west, illustrating the ceiling slats that follow the arcs of the lower sides of the space-frame.

OPPOSITE, TOP The roof's slow curve demonstrates the continuation of the space-frame and slats across the huge overhang.

OPPOSITE, BOTTOM Detail of the space-frame.

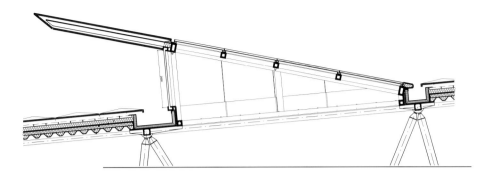

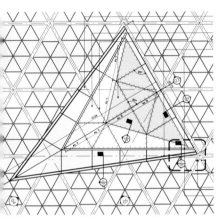

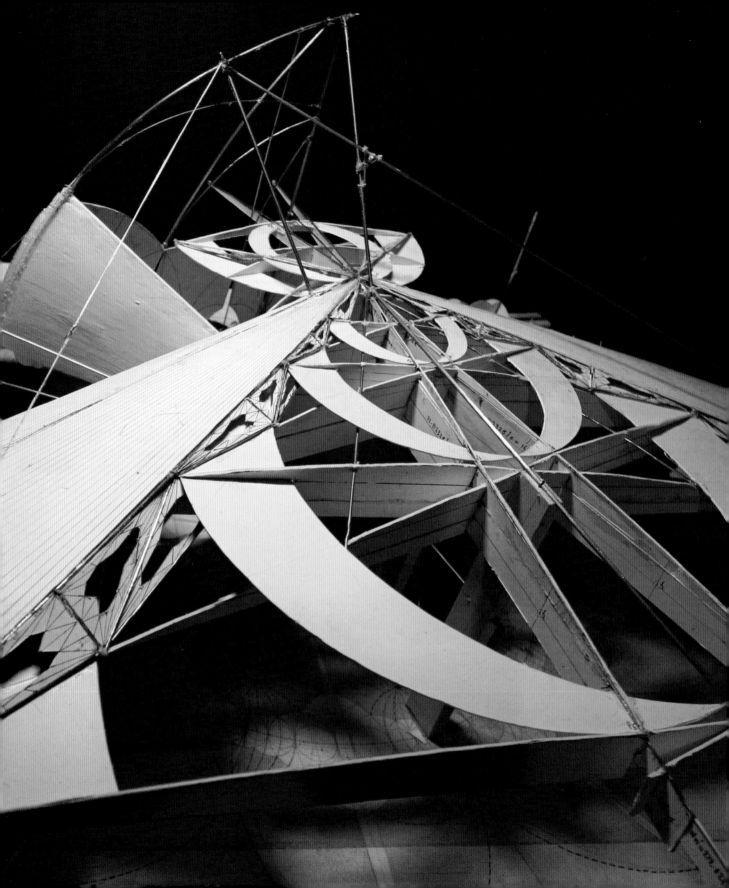

Inversion Modelling
JOHN PICKERING
Wolverhampton, UK

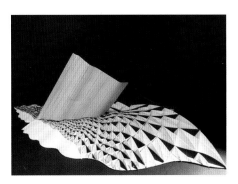

British artist John Pickering has devoted much of his career to working with just one particular mathematical transformation inversion with respect to the sphere – to achieve diverse compositional ends in his sculpture. In 2006, he collaborated with architect George L. Legendre on a monograph devoted to his work, in which Legendre described the artist as one who uses mathematics to produce small, finely wrought sculptures brimming with architectural qualities'.[10]

The book led to further collaboration with Legendre's practice, IJP, to explore the feasibility of developing two of Pickering's earlier sculptures as large-scale constructed pieces: *Inversion of cylinder with sphere* (1988–90), or, to give it its full title, *inverting a cylinder, the centre of inversion not lying on the cylinder, also connecting ellipses by projection*; and *Inversion of intersecting spheres, whose centres lie on the*

axis of a cylinder (2002). The partnership with Legendre and IJP led to the detailed geometrical interpretation of Pickering's method to reproduce his sculptures as digital models, and from these physical rapid prototyped versions that would inform the material interpretation of the artworks for large-scale construction.

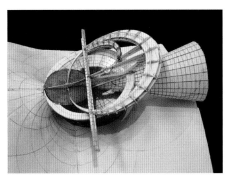

In 2008, Barry Phipps of Kettle's Yard Gallery in Cambridge invited Pickering and architects Foster + Partners to participate in a forthcoming show, *Beyond Measure: Conversations Across Art and Space,* and exhibit work that would demonstrate the use of mathematics and geometry in art and architecture. Pickering's subsequent collaboration with Foster's Specialist Modelling Group (SMG) began with a blank slate on which to apply the artist's methodology to a possible architectural outcome. In preparation for their first face-to-face meeting, SMG's Brady Peters had

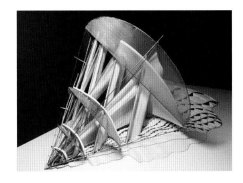

OPPOSITE Model developed on a 'faulty' hyperbolic plane, exploiting holes in the compact tiling of the surface.

RIGHT, TOP Inverting a corrugated cone with a sine wave profile with respect to a point not lying on any part of the cone or sine wave.

RIGHT, BOTTOM The part cyclide is repeated at a ratio of 2:1, decreasing and increasing; the radius of the sphere of inversion also increases 2:1 around the same centre. The surface of the intersecting part cyclides are triangulated to give a more rhythmic flow.

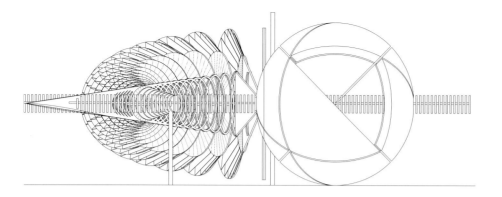

THESE PAGES All of the drawings and the render below were produced by IJP from Pickering's models for the purpose of representing the geometry for constructi... as large-scale installations.

LEFT, BELOW AND OPPOSITE, TOP *Inversion o... cylinder with sphere* (1988–90).

OPPOSITE, BELOW *Inversion of intersecting spheres, whose centres lie on the axis o... a cylinder* (2002).

...pression', John Pickering 2008

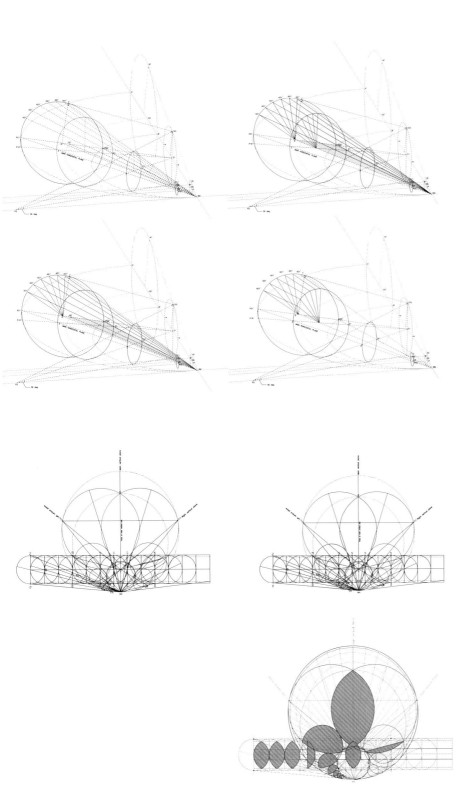

written a Visual Basic script to automate the inversion of geometry, while his colleague Xavier De Kestelier had created a similar, parallel process in Bentley Generative Components software. Peters and De Kestelier were nervous about the potential implications of juxtaposing months of Pickering's meticulous manual calculation and hand-crafted modelling with seconds of computation. Pickering, however, was delighted at the opportunity for rapid experimentation. Over the course of a series of meetings, a collection of interesting inversion experiments developed. Within the computational 'inverter', it was possible to move the centre of inversion relative to the parent form in real time and watch the morphing result on screen. Soon it became apparent that inversion was possible through any surface, not just the sphere. Variable radius and curvature produced more surprising results.

During the ensuing weeks, many discoveries but no architectural project emerged from this process. The final exhibit became a cabinet of arresting prototyped geometrical curiosities: three-dimensional objects that acted as diagrams of inversion, demonstrating geometrical starting and end points, awaiting their architectural day in the sun – a fascinating counterpoint to the spatial worlds of their richly crafted card, board and paste predecessors.

• Inversion (p. 260)

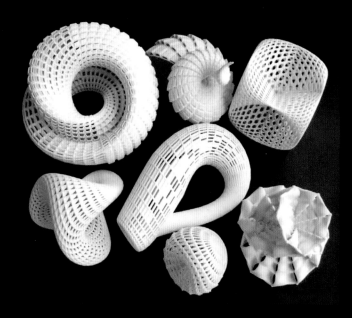

LEFT Earlier speculative geometrical models developed by the SMG prior to their collaboration with Pickering.

BELOW 'Sea Urchin', actually an inverted icosahedron. Xavier De Kestelier of SMG inverted a regular polyhedron, then inverted each resulting individual surface. Colleague Brady Peters then populated these surfaces with architectural components (using a VB script), and applied a third inversion of the whole with an off-centre inversion point in the VBA inverter, before colouring the result, again using a VB script.

BELOW, LEFT AND OPPOSITE The cross-cap, inverted from two centres.

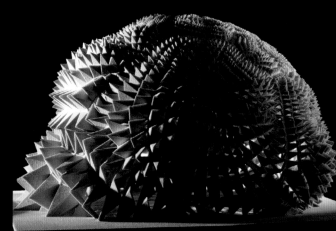

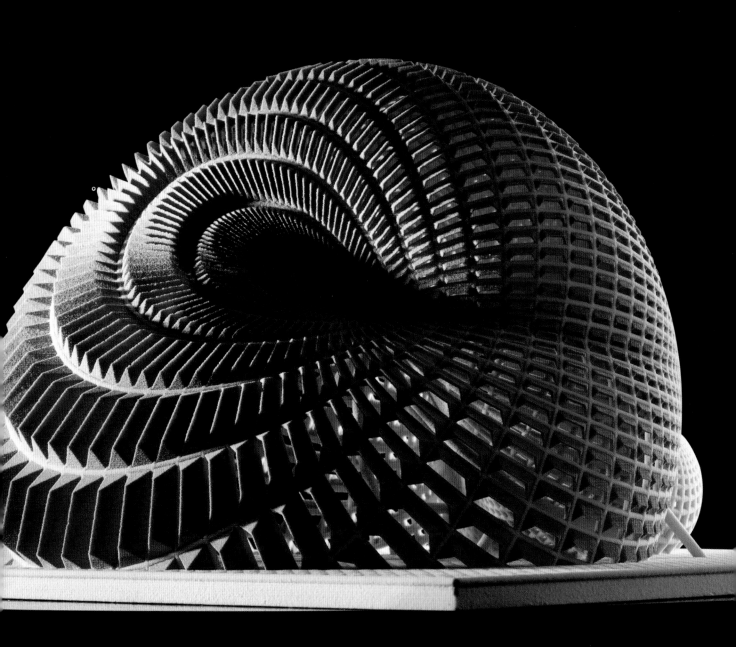

Sagrada Família

ANTONI GAUDÍ
Barcelona, Spain

THE PASSION FAÇADE: MATHEMATICAL SEQUENCE AND THE PATTERN THAT CONNECTS

Antoni Gaudí was already using a system of doubly curved, ruled surfaces in his design for the church of Sagrada Família almost a century ago. His work shows a profound grasp of concepts that underlie naturally occurring form, both organic and inorganic. Through a combination of intersecting ruled surfaces, Gaudí was able to work in a fluid way while finding a strong, systematic rationale to make the work transmissible and buildable, communicating to model-makers and stonemasons both of his own time and of the future the means with which to continue the work and realize the church.

A colonnade of inclined, bone-like columns and a stepping pediment that sits over the main portal in the west transept, part of the façade dedicated to the Passion of Christ, combine an intriguing intersection of geometries. The colonnade supports a frieze

of hexagonal prisms, reminiscent of the basalt monoliths used by Gaudí as columns in the crypt of his Colònia Güell chapel. Above is a sloping cornice of blocky steps, like a giant causeway topped with paraboloid pinnacles. Many of the examples in this book are concerned with breaking from the regular, repetitive Cartesian grid in space as the main mathematical organizational strategy for architecture. At Sagrada Família, Gaudí tackled the complexity of spatial subdivision strategies without the aid of digital computation, but computers can now be useful tools for interpreting the church's naturalistic geometrical complexity.

To build the colonnade, the detailed geometry of the composition must be interpreted from a single surviving photograph, taken in 1917, of the original drawing for the elevation. Gaudí worked

OPPOSITE The Passion Façade of Sagrada Família.
RIGHT, TOP The 1917 photograph of the elevation drawing of the façade.

RIGHT, MIDDLE AND BOTTOM Perspective-corrected photographs of the west elevation for use in the design process with three temporary full-scale prototyped columns.

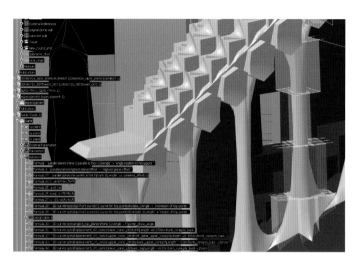

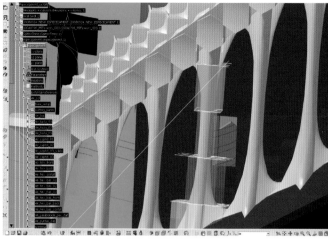

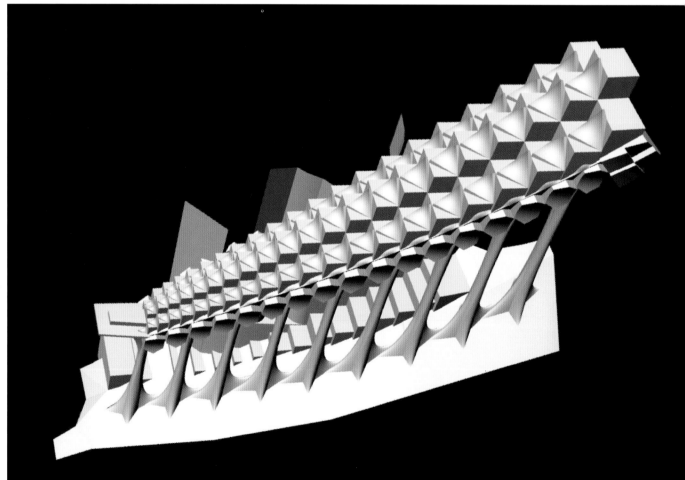

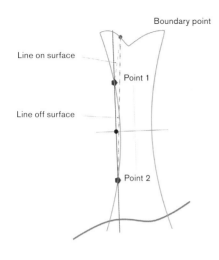

Boundary point

Line on surface

Point 1

Line off surface

Point 2

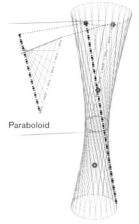

Paraboloid

Hyperboloid

OPPOSITE, TOP Virtual stonecutting.

OPPOSITE, BOTTOM Virtual model, showing the growth in the steps of the crowning 'crestaria'.

BELOW A piece of virtual stone.

ABOVE Each column is based on the intersection of an elliptical hyperboloid (a cooling-tower shape with a non-circular section) and eight hyperbolic paraboloids (a saddle shape). The two geometries meet along straight ruling lines that occur on both surfaces. They can vary infinitely in shape through altering the shape parameters and critical points of intersection.

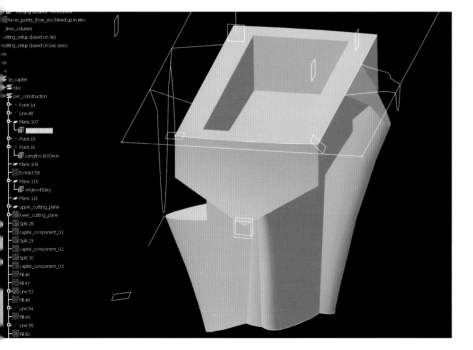

principally through the use of 1:25- and 1:10-scale gypsum plaster models; the colonnade is one of the first parts of the church to be built for which no such models have been found.

A sequence of elements is found here that share a genetic blueprint, yet each element is unique. The columns are similar to one another in shape, but cannot be transformed one into the next through scaling, translation, reflection or rotation. What is the basis, to use anthropologist Gregory Bateson's words, of this 'pattern that connects'? The stepping cornice appears even simpler conceptually: repetitive rectilinear shapes lie on a straight pitch line in elevation. Yet even variation in shape through the curved plan, each appears uniquely sized, with some simple progression or growth algorithm controlling their increasing size towards the apex. The schematization of the geometry to replicate as closely as possible the architect's intentions, as seen in the photograph, becomes an exercise in forensics, uncovering the mathematical sequencing and its underlying algorithms, while trying to sense the degree of anomaly needed to replicate the powerful organicism of the original design.

This was negotiated through the use of parametric computational models to set up variable relationships on an underlying geometrical schema. The growth in the stepping cornice, for example, is controlled by a quadratic function that can be given different degrees of growth hormone in order to vary the rate at which the steps grow between base and summit (rather like adjusting the pleats of a curtain).

AN ARCHITECTURE OF REAL ABSENCE AND VIRTUAL PRESENCE: BOOLEAN SUBTRACTION

During the last twelve years of his long career, Gaudí moved away from his more free-form architecture to one based on a simple set of three ruled (second-order) surfaces, used in two distinct ways: real absence and virtual presence. He devoted these final years to concluding the design for the Sagrada Família church, to the exclusion of all other projects, using combinations of these surfaces – the hyperboloid of revolution of one sheet, the hyperbolic paraboloid, and the helicoid – in a rich interplay. When examining his work from this period closely, it is clear that Gaudí employed two distinct strategies: sculpting and sewing.

Gaudí's method was to make models in plaster of Paris to create rich combinations of these geometries, an effective but nevertheless highly laborious strategy. The digital equivalent to 'sculpting' and 'sewing' in plaster are distinct from each other. Digital sculpting relies on Boolean solid modelling operations, whereas digital sewing depends on working around a virtual armature to which the associated surfaces are made to conform. Gaudí's own approach to sculpting is understood through the plaster model-makers working on site today, who bear witness through their uninterrupted apprenticeship to the master's tutorage prior to his death (Gaudí died in 1926, aged 74).

Digital sculpting via Boolean subtraction involves conceiving what is not wanted in order to use its removal as a means to obtain what is actually

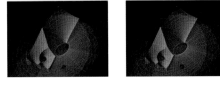

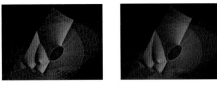

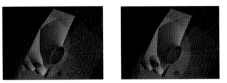

ABOVE The vaults of the central and lateral nave.

ABOVE, RIGHT The 1:1-scale model.

RIGHT Digital sculpting, showing the ghostly subtracted forms.

OPPOSITE, TOP LEFT AND BOTTOM Gaudí's original model for the upper nave window, restored after damage sustained during the Spanish Civil War.

OPPOSITE, TOP RIGHT Comparing digitized measured surfaces with geometrically generated surfaces in the virtual model.

OPPOSITE, BOTTOM RIGHT Detail of model.

sought: the residue from that removal. When working with hyperboloids, for example, the first step is to make a convex hyperboloid master. The sculpted effect of removing this convex master from a notional solid is a residual concave hyperboloid 'soup plate'. The concave hyperboloids are then selectively cut away and joined together to reveal subtle 3D curves of intersection between adjacent surfaces with key triple points – the intersection of the minimum three surface intersections that characterize this approach. Gaudí's latter-day collaborators employ the same series of moves digitally to form the church walls. Ultimately, like the ceiling vaults, the ceiling defined through such sculpting is supported by the columns beneath, ending in capitals made as concave hyperboloids and attached through Boolean intersection.

Complementing this architecture of 'real absence' – defining what is not wanted and subtracting it from the wall and ceiling mass – is the architecture of 'virtual presence'. Here, there is an implied guiding armature made from straight lines, each of which are the common directrices of hyperbolic paraboloids joined in space. In many cases, only a portion of the surface geometry is retained; the rest is invisibly excised in space, conforming to a geometrical framework that is implicit but not left whole in the resulting architectural fabric.

• Hyperbolic geometry (p. 260)
• Ruled surfaces (p. 264)
• Series and sequences (p. 264)

Main Station Stuttgart
INGENHOVEN ARCHITECTS
Stuttgart, Germany

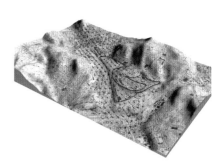

This competition-winning proposal for a new main station for Stuttgart addressed the requirements of the European fast-rail network by proposing a solution for siting a through-station in the heart of the city, along with one of the issues that result from Stuttgart's location in the basin of a long, narrow valley. The railway currently enters the valley from the north and proceeds southward to a terminus in the city centre, bringing every journey to the end of a narrow cul-de-sac, while the railway lines carve the city in two. 'Stuttgart is a city that a king ordered next to his castle,' notes architect Christoph Ingenhoven. 'We don't know why the king loved this valley, but we do know this place is not well suited for a city.'[11]

The proposal placed the new station at 90° to the existing one, oriented to new railway tunnels through the sides of the basin, which were themselves oriented across the valley. The monumental hall would be sunk below

ground, enabling land to be given back to the city as green spaces and freeing up an area that would house 11,000 people and where a further 24,000 people would work as part of the Stuttgart 21 masterplan. At its heart, this grand project is a story of using surface, found physically but understood mathematically, to solve two problems simultaneously. The first is the matter of structural and material economy, and the second is the provision of light and air to the vast underground space, without creating significant energy consumption or carbon pollution. The main hall is a 420m-x-80m public space where up to 300,000 commuters gather each day, slipped beneath the city's gaze.

In the spirit of the disappearing dimension (the thinness of surface), a concrete shell structure was developed that could span 36m at a depth of just $1/100$ of its span.[12] Its conception drew on work that has been undertaken at the University

OPPOSITE Detail of the 'eyes', in the proposal for Stuttgart's main station.

RIGHT, TOP TO BOTTOM Aerial views of the city's topography; the position of the new train hall, superimposed upon the existing station; the area of mineral springs that need to be protected during and after construction.

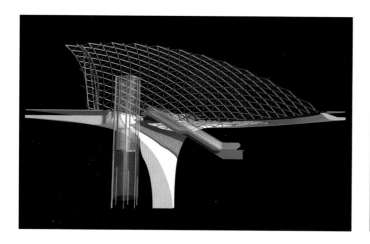

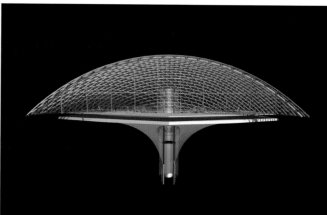

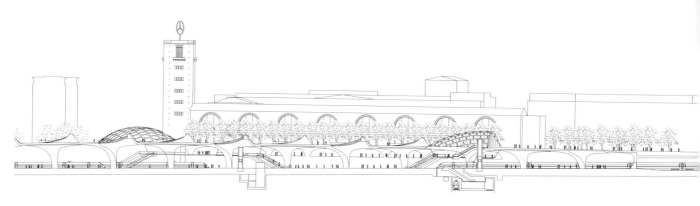

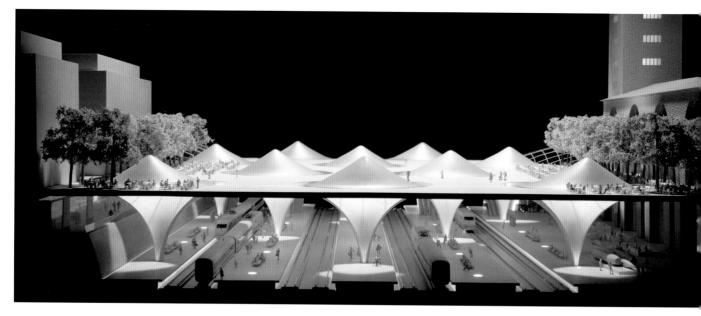

of Stuttgart's Institute for Lightweight Structures since 1963, using soap-film membranes, in which the stresses are tensile, isotropic and evenly distributed. Point loads can be supported by these membranes without a local stress peak. These minimal surfaces can be formed around a hole, called an 'eye', where the smooth flow of tensile stresses means that the eye forms a loop within the membrane. From this principle, a funnel-like chalice is formed as a modular prototype unit that combines roof, vertical support and opening to the sky in a single, minimal surface.

A continuous shell roof would cover the whole underground space, everywhere admitting natural light and ventilation via the chalice eyes. This space would draw on the Earth for heating and cooling, and the tunnels for ventilation. A way of finding out how multiple chalice supports and trough walls would interact together in a continuous roof structure was to construct a physical suspended chain model. A chain net with quadrilateral mesh was anchored at the high and low points, and allowed to deform under its own self-weight to give a form in pure tension. (This hanging chain model is in the tradition of the funicular model employed by Gaudí to find the tower forms for the Colònia Güell chapel.) When inverted and made rigid, this same surface shape distributes forces in pure compression, minimizing both the depth and the need for steel reinforcement in the shell.

OPPOSITE, TOP Details of the dome for the entrance and main vertical circulation.

OPPOSITE, MIDDLE Lateral section.

OPPOSITE, BOTTOM Perspective section.

ABOVE One of the proposed light-scoop 'eyes', lighting the station hall below.

BELOW View of the 'eyes' in the underground station.

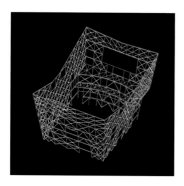

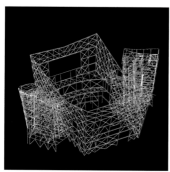

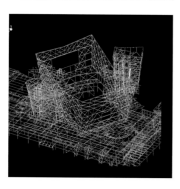

Disney Concert Hall
GEHRY PARTNERS
Los Angeles, California, USA

The story of the development of the Disney Concert Hall in downtown Los Angeles is a long one, from the winning of the competition by Gehry Partners in 1988 to the first performances in 2003. As the design evolved in collaboration with the acousticians, the hall became the central organizing force for a project that aimed to extend the building's remit: the idea of the audience at home, embracing the performers. Within the Gehry repertoire, the design was in the tectonic lineage that had begun in the 1980s with the Vitra Design Museum in Weil am Rhein, developing ideas that were given fuller expression during the realization of the Bilbao Guggenheim in 1997.[13]

All built architecture embodies a process of translation, from its abstract conception through various modes of representation of ideas and intention (generally iterative), to description for construction, to constructed realization. In Frank Gehry's architecture, adhering to the nuances of the idea as represented in early design models has been the challenge facing those traversing this treacherous series of translations. Dennis Shelden, founder and CTO of Gehry Technologies, has a clear theoretical framework in which to view these translations. He considers them mappings, or well-defined mathematical transformations, between different but related geometrical or topological spaces.

The sinuous, metallic surfaces leading into curving interiors were becoming a Gehry signature. To realize these surfaces with the scale, structure and constructability necessary for a building like the Disney Concert Hall became a fascinating journey into the geometry of surface itself. Surfaces have their own inherent characteristics, onto which a different constructional geometry must be mapped that makes sense of the unitary building elements that have to come together

LEFT Digital model of the structure, showing the hall as the central organizing element.
OPPOSITE, TOP Model exterior.

OPPOSITE, BOTTOM The interior is the result of a long series of models to reconcile the architects' 'vineyard' seating aspirations with the acousticians' need for a box to guarantee sound quality.

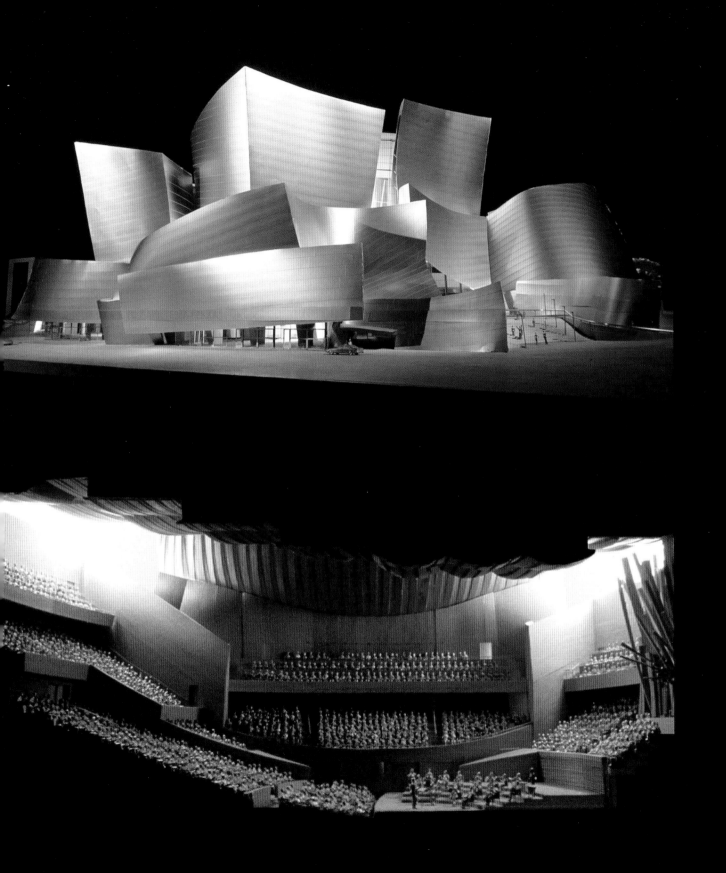

according to various ordering rules, to support and shelter the building and conform to the conventions of gravity and directionality in the physical world.

According to Shelden, surfaces aren't just surfaces: they are fields embedded in R3. What their interpreters care about is the Gaussian curvature, or the derivatives in two dimensions mapped to their equivalents in 3-space. They must consider the reason why two ants drift apart when walking in parallel on a curved surface. The three-dimensional parametric surface can be seen as a subset of the product of a 2-space and a 3-space. These surfaces use implicit, rather than explicit, functions. Each point on the surface has an X, Y and Z parameter that is a function of its U and V parameters. Mathematically, there is a view that sees this space as a point in five-dimensional space.[14]

The physical modelling must adhere to a language of sheet materials, but computational surfaces are nothing like the physical. One can work with paper unaware of the constraints that are being imposed. In other words, developable surfaces (surfaces with another mathematical overlay) can sneak up on you.[15] Fortuitously, the characteristics of the developable surfaces – being of single-curvature and able to be unrolled onto the plane – can be exploited directly for finding supporting structures and for constructability in the building.

RIGHT The Disney Concert Hall during construction.

BELOW The contrasting geometries of the metal cladding tiles and the underlying structure are revealed – one exploiting the principle line of curvature, the other the ruling lines through the conical arcs of the surface.

OPPOSITE, TOP Interior of the concert hall.

OPPOSITE, BOTTOM Baroque space.

Abu Dhabi Airport

KOHN PEDERSEN FOX

Abu Dhabi, UAE

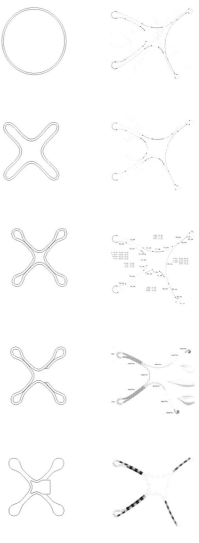

This ambitious and complex terminal building follows on the development of a second runway and the rapid, provisional expansion to Terminal 3. The first phase of the project caters for 20 million passengers per annum, and will have forty-two gates, with projected expansion in the second phase to ninety gates and 50 million passengers and two tons of cargo a year. Conceived to echo the undulating dunescape of the surrounding desert, and to create a structure in which daylight can be harnessed yet modulated and heat passively controlled, the terminal's shape has a complex yet highly explicit underlying geometrical schema. Parametrically driven computing was used to create the folding form, and to achieve the standardization, modularization and prefabrication of the components necessary to control costs and cater for long-term serviceability.

The designers make reference to the work of artist Marcel Jean, whose Utopian architecture embraced abstract geometrical processes in order to create buildings that were responsive to fantasy and emotion, and to that of psychoanalyst Jacques Lacan, who, in relation to certain mental processes, harnessed the possibilities of mathematical logic to recreate an intangible dimension, also related to emotion and intuition.[16] In the present design, mathematical operations were used through computation to marry the resolution of functional requirements to the qualification of a particular aesthetic response and experience.

The first geometrical move was to depart from an ideal circle to a quatrefoil, thus providing one central and four peripheral spaces, while still minimizing the walking distances between check-in and gate. The quatrefoil was slightly distorted in response to the site, and its curving perimeter defined as a series of cotangential arcs of variable radius. In this way, the shape could be adjusted to

OPPOSITE Bird's-eye view of the quatrefoil.

RIGHT The circle transformed to a quatrefoil: extremities are aligned with the runways; curvature is determined by air-bridge spacing, and points of inflection are located between bays.

accommodate the first spatial parameter – the number of adjacent parking bays needed for the plane fleet at the gates. Each point of inflection between concave and convex arcs occurs at a bay division.

The main goal was to achieve spatial and material continuity.[17] To this end, the main hall has a huge, continuous curving roof, supported on a series of long-span, arching parabolic steel trusses, which leave a flexible footprint for planning and changing the functional layout of the hall. Smooth, longitudinal curvature in the departures hall – governed by a series of law curves, variable during the design process – was used as a guiding and orienting device for passengers and for setting up other geometry. Each lateral line of leaning parabolic arches is unique, as are their springing points, which are also set up to be variable in the design model. The lateral roof profile is a series of opposed cotangential arcs, supported on the structural arches.

The four piers of the quatrefoil plan are roofed by a parametric surface with a radial argument in the transversal direction (intersecting arcs), and a sinusoidal argument in the longitudinal direction. The roof and façades are one continuous surface, which repeatedly dips down almost to apron height in order to allow connections to the gates, and lifts up to accommodate large view windows in an undulating, periodic pattern. The windows in the façades are inclined at 14.75° towards the exterior, reducing the incidence of direct sunlight.

• Curvature (p. 255)
• Functional surfaces (p. 259)

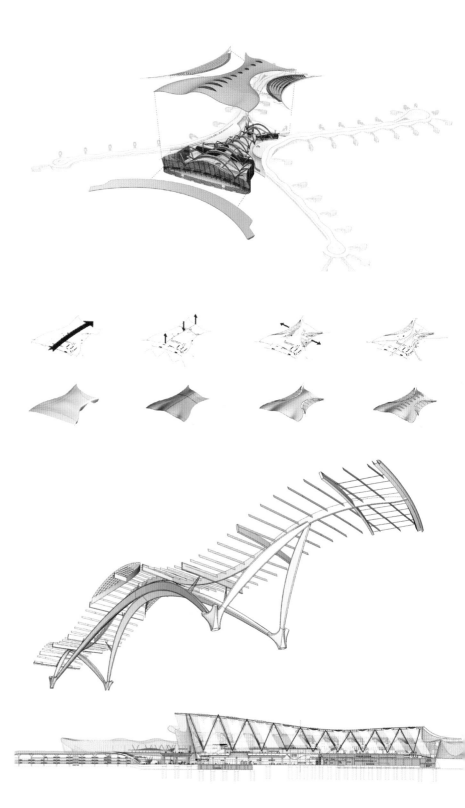

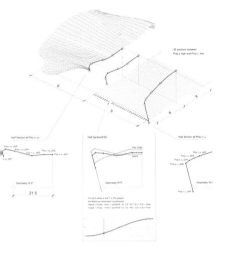

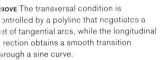

ABOVE The transversal condition is controlled by a polyline that negotiates a set of tangential arcs, while the longitudinal direction obtains a smooth transition through a sine curve.

ABOVE, RIGHT The leaning parabolic arches of the structure of the main hall.

RIGHT Periodic envelope.

BELOW Roof section.

BELOW, RIGHT Entrance to the terminal.

OPPOSITE, FROM TOP The central massing and its principles; the architects' primary and secondary structural proposal; section, showing the arches.

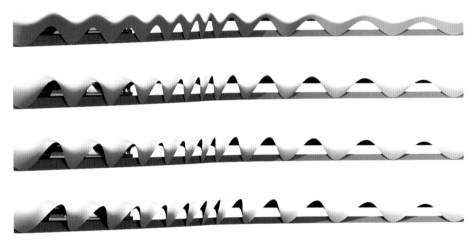

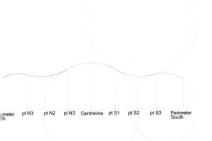

2 CHAOS, COMPLEXITY, EMERGENCE

'Complexity' is a term that has been widely used to mean anything that is not simple, but it does have many discipline-specific definitions. In this chapter, we focus on the behaviour of complex systems when applied to architecture. A key idea in complexity theory is that of small, simple parts, which are replicated, combined or changed, following simple rules. After a number of iterations, the result is a diverse system whose future state is not easily predictable. The system itself gives back new information from simple inputs. In architecture, this idea provides opportunities for analogical inference directly from other processes, including self-organizing systems in nature that result in spatial form and materiality. Architects look to living organisms that acquire their complex forms and behaviour patterns through the interactions of their components in space, sometimes over long periods of time.[1] D'Arcy Thompson famously demonstrated the convergence between the physical and biological sciences through the mathematical processes that govern form, shape, growth and scale. Architecture takes up these processes in bio- or geomimesis, but the mathematical principles can be abstracted to be applied in ways not dependent on the direct analogy, allowing system descriptions without direct metaphorical or geometrical reference to nature. Indeed, emergence is a key concept in disciplines outside the natural sciences that are grounded in empirical knowledge.

In architecture, complexity is not just a mathematical idea to be appropriated from science and the natural world or systems theory, and reapplied in design. It is also an inherent quality of the constructed world, most apparent in the patterns of growth and development of human settlement. These patterns may be ancient, but this mathematical approach to seeing and understanding them is more recent. In city-making, it is an interesting cosmological, organizational and geometrical shift in perspective to engage with the city bottom–up, from the discrete granular forces from which it unfolds, rather than top–down, in the manner familiar from 19th-century planning and, even more so, Modernist planning.

Michael Batty observed that, since 1990, the concern for more micro-issues, for thinking of cities in terms of the actions of individuals, came from another area entirely: ideas about disaggregation and heterogeneity.[2] Batty uses these ideas in city simulation, studying emergence through cells (representing the physical and spatial structure of the city), and through agents (representing the human and social units that make the city work). He argues for the existence of the fractal city, hallmarked by self-similarity and order on all scales, and links city growth explicitly to sensitivity to initial conditions, to bifurcations and chaos theory. This is qualified, however, by the observation that the rates of growth are generally too low to exhibit the dramatic manifestations of chaotic behaviour that might be seen in other systems. The point is that the systems' mathematics and the speed of digital computation have provided a new power with which to simulate the complex evolution of settlement patterns, even in the multifarious modern city. Such an approach has both analytical and generative potential. What does a similar focus and process mean, in terms of aesthetics, materiality and responsiveness, at the scale of the individual architectural project?

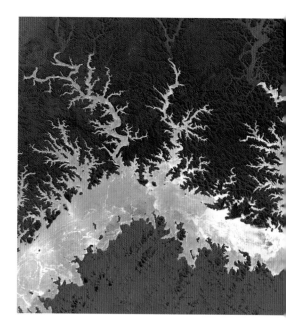

- Aesthetics: Pattern is our currency in understanding and interpreting the world, and there is an argument that the fractal dimension of pattern, its number of self-similar levels of scale, has value for our own spatial and intuitive mathematical engagement and enrichment.[3] Complexity in architecture returns to the senses (and to the intellect via the senses) what the reductivism of Modernism and the aesthetic of machine production has stripped away.[4]
- Materiality: There is a sophisticated argument that is well articulated by Michael Hensel, Achim Menges, and others about the lessons to be learnt from the efficiency and economy of material production from natural systems. Every child knows that a spider's silk is far stronger in relation to its diameter than a steel cable. Natural systems display higher-level integration and functionality, evolving from a dynamic feedback relationship with a specific environment.[5] They are our first recourse in generating new materials.

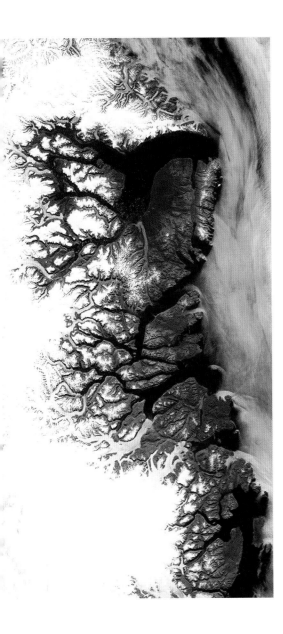

- Responsiveness: Emergence and optimization are not always distant cousins. A system in which the inputs and initial conditions can be adequately represented, and an appropriate procedure defined, will reveal formal and spatial relations that are not premeditated. This promises potentially novel environmental responses. The trick would be in being able to design a system that truly represents the systems of the environmental performance being investigated.

Self-organization raises the question of control. Where is the designer in a self-organizing system? The designer is, of course, the genetic engineer. Tinkering with the system, designing through iterative modification of the genetic algorithm (the procedural component), he shapes the process rather than directly determining the outcomes. This raises questions about discrimination. If the designer is designing the design of the design, how does he discriminate between the different results of this process?

Mathematical concepts

Chaos theory is far from the theory of total disorder that its name suggests. The so-called chaotic behaviour of systems was first discovered in the 1890s by Henri Poincaré, who, while studying the problem of three attracting and repelling bodies, found orbits that were neither periodic nor ever-increasing, nor approaching a fixed state. At around the same time, Jacques Hadamard published a study of the chaotic motion of a free particle gliding without friction on a surface of constant negative curvature.

Perhaps the best-known actor in the drama of chaos theory is Edward Norton Lorenz. In the 1960s, Lorenz created a simplified model that represented predictions about air flows causing weather. It was a recursive system with variables, and could be left to run overnight. In attempting to repeat a particular cycle, Lorenz discovered the significance of small changes to the starting values: the input of a reduced number of decimal places for the value of a particular starting value resulted, after many iterations, in completely different weather predictions. This phenomenon has become known as the 'butterfly effect', from the idea that the beat of a butterfly's wing in one part of the country could result in the formation of a tornado in another, at another time. Chaotic systems have a number of general characteristics: they are non-linear; deterministic, rather than probabilistic;[6] sensitive to initial conditions; and exhibit sustained irregularity (order in disorder).

One of the most important concepts in complexity is recursion, a method of defining functions in which the function being defined is applied within its own definition. Thus within a procedure, one of the steps is to run the whole procedure again; in other words, the output of applying the function becomes the input of the next iteration. The Fibonacci sequence

CLOCKWISE, FROM TOP LEFT Satellite views of the fractal water course and land formations of Lake Nasser, Egypt; the fractal coastline and river system of Greenland; Muscat, Oman.

PRECEDING PAGE Klondike Gold Rush National Historic Park, Alaska and Washington.

is a well-known mathematical example in which a number is the sum of the two previous numbers in the sequence, each of which is the sum of the two before it, and so on.

The term 'fractal' was coined by Benoît Mandelbrot to describe the geometry of the highly fragmented forms of nature that were perceived as amorphous (such as trees and clouds), and not easily represented in Euclidean geometry. A second aspect of fractal geometry is its recognition of the practically infinite number of distinct scales exhibited by units of length in patterns in nature. Thirdly, fractals involve chance, their regularities and irregularities being statistical. And finally, they engage the Hausdorff-Besicovitch dimension, an effective measure of complexity, scalar diversity or fragmentation. (The mathematical definition of a fractal is a set for which the Hausdorff-Besicovitch dimension strictly exceeds the topological dimension.) Emergence is very evident in the behaviour of cellular automata like John Horton Conway's Game of Life (1970), a game without human players that is played by establishing initial conditions and standing back to see how it evolves. The key idea of emergence is that it gives something new, more than that which is put into it.

Complexity in architecture

The interest in complexity science and fractal geometry in architecture dates back to the translation into English of Mandelbrot's essay *Les Objets fractals: forme, hasard et dimension* (1975), and subsequent book *The Fractal Geometry of Nature* (1977), in which he combined intuitive metaphorical description with a highly mathematical text. In the 1980s, architect Peter Eisenman adopted the idea of fractal geometry in metaphorical and iconic ways in his Biocenter for the J. W. Goethe University in Frankfurt. While the building has no obviously fractal aesthetic or extrinsic reading, it makes reference to an abstract idea of fractal ordering in its design process.

It is the architects of more recent years who have taken up not only complexity theory, but also the underlying principles of complexity and fractal geometry directly in the generation of systems. These systems are practically buildable based on a recent, more engaged approach in architectural design to digital computation and the possibility of rapid iteration. But the complexity in the projects in these pages is not born exclusively of digital engagement. In some cases, it is a deep faith in this bottom–up, systemic approach to meaningful pattern-making.

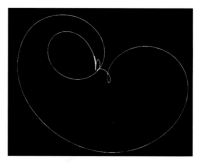

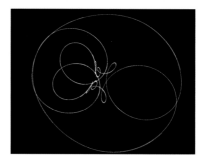

ABOVE AND OPPOSITE Edward Norton Lorenz's beautifully simple equation to demonstrate the chaotic behaviour of dynamic systems. Although moving the initial orbit won't affect the shape of a strange attractor, the position of the orbit on the attractor after several iterations will vary considerably from one position to the other.

There are four parameters: A, B, C and dT. Interesting attractors can be found with a relatively high value for dT, i.e. dT > 0.3.
1. A. 0.611211 B. 6.102531 C. 2.405063 dT. 0.357994
2. A. 0.611211 B. 6.202531 C. 2.405063 dT. 0.357994
3. A. 0.632911 B. 6.202531 C. 2.405063 dT. 0.355794
4. A. 0.632911 B. 6.202531 C. 2.405063 dT. 0.357994

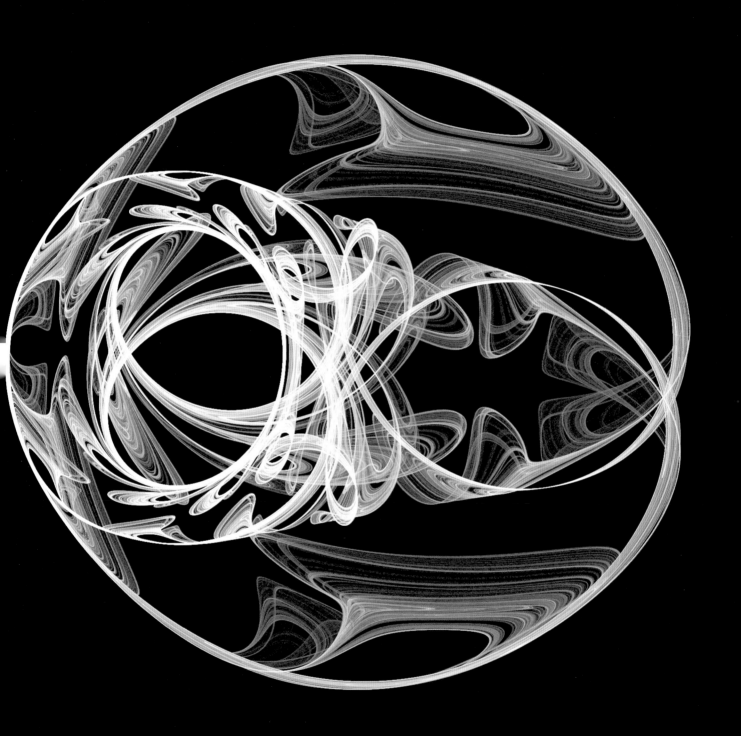

Federation Square
LAB ARCHITECTURE STUDIO
Melbourne, Australia

This design for a public space to mark the centenary of the federation of Australian states (an important step in creating a nation from its parts) is a story that reflects at every level the shift in geometry from top–down to bottom–up, encapsulated by complexity theory and fractal geometry. Melbourne-based Lab Architecture Studio's entry was one of five short-listed designs in the first stage of an international design competition in 1996; the firm partnered with the Australian practice Bates Smart to win the second stage the following year. The finished space opened in 2002, the year after the centenary.

'Architecture's desire towards geometry', wrote Peter Davidson and Donald Bates of Lab, 'is for substantiation by both a material and sensory discourse, and at the same time by an abstract and cognitive formation'.[7] Out of their research for the Federation Square design grew an investigation into

geometrical patterns that allowed for repetition (in terms of constructional elements), as well as differentiation in the composed surfaces of the building. The fractal self-similarity of the panels became a vital quality in achieving coherence and difference to the façades.[8] In the façades of those buildings that define the public spaces there is an almost iconic representation of self-similarity: the $1:2:\sqrt{5}$ triangles that combine in 5s to create larger triangles and, therefore, five of these into the next scale of the same proportion, are an intellectually graspable and simply constructable motif that is nevertheless combined in ways that generate relentless difference and absence of repetition across the whole site.

In the plan and programmatic distribution – the 'square' is surrounded by a host of offices, cultural institutions (including the BMW Edge performance space), restaurants, bars and specialist

LEFT Conceptual pencil sketch by Donald Bates: 'A notation for a new type of spatial ordering.'

OPPOSITE South façade.

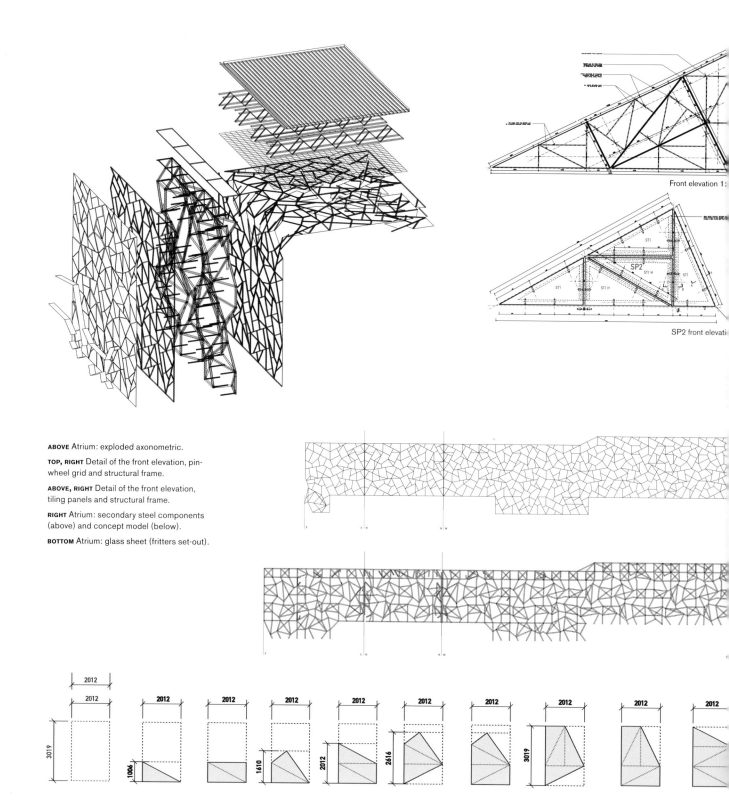

ABOVE Atrium: exploded axonometric.

TOP, RIGHT Detail of the front elevation, pin-wheel grid and structural frame.

ABOVE, RIGHT Detail of the front elevation, tiling panels and structural frame.

RIGHT Atrium: secondary steel components (above) and concept model (below).

BOTTOM Atrium: glass sheet (fritters set-out).

Front elevation 1:

SP2 front elevati

shops – this complexity and multiplicity from simple component elements is less easily read, but powerfully felt. Geometry as the 'measure and image of a sensate world'[9] and geometry as the 'conceptual ordering that affirms its relevance in spite of the sensory world'[10] are almost tangibly present and experienced through the senses as much as through the intellect.

In the glazed, covered atrium that provides the cool counterpoint to the plaza, and in the BMW Edge amphitheatre, the same geometrical motif continues in the internal and external steel structure that supports the glazing. But here the unitary nature of the generative component is less readable: every edge is not present. The variation between the internal and external patterns and between the elements that link their nodes creates, in the steel square sections that mark these geometrical etchings, a boscage through which light is filtered in a way that is powerfully suggestive of the complexity or organic precedents cited by Benoît Mandelbrot as calling for fractal geometry for their description.

• Fractals (p. 258)

TOP Night view of the BMW Edge from the bank of the Yarra River.

ABOVE The glazed façade of the BMW Edge, showing the arboreal effect of the offset of the internal and external glazing set-outs and web members.

RIGHT Concept model of the atrium.

Louvre Abu Dhabi

ATELIERS JEAN NOUVEL
Abu Dhabi, UAE

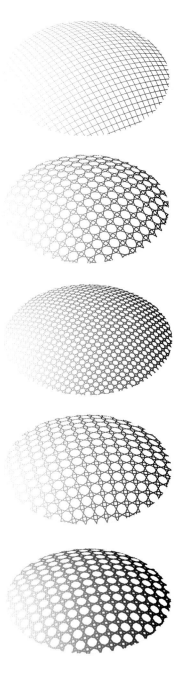

The Louvre Abu Dhabi is planned as the centrepiece of a new tourist and cultural development on Saadiyat Island, opposite the city. The French government has agreed to provide the Louvre's name, as well as art loans, special exhibitions and management advice. Earmarked as 'a world-class destination that bridges global cultures', the new building has been conceived, by the architects, as a lost city recovered archaeologically from the sands, a cluster of simple buildings that will give visitors the sense of entering another world.

A large, shallow dome, 180m in diameter, floats above the collection of buildings, with only four support points around its perimeter truss. The dome unites this micro-city, and takes up the Islamic tradition of the perforated screen and the use of self-similarity and fractal organization of patterning to create a special micro-climate below. The space beneath is animated by

the shadow play caused by the modulation of light by the complex, lacy mesh of small openings across the dome's surface, reflected on the buildings and the water of the inlet.

The exploration and design development of the dome's patterning and relationship to the environment it creates, as well as the lighting levels, shading, structural performance and variation of density across the surface, is an interesting tale of integrated modelling, analysis and optimization. The pattern results from the superimposition of the layers of the structure and the external and internal cladding. Within the parametric design model developed by the SMART group at Büro Happold, it was possible to play with the relative scale and rotation of each pattern overlay to vary the overall outcome. Based on a rectilinear grid across the dome surface, each layer (the structural space-frame and the four layers of cladding) have

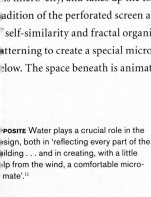

OPPOSITE Water plays a crucial role in the design, both in 'reflecting every part of the building . . . and in creating, with a little help from the wind, a comfortable micro-climate'.[11]

RIGHT, TOP TO BOTTOM The Great Circle grid and primary parameters: basic pattern element; rotation; scale; and member width.

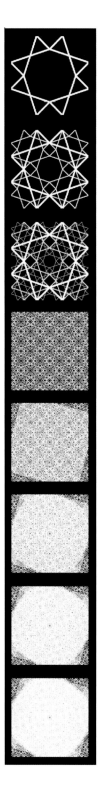

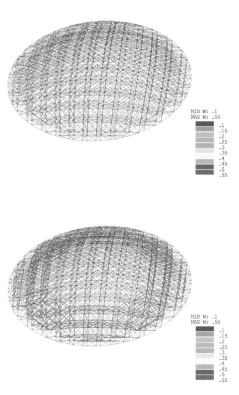

MIN W: .1
MAX W: .55

.1
.15
.2
.25
.3
.35
.4
.45
.5
.55

MIN W: .1
MAX W: .55

.1
.15
.2
.25
.3
.35
.4
.45
.5
.55

FAR LEFT Fractal pattern.

LEFT Structural optimization ensures that just the right amount of material is placed where it is needed.

RIGHT Exploded construction section, detailing the relationship between the primary structural space-frame and the multi-layer façade.

BELOW Illustration of the automated pattern-generation process and translucency analysis.

OPPOSITE Comparison of two generated dome models, with varying levels of light transmission.

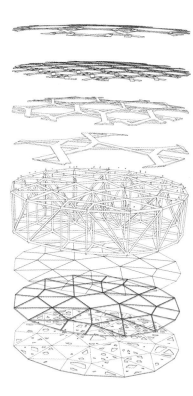

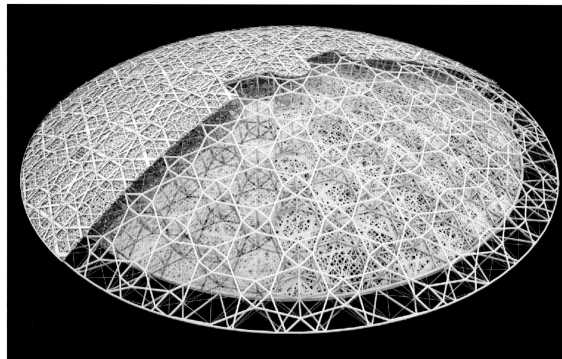

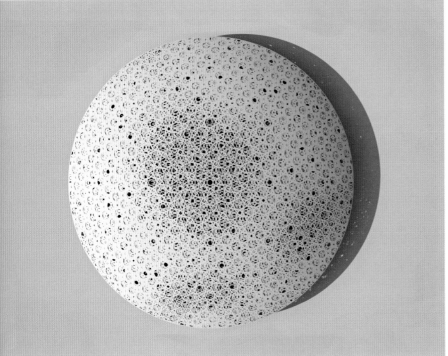

a basic pattern schema. In each case, the orientation and scale can be varied. The widths of the solid pattern members can be varied to alter the occlusion of light, as well as differentially across the dome to graduate the opacity between the different areas. Each of these separate elements inherits from the same base pattern, with their precise geometry controlled through the five primary parameters: grid, base pattern, rotational orientation, scale and member thickness. From this base pattern of simple geometric elements, a rich, aesthetic complexity emerges. Here, it does so in response to the optimization for the lighting levels beneath the dome and the structural sizing of the members.

The seemingly complex and random geometry of the perforated dome is achieved, and, in fact, emerges naturally, from performance criteria, the standardization of components, and consideration of fabrication constraints. This complex aesthetic is an expression of its performance in occluding light and economy of support,[12] and is designed to work in tandem with the natural environment.

• Chaos theory (p. 254)
• Complexity theory (p. 254)
• Emergence (p. 256)
• Fractals (p. 258)

The simulated effects of
light through the dome.

Jyväskylä Music and Arts Centre

OCEAN NORTH

Jyväskylä, Finland

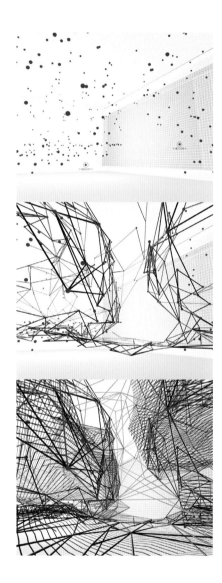

The aim of this project was to create a differentiated event space and extend the landscaped town square into an animated interior that catered for music events, art exhibitions, and other cultural activities. The lattice structure and surfaces that define the building's interior allow for ad-hoc stages, seating and exhibition areas, while creating a dynamically articulated space of acoustic and visual intensities. The lattices are locally sound active, extending the acoustic experience beyond the music hall and rehearsal rooms into the interior landscape of the building volume.

The layered envelope consists of a transparent and reflective skin. Light conditions affect the layered gradients of reflection and transparency, which yield the perception of an area that is deep and boundless. The directionality, density and layering of the lattices, and the surfaces and volumes that evolve from it, result in

a locally differentiated yet vast space. The architects deployed an iterative growth process to articulate the lattices, informed by rules pertaining to the location, orientation and density of the struts that make up the lattice systems; the structural, sonic and luminous performance requirements; and the spatial design guidelines. The resulting systems informed the geometries of the terrain, structure and envelopes of the primary and secondary spaces and surface areas, the circulation pattern and the sound active system.

The growth process began with the definition and distribution of the virtual volumes. A series of gradient maps, organized along the X, Y and Z planes that delimit the growth area for the various lattice systems, informed the process with performative requirements. Such maps constrain the local search space for each strut of the system in terms of size and

LEFT Animated sequence showing the development of the lattice structure.

OPPOSITE Laser-cut model of the design study.

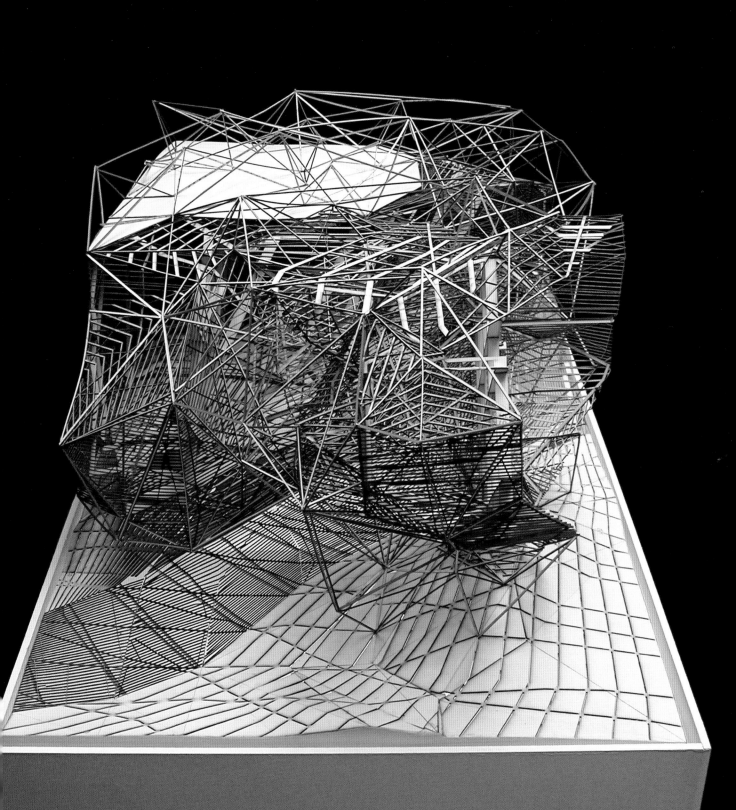

search angle. Here, the gradient maps were based on structural performance, as well as on the modulation of the micro-environments of the interstitial space between the outer envelope of the building and the envelopes of the various spaces not to be intersected by the lattice system. Subsequently, a first set of definition points and search rules were defined, which distributed and oriented the struts that make up the primary system in response to the outlined rule-set. From this system, a second set of virtual surfaces were derived on which a new set of definition points could be defined. In further iterations, secondary and tertiary systems were evolved that defined mesh-like enclosures for the required internal volumes, circulation and sound-active systems.

While the iterative growth process was informed by performance requirements, the synergetic impact of the various systems working together needed to be analyzed in stages. Digital structural and luminous performance analysis was repeatedly conducted in order to evaluate the emerging conditions and synergies between the systems. From the differential density and angular variation of the lattice systems, together with the varied distribution of sound-active elements, a spatial and ambient differentiation of the scheme evolved: a heterogeneous space, in which the augmented differentiation would allow for choices between micro-environmental conditions, which in turn would provide for the time-specific requirements of the inhabitants.

• Complexity theory (p. 254)
• Emergence (p. 256)

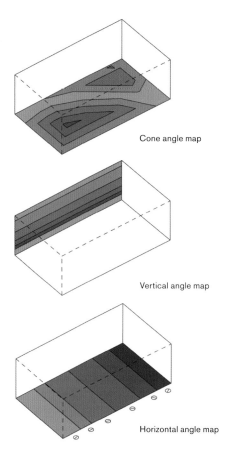

Cone angle map

Vertical angle map

Horizontal angle map

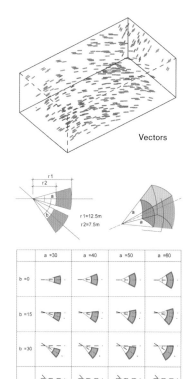

Vectors

ABOVE The diagrams show the strategic constraints of the growth process, including the local search windows that determine the angles of each strut of the lattice in relation to the connection with the neighbouring struts (right), as well as the gradient maps that allocate search window constraints to regions within the building envelope (left).

LEFT Perspective view of the interstitial space between and below the volumes of the music hall and rehearsal rooms along the main public circulation trajectory.

OPPOSITE Side view of the laser-cut model.

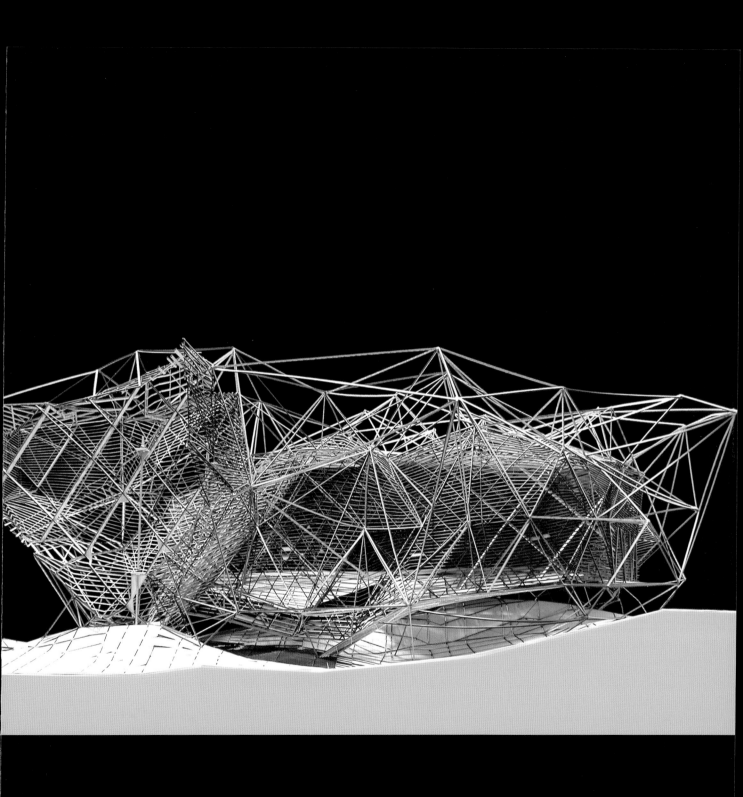

Seroussi Pavilion
BIOTHING
Paris, France

Alisa Andrasek's practice Biothing has engaged and sponsored a field of enquiry into emergence in architecture. There is no clear scientific definition of the concept, although its essence has been described by John Holland as 'a lot coming from a little'.[13] As with the concept of complexity, some very low-level rules can lead to high levels of sophistication through self-organization.[14] Once these rules have been instituted, formal organization emerges by letting the system run. Recursion and the interaction of networked, small systems can lead to surprising, unpredictable emergent results.

The originality of Biothing's work stems from their investigations into potential formal organization at macro-level, as well as the emergence of synthetic architectural matter. While 'emergent phenomena are always aesthetic phenomena',[15] there is an interest in the combined performative and expressive potential of this design approach.

The practice has explored the potential of recursive and responsive algorithms that mirror but diverge strangely from emergent processes in nature.[16] They generate new and mesmerizing systems and material outcomes from the seed of simple, computer-coded inputs and rules. While the work is not focused on static outcomes (rather, there is the sense of a potent and quasi-organic foment), its materialization is significant, and there is an important exchange between physical embodiment and its computational eye of creation. Ideas such as the 'gene library' and the contribution of atomic and sub-atomic interactions to the macro world are fundamental here. These experiments have engaged a variety of different software programming environments and collaborative team dynamics.

With the Seroussi Pavilion, the emergent outcome is indeed a building, one in which Parisian gallerist Natalie Seroussi can 'live

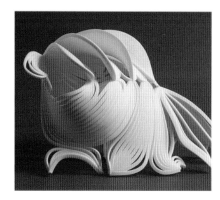

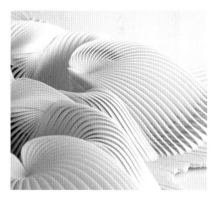

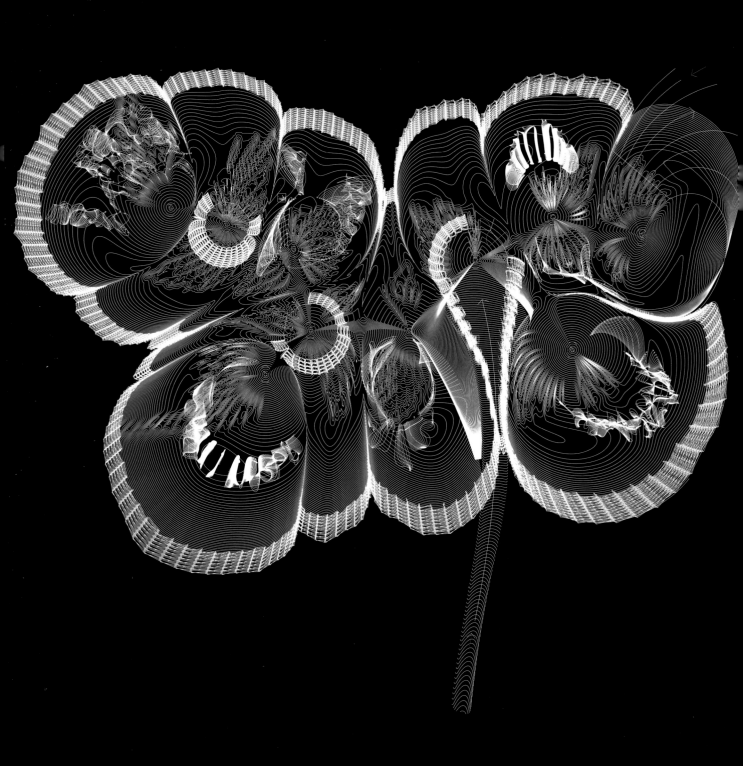

OPPOSITE Plan cross-section of the pavilion, showing the spatial differentiation within and the 'lemon fleshiness' of the formal outcome.

RIGHT Aerial perspective, demonstrating the varying densities of programme.

BELOW Details of the physical models with differing textures in surface skins.

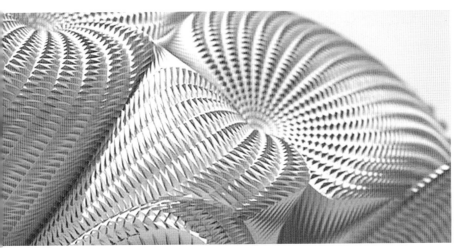

with art'. Living with and the exhibition of art were to be interlaced in changing and fluctuating rhythms. This rich programmatic density is translated to material expression through a scripted, computer-realized design process. The programme itself models self-changing electromagnetic fields, the interaction of attractions and repulsions from which the plan emerges.

This is an idea inspired by subatomic physics and the existence of mesons (unstable particles comprised of a quark and an antiquark combined, and predicted by the theoretical physicist Hideki Yukawa – work for which he won the Nobel prize in 1949). Appropriated from physics to architecture, the meson becomes a metaphor of in-between states, potentials and intermingling relationships. Within the computer script, the plan that emerges, likened by its author to the density and consistency of fruit flesh, is integrated with sinusoidal functions of different frequencies that govern the section through the building. The script also implants the structure responsively onto the profile of the steep, hilly site.

• Complexity theory (p. 254)
• Emergence (p. 256)

3 PACKING AND TILING

The two mathematical ideas in the title of this chapter are closely bound together by two more generic considerations: space-filling and symmetry. Space-filling is really about subdividing space in ways that leave as little as possible, or nothing at all, unaccounted for, even if that subdivision continues to infinity. And symmetry takes on its most encompassing meaning – rather than just its most familiar manifestations in Euclidean geometry (mirror, rotational and translational symmetry) – when size does not matter, when the same parts repeat, the same shape is found at many scales, and there are underlying patterns that bear witness to the deeper connections between things. As is frequently the case, mathematics seeks out the hidden truths, while architecture applies this knowledge, flirtatiously exploiting and subverting.

The interest of mathematicians in packing has little to do with the heterogeneous packing of disparate objects in suitcases and fridges, as Denis Weaire has pointed out, or even with the spaces in architectural plans and sections, but is motivated from two directions: being able to establish the number of similar objects in a stack of the same (the cannon balls on Sir Walter Raleigh's ships, for example), and to develop a better understanding of the structure of materials at molecular and atomic scale.

When shuffling similarly sized coins on a table top, we can quickly arrive at the triangular/hexagonal, two-dimensional pattern that covers the smallest part of the table (the densest packing), but it is not so easy to *prove* that this is a general global result. Here lies the mathematical challenge. Stacking oranges results in the elegant tetrahedral structures displayed at a traditional greengrocer's. But the tetrahedra themselves do not tessellate in three dimensions; the angles of the planes intersecting in each apex do not allow them to meet without interstitial space, so there is no close packing for oranges stacked in such a way that can be extended infinitely in three dimensions. The ratio of orange to space is reduced in extending the packing beyond the tetrahedron. These are the concerns of mathematicians who strive to be able to determine such ratios at a fine level of precision.

What has this to do with architecture? Architects, too, have to find ways of subdividing space that leaves nothing within the boundaries unused. The constraints are different, and as related to the substance and fabrication of spatial partition as to the precise repetition of shape or volume within the individual cells. The cells themselves may be the habitable spaces of the building, as in the auditorium proposal for the Battersea Power Station (p. 82), or the cells of a structural space-frame that give back and allow for the servicing of large, enclosed spaces, unencumbered by structural support, such as those of the Water Cube for the 2008 Beijing Olympics (p. 86). In architectural design, there is a long tradition of harnessing relatively regular periodic packing regimes: orthogonal structural grids, repetitive space-frame units. This chapter exposes how recent architecture has explored the adoption of some younger mathematical discoveries, including aperiodic tiling (patterns that have a small number of repeating units, but whose arrangement is such that the resulting pattern, unlike orthogonal or hexagonal grids, cannot be superimposed upon itself through translation). Here is an element of mystery and wonder, of intrigue and hope: patterns that can be known by their generators, but never known top–down in a stultifying or all-encompassing way – their manifestation by its nature unpredictable, offering visual and aesthetic sustenance. This is new food for the senses and the intellect.

Tiling is an architectural tradition too ancient to confidently identify its earliest origins, where two-dimensional shapes (and two-and-a-half-dimensional shapes; relief is also a feature of sophisticated tiling traditions) are used to cover the surfaces of built interiors and exteriors. Ceramic, plaster, brick, stone and timber, repeating regular units and collections of shapes, or irregular elements resolved within a jigsaw composition: these are all familiar elements in architectural spaces. Small collections of regular tiles that cover the surface to infinity without gaps in aperiodic patterns have been adopted from the published work of Roger Penrose

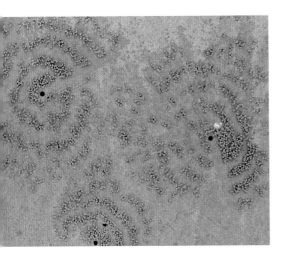

and Robert Ammann to apply creatively in design for the built world and, in some instances, corrupted to enjoy its flawed nature. There is another line of inquiry seen in these projects: the symmetry that transcends scale and metrical dimension. In fractal subdivision, shapes can be subdivided into smaller-scale tiles that replicate the shapes found at the starting scale. Conversely, this can manifest through the assemblage of tiles of one or a small collection of shapes to reform their shape at larger scale. Many of the projects in this chapter engage either aperiodicity or fractal geometry, or combine the two to enrich the level of surface variability; Daniel Libeskind's Spiral Extension (p. 98) for the Victoria & Albert Museum in London is a striking example.

The built projects here tell a further spatial, or surface, subdivision story. It is a highly generic tale: the definition of cells or tiles associated with points scattered or patterned across two-dimensional or three-dimensional spaces. A set of points has an associated pattern of cells for which every point within a particular cell is closer to one of the points than to any other point. This subdivision of space can be a two-dimensional net of polygons, or may need more complex spatial representation if it represents, for instance, the intersecting fields of gravitational attraction of neighbouring objects in space (such as the field of shapes that sand falls into around neighbouring holes created by burrowing crabs). Every point within a given cell is not equivalent; there is a sense in which the points closest to the cell boundaries are associated with greater potential energy than those close to the gravitational centre of each cell. These patterns collectively belong to a theory of mathematical subdivision known as Voronoi patterns, after Georgy Voronoi (1868–1908), or Dirichlet tessellations, after Lejeaune Dirichlet (1805–59). While they were formalized (in n-dimensions, just to illustrate what a mathematical business this was) by Voronoi, they had been known and used earlier, including informally by Descartes. In this case, it is not the tiling or subdivision of a repeating shape or group of shapes that is the issue, but the mapping of a distribution of points (regardless of whether they are located as singular sites of particular significance, or organized according to an overriding pattern) to a subdivision of a two-dimensional surface or three-dimensional space into contiguous cells related to those point sites. At Minifie Nixon's Centre for Ideas (p. 112), in Melbourne, Australia, we see the theory taken up in the façade and interior composition. But it might equally be applied to relationships of space-planning to social spatial behaviour in building and urban design.

Packing has already been referred to as the subdivision of space in which as little space as possible, or none, is left over. This is an intriguing idea that alludes to an aspiration to perfection, and perhaps spawned the title of Denis Weaire and Tomas Aste's book, *The Pursuit of Perfect Packing*. One of the topics the book describes is the move of mathematical investigation away from defining the densest packing as that which achieves the greatest density in a three-dimensional array of similar objects, to the more subtle question of how deformable bubbles of fixed and similar volume might comport themselves in space to minimize their collective surface area. In other words, how would a foam of similar adjacent bubbles, sharing surfaces, fill all the space while the individual cells remained as close as possible to spherical? This question was effectively posed by Sir William Thomson (later Lord Kelvin) in 1887. In 1900, David Hilbert's eighteenth problem, among twenty-three, asked: how can an infinite number of equal solids of given form be arranged most densely in space, or, how can they be fitted together so that the ratio of the filled to the unfilled space may be as great as possible? Johannes Kepler had conjectured that no other arrangement of regular spheres in space would have a greater average density than cubic close packing and hexagonal close packing (a little over 74 per cent). What is interesting is that the solution to these problems is far from absolutely resolved. Many have attempted to find one, and proofs have run to so many pages as to be unverifiable. The Weaire-Phelan packing model improved on Lord Kelvin's proposal by only 0.3 per cent, a figure that immediately highlights the greyness of the area in which that problem lies. So, even proposed packings of objects or shaping of space-filling spaces idealized to be regular are lacking in the sort of rational perfection sought by the mathematicians of Ancient Greece. Rather than perfection, we see improvement by subtle measures.

Architecture, while it is less concerned with generalizability than with mathematics, has had a close interest in standardization to satisfy the industrial thirst for regular components. But as we see in some of the projects that follow, it is the expressive potential of imperfection and of breaking rules often exploited in built work that draws on mathematical ideas of composition. Information is in difference; we are intrigued by the crystalline in the context of its mineral faults and disorder.

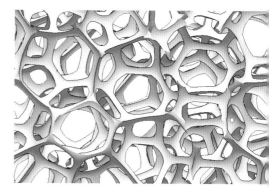

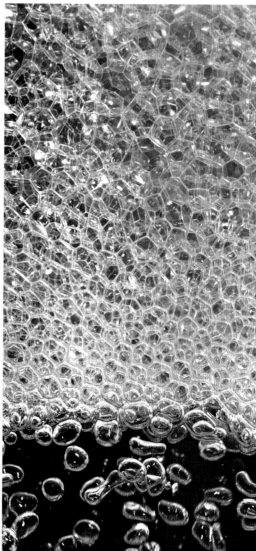

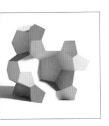

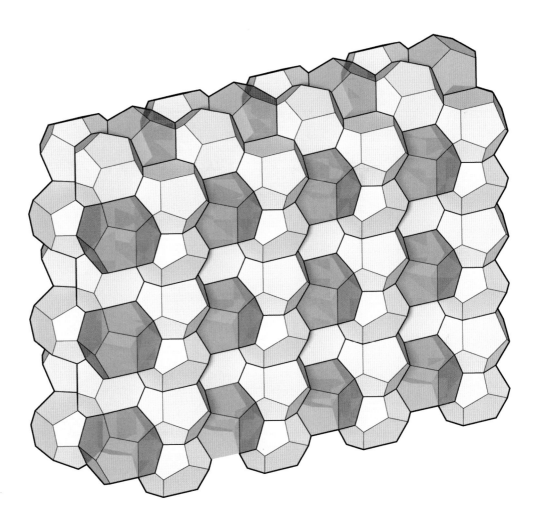

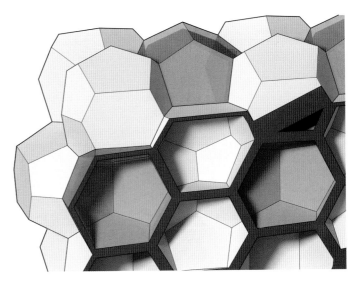

THIS PAGE Weaire-Phelan packing: the 14-faced tetradecahedron, with its two hexagonal and 12 pentagonal faces (grey); the 12-pentagon-faced dodecahedron (pink); and the packing in which they fit together in units of six and two, respectively.

OPPOSITE, TOP Digital representation of the structure of liquid film shapes between gas bubbles in foam.

OPPOSITE, BOTTOM One of Professor Jan Cilliers's photographs of foam.

PRECEDING PAGES Examples from the animal and plant kingdoms reveal nature's propensity for efficiently subdividing space and surfaces.

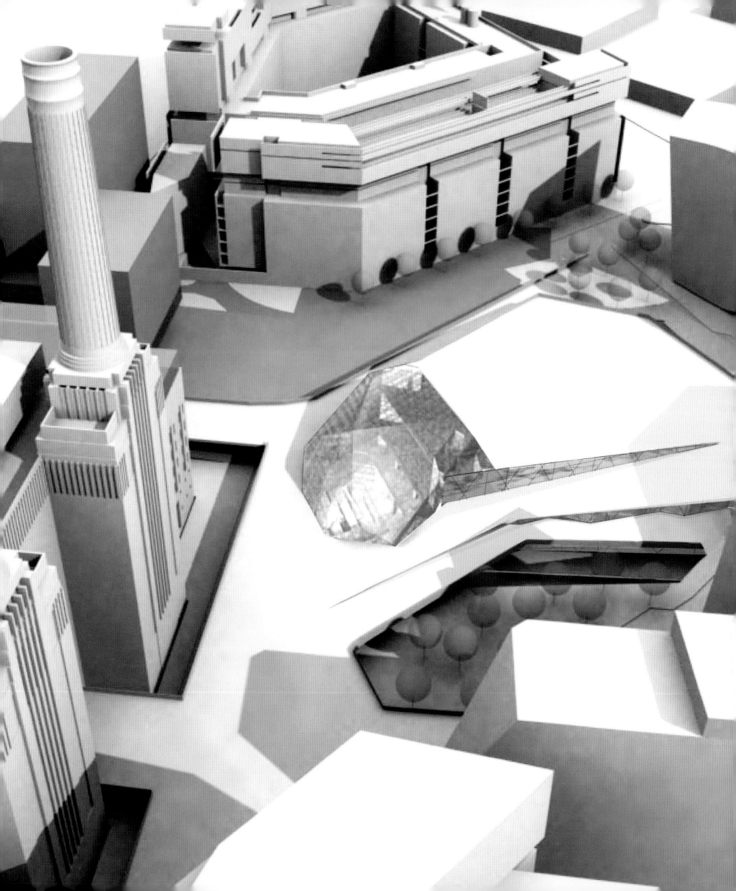

Battersea Power Station
ARUP AGU
London, UK

Arup AGU's proposal for a hexagonal auditorium, sunk into the grounds of the long-obsolete Battersea Power Station, gave full rein to ideas that had been introduced in earlier projects. This was a masterplan relatively unconstrained by site, contextual exigencies or budget. Set against the monumental language of Sir Giles Gilbert Scott's 1930s building, the proposed theatre and surrounding car park would be buried beneath a sloping landscape, with the translucent crystalline eruption from the landscape of the theatre roof and foyers providing an energy-focusing counterpoint.

The form and setting-out of the project combined a number of ideas appropriated from science with respect to the packing structures found in crystals and quasicrystals.[1] Whereas Robert Ammann's aperiodic tiling was deployed in Daniel Libeskind's extension for the Victoria & Albert Museum (p. 98), here the planes were combined with Danzer aperiodic packing, moving the ideas of non-repeating pattern fully into three dimensions. Quasicrystals exhibit long-range orientational order, but no translational symmetry. Taking the traditional practice of designing a building on a grid generated by three sets of intersecting rectilinear planes, a new type of grid was generated with many more planes and unpredictable intervals between them.

The Golden String was used to set up the set-out grids for the auditorium. This is non-periodic. Although recognizable patterns reoccur, the sequence is non-repetitive and, when viewed locally, appears unpredictable. There are two modules in the pattern. A 'short' module will always be flanked on either side by a 'long' module, but it is unpredictable whether long modules will appear in pairs or individually. The short and long modules in the Golden String occur in the ratio of 1 to Phi (the Golden

OPPOSITE Crystal foyer and auditorium: three-dimensional model in context.

RIGHT The crystal's structure consists of load-bearing members of laminated toughened glass. The space-frame is represented as 14 solid polyhedra, with glass on all faces. There are 10 panel types in the external skin and 10 web panel shapes.

Ratio). The resulting grids share the characteristics of musical patterns, being clear and understandable while remaining unpredictable and engaging.[2]

The faceted crystalline patterns of the auditorium roof and foyer can be imagined as being set out from a dodecahedron, which has twelve faces (or six parallel pairs of faces). There are fifteen ways to select a combination of two out of these six, with a choice of one of six planes for the first option, and the five remaining for the second. Half the possible combinations are equivalent, just chosen in the opposite order so that the number is $(6 \times 5) / 2 = 15$. Fifteen new planes are set up, each bisecting one pair of dodecahedron planes, which are intersected with Ammann planes that occur at aperiodic intervals in space. The result is used as the structural setting-out grid for the building, including the glass space-frame of the foyer roof.[3]

The site is set up on an 18m equilateral triangular grid, with one axis aligning with the power station and with the idea of rotational opportunities. The 120° angles are very close to those between the dodecahedron faces. The regular periodic crystalline nature of these areas is set against the quasicrystalline structure of the building. The building and car park, and hence the crystalline and quasicrystalline grids, are separated by deep vertical chasms, bridged at entry points.

• Ammann tiling (p. 253)
• Danzer packing (p. 255)

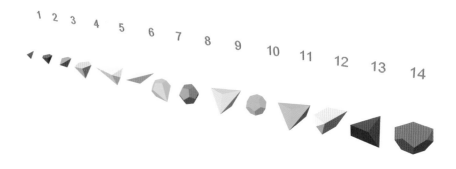

ABOVE The shapes of the 14 solid polyhedral tiles were created by partitioning up the space with the Ammann planes.

BELOW The 14 polyhedral tiles in a tiling.

OPPOSITE, TOP Section.

OPPOSITE, BOTTOM Interior of the foyer.

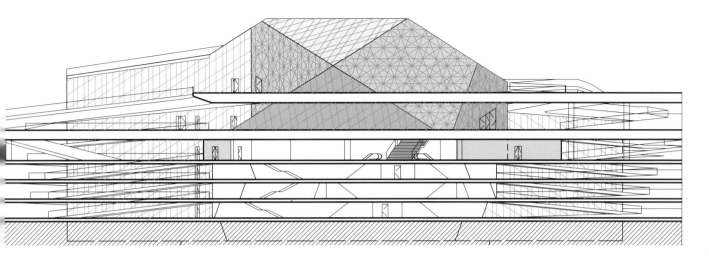

The Water Cube
PTW ARCHITECTS
Beijing, China

Olympic buildings are slaves to the camera. The aquatics centre for the 2008 Beijing Olympics was the subject of an international competition that was won by PTW Architects, who headed a team that included Ove Arup Australasia, the China State Construction Engineering Corporation and the Shenzhen Design Institute, and understood the need for a powerful and iconic aesthetic. The architects proposed a simple symbol for a building that would express water, as well as recycling it: a box of bubbles. It would be a blue box, the counterpart to Herzog and de Meuron's red 'bird's nest' stadium nearby.

Arup drove a compelling technical agenda, proposing an insulated greenhouse clad in Ethylene-tetrafluoroethylene (ETFE), which would minimize the use of energy needed to heat the pool throughout the year.[4] The light weight of ETFE, at 1 per cent of the equivalent weight of glass, would eliminate the need for a secondary structure, further reducing the weight and embodied energy of the building materials. The bubble-like ETFE cushions would passively 'collect' 20 per cent of the solar energy falling on them, the equivalent energy gain of cladding much of the building in photovoltaic cells. The greatest challenge was to find a structure that would uniformly fill the three-dimensional space between the external and internal skins, without resorting to the familiar triangulated space-frame: a new type of frame geometry, resulting in a naturalistic sea of bubbles of varying size and shape on the cladding.[5]

Intriguingly, the designers found a partial answer to this problem in an idea about uniform crystalline packing, borrowed from mathematics. Soap-film bubbles were the starting point, the inspiration for the question posed by Lord Kelvin in 1887: what space-filling arrangement of similar cells,

Exterior of the Water Cube, clearly showing the packing of the ETFE cushions.

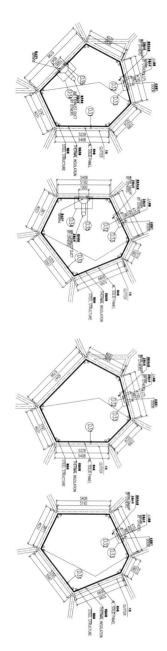

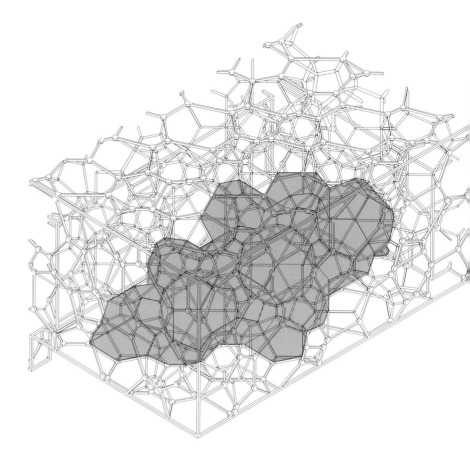

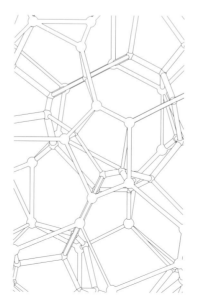

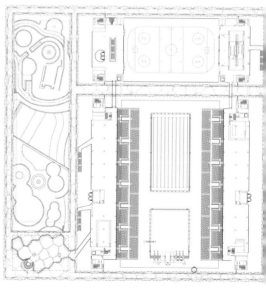

ABOVE Construction drawings showing variable dimensions of individual 'cells'.

ABOVE, RIGHT Restaurant zone isometric.

RIGHT Weaire-Phelan model packing.

FAR RIGHT Plan.

OPPOSITE, TOP The steel space-frame.

OPPOSITE, BOTTOM Interior view of the restaurant.

of similar volume, has minimal surface area? The latest in a long line of solutions is Denis Weaire and Robert Phelan's 1993 model, a repeating unit of eight irregular polyhedra, six fourteen-faced and two twelve-faced. Here, the edges of these polyhedra became the centre lines of the steel structural members of a Vierendeel space-frame.[6] The polyhedra were modified from the strict Weaire-Phelan model, exchanging cells of equal volume for a simpler, more repetitive arrangement of edges and nodes.[7]

In the virtual design model, the polyhedral bubble cells were arrayed in a horizontally and vertically oriented packing, which was then rotated by 60° on a diagonal axis. From this extensive tilted packing, a horizontally and vertically oriented box was carved. From the interior of the box, the occupiable internal spaces – swimming and diving areas, leisure centre and water-polo pool – were then excised as simple rectilinear volumes. The planar cut sections through the packed polyhedral cells created an apparently naturalistic, random, non-repeating, organic pattern of structural polygons on the outer and inner façades, with the remaining edges of the polyhedral cells forming the web of the space-frame in the 3.6m-deep walls and ceiling space. Only in the second-floor bar do the bubbles of the foam effervesce into three dimensions.

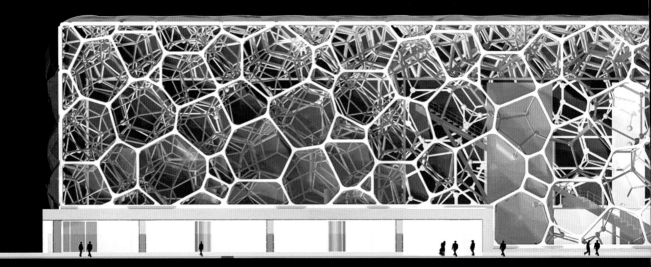

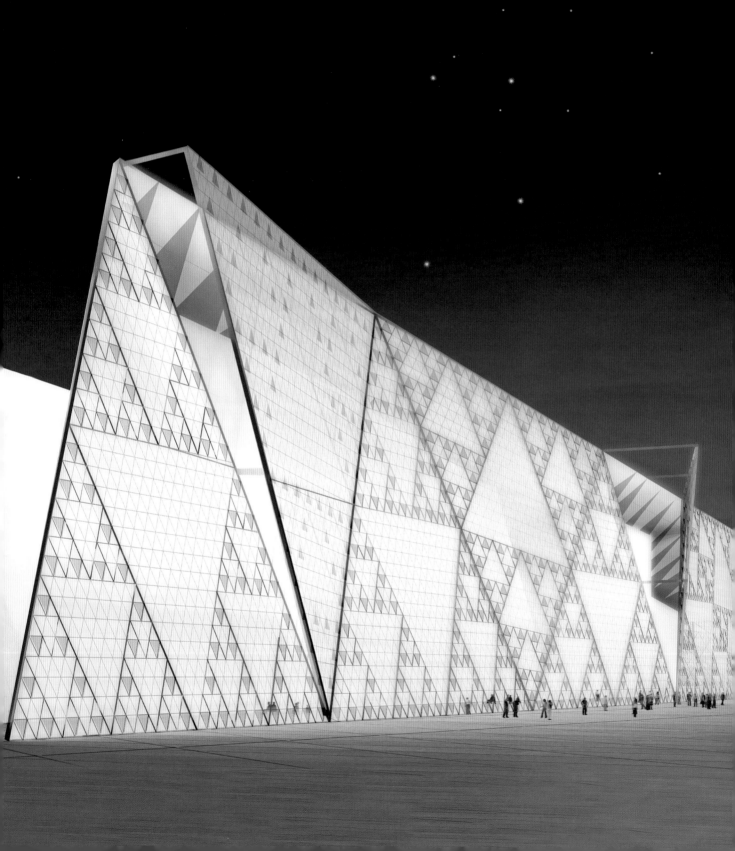

Grand Egyptian Museum

HENEGHAN PENG

Cairo, Egypt

The Grand Egyptian Museum project, led by Egypt's Ministry of Culture, was the subject of a UIA-supervised, UNESCO-sponsored international competition in 2003, won by the architectural practice Heneghan Peng. The design brief was for a large-scale repository that would be devoted to the last 7,000 years of Egyptian history and house over 100,000 artifacts, situated within sight of the pyramids at Giza. The architects cited three significant elements that organize the museum within the site: the 'Plateau Edge', the view to the pyramids, and the Cairo–Alexandria approach. The museum is built against the Plateau Edge, which, like a cliff, divides the site into higher and lower sections, causing the building to become part of the extended plateau.[8]

This new Plateau Edge was designed as a vast, sloping, translucent stone wall, inscribed with fractal patterning. Behind the wall, the building is divided internally by walls set along significant sight lines to allow views of the pyramids from the galleries. The translucent stone wall, 750m in length, is the main tectonic and iconic event, wrapping around the building and extending beyond it, tapering down from a height of 46m to approximately 8m to reflect the perspective of the sightlines. It is composed of forty-three 'mega-frames' that divide the equivalent space within the galleries along chronological lines.

For its subdivision, the wall adopts a fractal described by Waclaw Sierpiński in 1915 (it also appeared in 13th-century Italian art), known as the Sierpiński sieve (or gasket, or triangle). It is a recursive subdivision of triangles by sub-triangles with the new vertices in the centre of each edge, in which one component triangle – the central one – is omitted in each generation, or iteration (the holes in the sieve). It is a figure that can be produced in many

The wall.

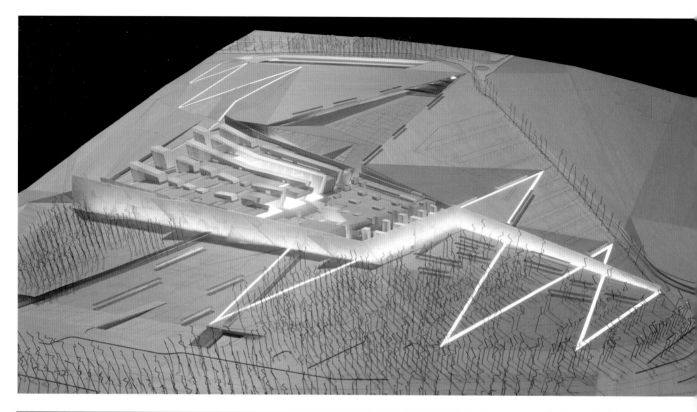

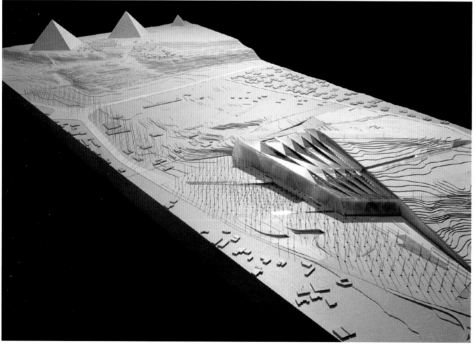

ABOVE The fractured wall by night.

LEFT The museum built into the escarpment, looking towards the great fractal wall, as though approaching from the city.

OPPOSITE, TOP The relationship of the wall to the museum.

OPPOSITE, BOTTOM LEFT The mega-frame, with the fractal revealed in relief.

OPPOSITE, BOTTOM RIGHT Cable systems in the upper three cladding panels.

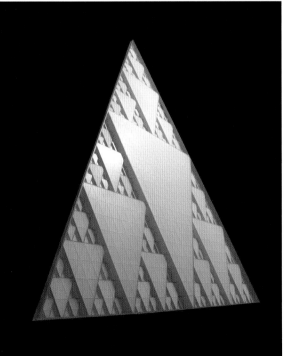

different ways computationally, and is a potentially infinite and scaleless system. In its application in the wall, there is a hierarchy of up to six iterations expressed in relief, with differently sized triangular panels on different planes relative to the plane of the wall surface. The smallest triangles are the individual stone panels. The mega-frames vary in size and aspect, but are largely similar geometrically. Each is a structure of large, fabricated steel members and prestressed cables on a triangular grid, supporting the onyx panels.

The design is dominated by the sightlines from every gallery to the pyramids, whose rigorous geometry informed the design, conception and the adoption of the Sierpiński triangle as the motif for the wall. According to Francis Archer of Arup AGU, who co-developed the detailed proposal for the wall with the architects, there was no direct route to this decision.[9] It was the Great Pyramids themselves, perhaps, that inspired the grandeur of the gesture of the wall, and the early description of the geometry of the building.

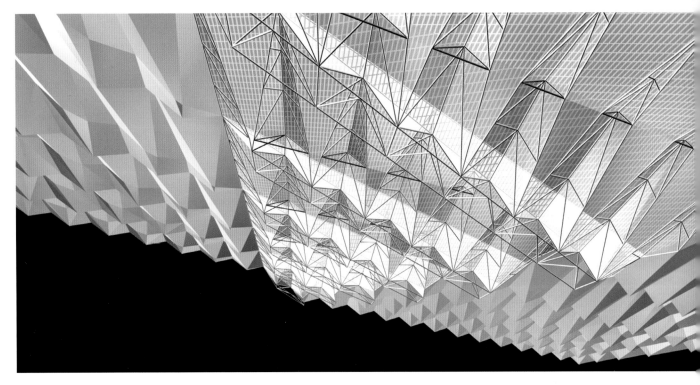

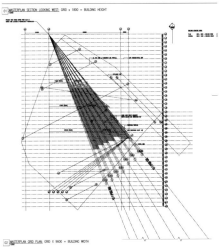

01 MASTERPLAN SECTION LOOKING WEST: GRID x 1800 = BUILDING HEIGHT

02 MASTERPLAN GRID PLAN: GRID X 9600 = BUILDING WIDTH

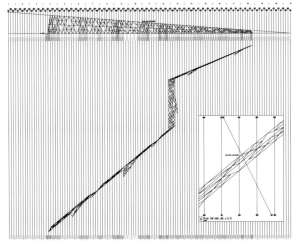

ABOVE The folded roof.

FAR LEFT The galleries, in grey, extend towards the view of the pyramids and the plan of the fractal wall.

LEFT Geometric grid and setting-out.

BELOW Masterplan.

OPPOSITE View from the gallery.

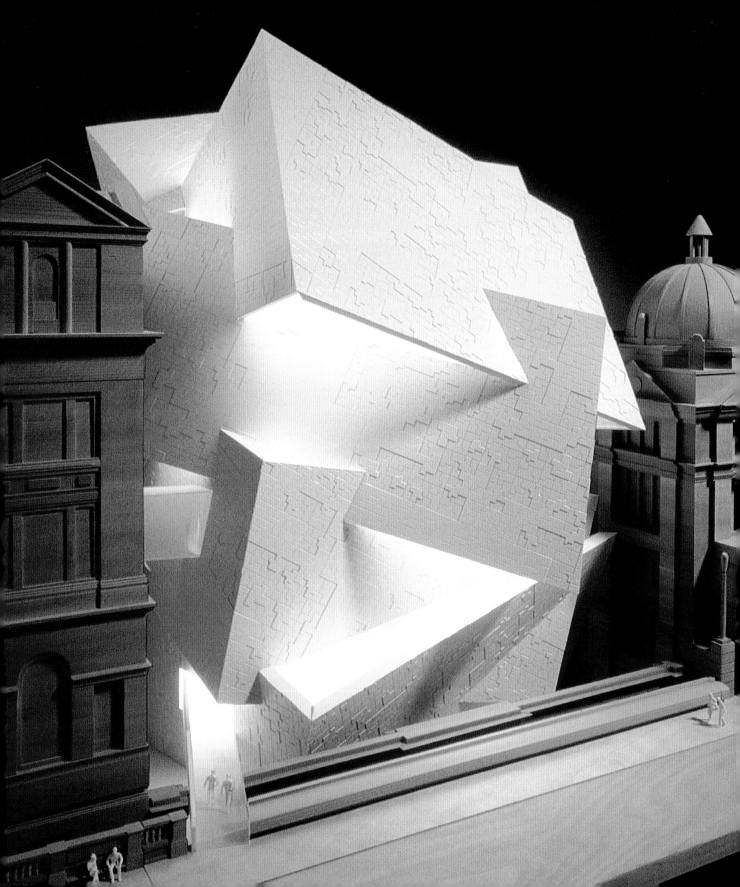

The Spiral Extension

DANIEL LIBESKIND

Victoria & Albert Museum, London, UK

Daniel Libeskind's unbuilt competition-winning proposal for an extension to the Victoria & Albert Museum in London is redolent with mathematical references and manifestations. The walls of the extension are generated by a chaotic spiral – the spiral of history, a spiral in which not only the radius, but also the centre shifts as the building rises out of the ground plane. 'Fractile' is a term coined by the design team for the scaleless, self-similar patterning of the building surface, deploying Ammann periodic tiling that would tile the planar surfaces infinitely, unceasingly, evenly, without repetition, were it not disrupted by a fractal tile subdivision.

Engineers Arup AGU proposed a number of possible tilings, including Robert Ammann's aperiodic tiling, the rectilinear nature of which was admired by the architect. The tiling was enriched tectonically through the creation of a fractal via selective subdivision. In the Ammann set used, there are three differently shaped tiles. Each one of those three tiles can subdivide perfectly into copies of the same three tile shapes, scaled down exactly by the Golden Ratio. 'Selective subdivision' means subdividing the tiles in this way, but choosing to subdivide some and not others as the subdivision proceeds. Each time a particular tile of the set of three is created – the 'R' tile – the subdivision is stopped for that tile. This creates a fractal that is especially rich because it, too, is aperiodic, and does not repeat in a way that would allow it to be mapped to itself through translation. This is the geometrical underpinning of the 'fractile'.

Just as there are infinite straight, parallel diagonal lines through the vertices in a simple, repetitive square grid, Ammann discovered that there are infinite straight, parallel lines through the vertices of his

OPPOSITE The model, showing the fractal tiling that divides the façade in relief.

RIGHT The Ammann tiles, showing how they tile one another with the copies scaled down by the Golden Ratio.

aperiodic tiling (now known as Ammann bars). These lines are spaced at a distance of either one unit apart or Phi (the Golden Ratio) apart in the same units. The sequence of the spacings of adjacent lines is aperiodic, a never-repeating series known as the Golden String. If Phi is represented by nought, this gives a binary sequence (such as 0110011, etc.) to represent the sequence of line spacings running in two different directions through the 2D tiling. This Golden String is an irrational number like Pi, which when expressed as a number is an infinite sequence of digits, and will never allow the prediction of the full sequence of digits through repetition in that sequence.

The fractal subdivision results in variable density of tiles and lines at different locations across the tiling pattern. When the pattern is wound onto the spiral walls, the result is different densities at different locations in the building. By having the unfolded building slide over the fractal tiling pattern, Libeskind was able to choose where these areas of greater density should occur. Finally, how should the graphical representation of the fractal be translated to the fabrication of the physical tiling itself? It was not practical to use different tiles at each of the different sizes. The answer was to raise the tiles in a relief, in which the varying depths represented the different scales in the fractal.

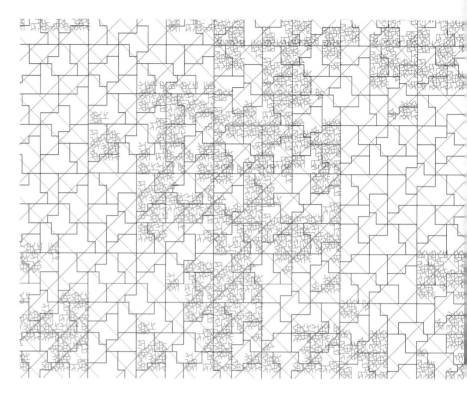

ABOVE The one-to-one mapping between the patterns of tiling and parallel lines extends infinitely in two dimensions, a counterintuitive discovery in an aperiodic, never-repeating pattern. The sequence of spacings between these lines conforms to two different possible spacings, but the sequence of these spacings is similarly aperiodic (see the sequences of green or blue lines).

BELOW Laying out the spiral on the tiling pattern. The spiral form of the walls is a developable form – the whole spiral can be laid out flat, showing the irregular fold lines of the corner and notches for the wall intersections between levels.

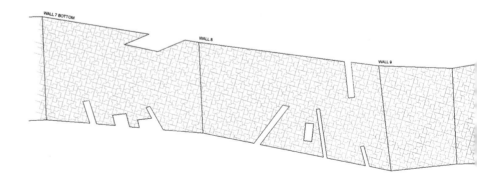

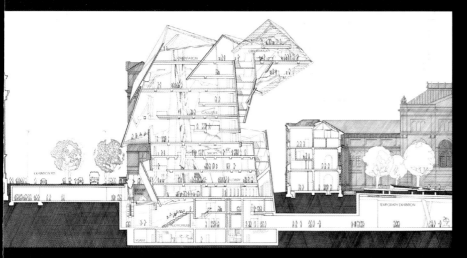

LEFT East–west section. The spiral walls appear and disappear unpredictably within the building.

BELOW, LEFT Competition panel, one of seven. This particular panel illustrates the concept of the spiral with the Ammann tiles in the background.

BELOW The spiral staircase.

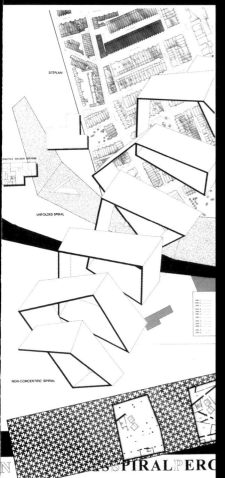

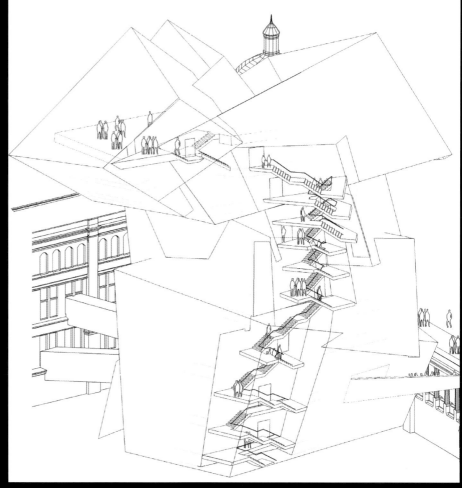

Storey Hall

ASHTON RAGGATT MCDOUGALL

Royal Melbourne Institute of Technology, Australia

n a visit to Melbourne in 2000, the
mathematical physicist Roger Penrose
ewed Ashton Raggatt McDougall's iconic
renovation and extension of Storey Hall, a
ublic meeting hall and traditional site for
ocial and political protest since the 1880s,
hich had been completed by the architects
our years before. Penrose 'politely identified
ome "mistakes" in the tiling,' recalls Howard
aggatt of Penrose's interest in the practice's
doption of his eponymous tiling.[10] The
egendary mathematician was intrigued
ather than inflamed by the architectural
nterpretation, which embraced the 'holes'
reated by misorienting some instances of
ne two tiles that Penrose had so surprisingly
iscovered would alone or in combination tile
ne plane aperiodically.

'Aperiodicity' is a pattern that when
xtended infinitely will never repeat in
 way that would allow the whole to be
uperimposed on itself through simple
translation. This underlying idea was a
significant note in the architecture, and
spoke to a more complex and immediate
contemporary world view than that
represented in the form of repetition of
elements in the 19th-century façade. The
radical new façade created next door to
the original building is, in fact, a blur of
this historic façade, 'smeared like lipstick'
across its polite front. The faceted, cave-like
entrance opens from Swanston Street onto
a new and imposing vertical entry sequence
to the original high-level hall. This faceting
extends into the theatrical interior, a space
that Raggatt calls 'purgatory' in reference to
Dante's *Divine Comedy*. (We do not explore
the circles of hell that this suggests are to be
found within either the building or the city
outside.) Tiling reappears, in another very
different manifestation, pentagons tipping
their hats once again to Penrose, in splendid
profusion in the hall itself.

he Swanston Street façade.

Raggatt sees the blanks in the tiling as analogous to physical consciousness. The tiling itself, materialized on the exterior of the building in textured verdigris, picks up a reference to an earlier decorative language, but also seems to make reference to nature and growth. So is the tiling about nature or about the city? '[Charles] Jencks saw it as about the city,' says Raggatt. 'We certainly saw it as about the city . . . This "creeper" is entirely going to take over our consciousness in the city.' In this way, Raggatt brings it back to a new way of thinking and designing that seems implicitly influenced by recent shifts in mathematics and science. Then he negates all that went before by commenting, 'I see meaning in architecture as a tragic failure. No one ever reads meaning in architecture.'

Raggatt emphatically distances the work of the practice from both mathematics and digital technology as generative forces. The very early interest that the firm took in the digital was a means of modelling and describing what could not otherwise be represented architecturally. The real focus of the practice's work, he says, is the human condition, tragedy and failure. This lends further explanation to the way that the mathematical resolution of the plane into two simple, tessellating, diamond-shaped tiles in an infinite pattern that never completely repeats is mutated and rendered flawed and enriched by failure and negation – the introduced 'mistakes' in the tiling – in the architecture of the renewed Storey Hall.

• Penrose tiling (p. 263)

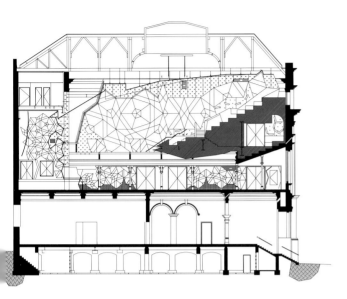

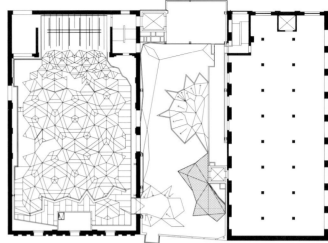

OPPOSITE, TOP Penrose tiling.

OPPOSITE, BOTTOM Tiling study.

ABOVE, LEFT Section, with interior wall tiling.

ABOVE Plan, showing the tiling in the ceiling.

BELOW Façade elevation.

Spanish Pavilion

FOREIGN OFFICE ARCHITECTS

Expo 2005, Aichi, Japan

The pavilion buildings for Expo 2005 all started out as similar, standardized blank boxes, for which the participating architects developed individual façades and interior environments. The Spanish Pavilion, designed by Foreign Office Architects, exploited both to give expression to the hybridization of Jewish–Christian cultures and the Islamic influence on the Iberian Peninsula, both so evident in the history of Spanish architecture. The architects identified characteristic architectural elements of this culture of synthesis, and played with them in the pavilion design. Those selected combined types of spatial organization (courtyards, churches and chapels), structural elements (arches and vaults), and enveloping and decorative elements (lattices and traceries).

The Spanish Pavilion was organized internally around a large, central space, itself connecting seven themed exhibition areas. This spatial sequence made reference to the nave and chapels of a cathedral, or the ecclesiastical courtyard and its cloisters. Ornate Gothic vaults, Islamic domes and faceted vaults were reinterpreted as more free-form structures, in which to contain the pavilion's different themes. Lattices, a traditional architectural element in Spain that reflect the fusion between Christian and Islamic architecture, as well as resonating with the Japanese concept of *engawa*, were adopted for the façades. The Islamic lattices and rose windows and traceries found in the late-Gothic cathedrals in Toledo, Segovia, Seville and Palma were important sources of inspiration for the lattice created here as the culturally appropriate cladding solution for the existing pavilion box.

The new lattice consisted of six different tiles, based in a hexagonal grid (like most of Gothic and Islamic tracery), coded with a colour. The specificity of these

The non-repeating lattice tracery on the pavilion façade.

pieces is that when they are assembled, they never repeat themselves, thus producing a continuously varying pattern of geometry and colour. The blocks were manufactured using glazed pottery, a technique common along the Mediterranean coast, but also present in the traditional ceramics of Japan. The actual process of making a ceramic façade also symbolizes the bringing of Spanish earth to Japan. The six colours of the tiles are variations of the red and yellow of the national flag, reflecting the colours of wine, roses, the blood of the bullfights, sun and sand – colours universally associated with Spain.

• Ammann tiling (p. 253)
• Aperiodic tiling (p. 253)

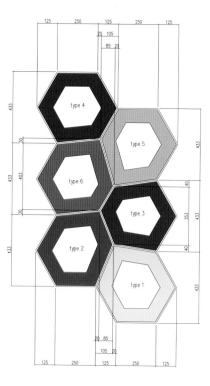

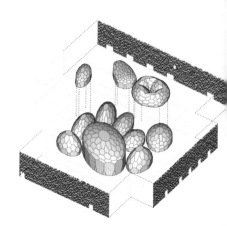

LEFT The non-repeating tiling was composed of six elements of distinct colour and shape.

BELOW Exploded axonometric drawing of the interior spaces.

BOTTOM, LEFT Construction detail of façade.

BOTTOM, RIGHT Cross-section of the façade.

OPPOSITE The façade and interior.

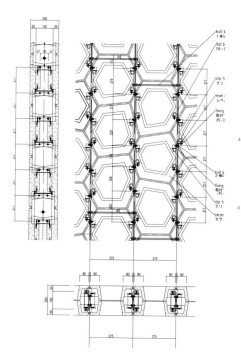

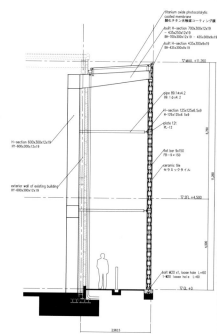

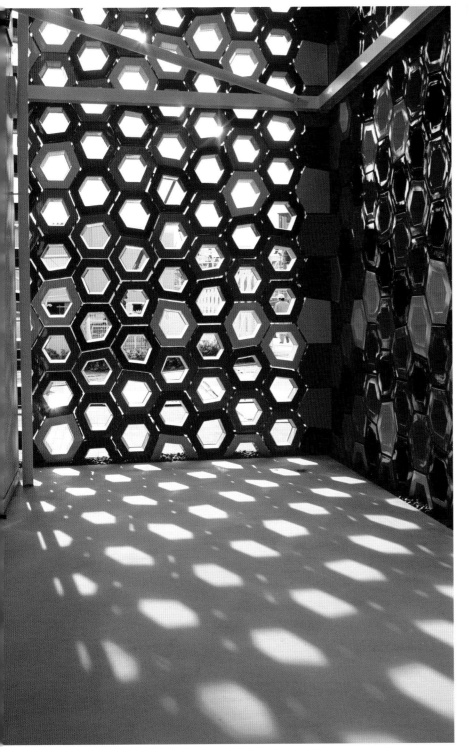

Centre for Ideas
MINIFIE NIXON
Victoria College of the Arts, Melbourne, Australia

Minifie Nixon's design for the Victoria College of the Arts incorporates a substantial extension to the library, café and student and staff lounges, and the addition of a Centre for Ideas. This last component is an ambitious cross-disciplinary, multimedia teaching facility, with a mission to foster critical cultural discourse and collaborative arts practice. The architects responded with an equally ambitious proposal for its home. The Centre for Ideas gives rich architectural expression to the abstract mathematical idea of the Voronoi decomposition. It is a building that celebrates its own design process: the transition from virtual to actual built fabric.[11]

At its simplest, the Voronoi diagram is the division of a plane into cells related to a set of points distributed in the plane. Every point belonging to a particular cell is closer to one specific point in the set than to any other. The nature of the distribution of the points determines the pattern and shape of the cells, which may vary from a random polygonal tiling to a highly ordered periodic pattern. This becomes more visually engaging when the plane acquires depth; this third dimension equates to an energy distribution within each cell. The reference point for each cell has a virtual gravitational pull; the closest points are also the deepest, and those furthest away remain near the surface. The point becomes the apex of a deep cone. Here, the virtual design process played the Voronoi diagram against the orthogonal composition of the façades; some of the Voronoi centres align with the fenestration pattern, and others float free. For each conical cell, the curved but (in elevation) apparently polygonal boundaries shift in response to the relative distribution of the generating points.

The intersecting cones are reminiscent, at one level, of naturally occurring Voronoi

Minifie Nixon's Centre for Ideas, at the Victoria College of the Arts.

distributions: patterns of crab holes in the sand. At another level, their materialization in this deep façade, in finely dimpled and highly reflective silver and bronze stainless steel, defies immediate association, and gives a powerful dynamic and iconic identity to the building that is not quite real. This suspension of material reality in favour of maintaining the associations to its process of coming into existence in transition from the virtual is consciously acknowledged by the architects.[12]

By contrast, the cones allow for a highly rational process of fabrication, each, when unrolled, conforming to a common planar module, but cut to its unique edge intersection profile, using laser-cutting technology from digitally generated profiles. The Voronoi idea reappears in the interior in the uppermost offices of the Centre for Ideas, where top-lit conical domes are subtracted from the mass of the white-plaster ceiling.

• Voronoi diagram (p. 266)

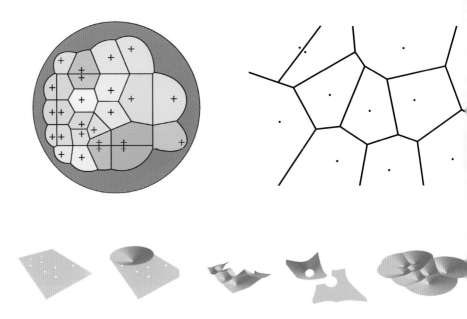

TOP Voronoi diagram with point distribution, resulting in boundaries forming regular quad.

TOP, RIGHT Voronoi regions in the plane around randomly distributed points.

ABOVE Virtual process of generation.

BELOW Holes in the sand.

OPPOSITE The reflective surfaces of the final building heighten the effect of complex geometries.

4 OPTIMIZATION

To 'optimize' means to find the best. In architecture, optimization speaks of a fitness for purpose that is in the nature of the thing, a special state of equilibrium, performance, or best-achievable economy of means. As is common with such concepts, it has made a fairly direct journey from the study of nature and natural systems. The word 'optimal', from the Latin *optimus*, has its origins in 19th-century biology, meaning 'most favourable', or 'desirable'. It speaks loudly of best, of a single goal within the ordered and rational Cartesian search for truth, and refers to the best conditions of, let us say, light, temperature, altitude for an organism to prosper.

The process of optimization describes the synthetic search for this best state within a model, whether of a biological system or architectural or structural system, usually under a set of restrictions, implied or expressed. These restrictions or conditions, the way that the optimal goal has been defined, and the nature of the model will all determine the outcome. In other words, no matter how deterministic the procedure or algorithm of optimization may be, the optimal state is always relative to the details of the system in which it is sought. The most materially economical structure may be nudged towards an architectural form that is favoured for other reasons through judicious changes to the overall structural context of loads and constraints within which the model is optimized.

Optimization has been used in architecture as a form-finding tool. Starting with the model in a state that is an approximate fit for purpose, adjustments are made to the geometry, and the form is assessed as to whether or not the overall performance has moved closer to the goal. Changes are made iteratively, and may or may not be recursive, looking for incremental improvement on the new temporary state of the model. Electronic computation offers high-speed, automated ways of deploying different families of algorithms to undertake this reversible form-finding exercise. Rivers sculpt the geology through which they pass over time, scouring and gouging out their path, depositing sand and silt in tireless small adjustments to the route. The rivers themselves have no goal, but the physicist will point out that they must always conform to certain laws of energy conservation and transfer, which, in a sense, defines their goal. The optimization model is a similarly restless creature that settles towards an unchanging, or less changing, state, moving towards some minimum. Like the river, it will respond to a change in contextual conditions by finding a new path when the process is rerun. Unlike the river, its goals (its laws of conservation) can be edited.

The art of architecture always engages, at some level, the search for an optimal formal, spatial, constructional answer to diverse aesthetic and performance measures, or a knowing compromise among the above. Trying to formalize this play-off between very different performative impulses, to search for several types of 'best' where each factor affects the others, is complex. It is known as multi-criteria optimization. It may be defined by a Pareto optimization, a state in which one thing can only improve at the expense of another. This rate of inverse change, however, may not be the same for all states of the model. Before the introduction of electronic computation in architecture, some architects and engineers used dynamic analogue (physical) models to compute optimal shapes and structural scenarios. The discovery that a hanging chain suspended from its two ends takes up in tension the shape that, when inverted, is optimal for a compression structure (such as a masonry arch of the same shape and same points of support) led to the use of hanging models for form-finding. The discovery itself has a long history; in 1675 Robert Hooke published a cryptic Latin anagram, having announced to the Royal Society four years before that he had discovered the optimal shape for an arch. The solution ('as hangs the flexible line, so but inverted will stand the rigid arch') was only published in 1705, after Hooke's death.

At around the same time, Gottfried Leibniz, Christiaan Huygens and Johann Bernoulli discovered the algebraic description of the curve of the hanging chain in response to a challenge by Bernoulli's brother, Jacob Bernoulli, and demonstrated that this shape was not, as Galileo had conjectured, a parabola but a catenary. (Although algebraically

ABOVE AND OPPOSITE Gaudí's hanging model for Colònia Güell, details and photograph inverted and rendered over to represent the form of the church.

different, the two are potentially very close in shape.) The parabola is also found among optimal structures; it is, for example, the shape taken up by the cables of a suspension bridge once they have been anchored to the bridge deck. The optimal arch is the shape that closely follows the line of compressive force, economical in its use of material, unlike the circular Roman arch, where the line of force does not follow the arch's shape or descend vertically from it. It must, in this latter case, be accommodated in the enlarged mass of the surrounding wall structure; the line of force passing outside the built matter spells certain structural collapse. Antoni Gaudí was the virtuoso in the expression of this principle, notably through the arches and single columns of the Convent of Santa Teresa and the hewn inclined columns of the Colònia Güell chapel. In the history of structural optimization, Gaudí is best known for extending the catenary principle to four dimensions in his funicular model for the unfinished chapel. He attached bags of sand to a web of strings, which hung in catenary curves, to represent the masses of the static loads of the structure, in order to uncover the shape and distribution in space of the towers of the chapel that would result from this loading, while at the same time being able to make live adjustments to the model.

Structural economy is one of the more familiar applications for optimization processes in architecture, but it is far from being the only one. In the race to reduce energy consumption and emissions attributable to the built environment, better ways of linking the analysis, simulation or measurement of various aspects more directly to synthesis in design are a focus of architectural research. Flows of air, heat, the best use of natural light and acoustic performance are all valid goals for optimization routines. Mathematically, optimization methods can be divided into stochastic and deterministic approaches. 'Stochastic' is derived from the Greek στόχος, to aim or to shoot with a bow at a target; in such an activity there is a spread of arrows, some of which hit the bull's eye, some that come close. A sequence that combines a random or probabilistic component with a selective process so that only certain outcomes of the random can prevail is said to be stochastic. In such methods of optimization, the current state does not completely determine the next. The same process run repeatedly under the same conditions will not necessarily arrive at the same outcome. In deterministic methods of optimization, there is no randomness: values are assumed to be precise. Each state and operation determines exactly the next state. So the same optimization routine repeated with the same starting conditions for the same number of iterations will result in the same outcome each time.

The optimization link to biology is more than merely etymological. Optimization techniques (particularly those that work by progressively adding and subtracting material to work through iterative analysis towards a form that better satisfies the desires and constraints) are closely analogous to the mechanisms of, for instance, bone growth. These ideas, taken up mathematically in post-digital times, owe much to the seminal work of D'Arcy Thompson. In this chapter, a range of different optimization applications are examined. Some are project-specific computer programmes, such as that used for the roof of the British Museum's Great Court (p. 122), which found a surface shape that represented a good fit between the architects' early proposal and the structural loading and bearing criteria. A second application considered the shape and distribution of the individual component facets of the roof that allowed the detailed design to meet the edge condition, size and regularity constraints.

At the Qatar Education City Convention Centre (p. 130), an extended version of evolutionary structural optimization was used to find the shapes of the Sidra 'trees' that formed the building. The trees were 'grown' via computer by progressively removing the smallest amount of stressed material from a block until the residual structure used the least material most efficiently. For Cox Architects' design for a rectangular stadium in Melbourne (p. 134), engineers Arup demonstrated another structural optimization procedure, in which each of the individual steel members was reduced to the optimal section for its performance in the whole structure, the form of which could also be varied to explore its relative efficiency. The hill-like greenhouses of Toyo Ito's Island City project (p. 138) deployed an evolutionary shape design process by sensitivity analysis to identify local and global minima of structural strain, as the shapes of the built hills were iteratively varied.

The last three projects in the chapter are examples of optimization techniques used for non-structural objectives. At The Pinnacle (p. 142), in London, it is the detailed ordering of the façade components and resulting building envelope that is optimized. Foster + Partners' Al Raha development (p. 148) draws on wind resistance and incidence of solar radiation to inform its form, while the Melbourne Recital Hall (p. 152) exemplifies the role of acoustic optimization in fine-tuning the exquisite detailed design of a sound interior.

OPPOSITE AND BOTTOM Two different sequences using evolutionary structural optimization to progressively subtract material, thus arriving at a more economical structure. The output from every twentieth iteration has been rendered from these sequences.

RIGHT Rapid prototype in wax.

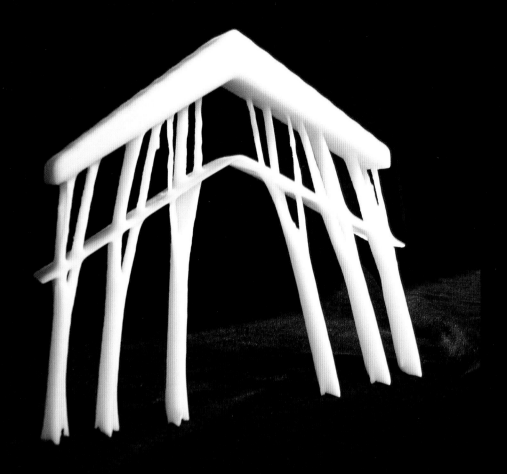

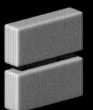 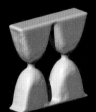   

British Museum Great Court
FOSTER + PARTNERS
London, UK

Level change function η

$$\eta = \frac{\left(1 - \dfrac{x}{b}\right)\left(1 + \dfrac{x}{b}\right)\left(1 - \dfrac{y}{c}\right)\left(1 + \dfrac{y}{d}\right)}{\left(1 - \dfrac{ax}{rb}\right)\left(1 + \dfrac{ax}{rb}\right)\left(1 - \dfrac{ay}{rc}\right)\left(1 + \dfrac{ay}{rd}\right)}$$

Function without singularity α

$$\alpha = \left(\frac{r}{a} - 1\right)\left(1 - \frac{x}{b}\right)\left(1 + \frac{x}{b}\right)\left(1 - \frac{y}{c}\right)\left(1 + \frac{y}{d}\right)$$

Function with singularity ζ

$$\zeta = \frac{\left(\dfrac{1}{a} - \dfrac{1}{r}\right)(b - x)(b + x)(c - y)(d + y)}{\left[\begin{array}{l}(b + x)(d + y)\sqrt{(b - x)^2 + (c - y)^2} \\ +(b + x)(c - y)\sqrt{(b - x)^2 + (d + y)^2} \\ +(b - x)(d + y)\sqrt{(b + x)^2 + (c - y)^2} \\ +(b - x)(c - y)\sqrt{(b + x)^2 + (d + y)^2}\end{array}\right]}$$

The design for the glazed roof that spans the British Museum's rectangular Great Court and circular Reading Room has proved to be highly influential. Here, Chris Williams and Paul Shepherd from the University of Bath compare the definition of the surface as built with an alternative proposal using subdivision surface techniques.

'The geometrical definition of the roof', writes Williams, 'consisted of two parts: the shape of the surface and the pattern of steel members upon that surface.'[1] To define the roof's surface geometry, the technique of NURB surfaces could have been used, but with boundaries of constant height that were both rectangular and circular in plan, a simpler approach was appropriate to generate the grid of members on the surface, and to have a singularity in surface curvature at the corners'. The reason for the singularity of curvature, Williams explains, is that the rectangular boundary was on

sliding supports to avoid horizontal thrust on the existing building'. The roof, therefore, could 'only be restrained horizontally at the corners where the resultant thrust is balanced by tensions in the rectangular edge beam. Functions without a singularity in curvature must be horizontal at a horizontal corner, like a ski jump, where the thrust has to change direction rapidly as the corner is approached, thus causing structural problems. But a cone lying on its side can have a slope even though it intersects two horizontal lines crossing at right angles.' A formula that created a cone with its apex at the corner was required, ensuring that there was a singularity in curvature at the corner.

The second part, says Williams, was 'the generation of the pattern of steel members on the surface, which produced the triangular faceting of the roof surface. The triangular grid was chosen because it is most efficient structurally, and because it avoids the need to produce either flat quadrilateral panels or curved glass. The grid was "relaxed" on the surface to remove discontinuities in geodesic curvature by moving each node to a point on the surface equal to the weighted average of its neighbours. The weighting functions were chosen to control the maximum size of glass panel, each of which were different, except for their mirror image on the opposite side of the north–south axis. The relaxation was done on a finer grid than the actual steel members and took many hundreds of cycles. Speed of convergence was improved by using Alistair Day's dynamic relaxation method.'

Colleague Paul Shepherd writes: 'Subdivision surfaces begin with a coarse mesh representation of a surface. Through a recursive process of splitting each mesh face into a number of smaller faces, and adjusting the coordinates of the newly created vertices (and possibly the original vertices also), a finer mesh representation is produced. This can be seen as a mesh-smoothing process, whereby each subsequent level of recursion results in a finer, smoother surface representation. The recursion process can be continued indefinitely and with careful choice of vertex positioning, the mesh can converge onto an underlying limit-surface with provably smooth properties (G2 continuity). The variable level of detail lends itself well to the application of optimization algorithms, which can manipulate the original control mesh and lead to more efficient geometries in terms of structural and environmental performance criteria.

'One disadvantage from a building

design point of view is that, by ensuring a smooth, continuous surface, control over the exact position of the surface at any one point is surrendered, and, in particular, it is difficult to specify the surface boundary . . . This problem was overcome by adopting a constrained subdivision scheme, whereby each vertex around the edge was snapped back to the constraining boundary after each subdivision step. The price paid for this extra control is a loss of smoothness around the boundary. However, since the effect is localized to the boundary, and results in a practical system of defining optimal surfaces for buildings, it is seen as a good compromise.

'Once a suitable surface is found, different options for applying a structural grid can be explored. While software tools for draping grids over the subdivision limit-surface, or for iteratively optimizing a grid for structural performance via dynamic relaxation or simulated annealing, are being developed, the most obvious choice is to use the subdivision mesh itself, which – as can be seen in these renders of the Great Court roof using subdivision grids – naturally leads to a smooth mesh with significant repetition of member lengths. Grids of various densities can instantly be generated, corresponding to various levels of subdivision from the initial mesh.

By adopting a subdivision surface modelling approach for the Great Court roof, many different options could be quickly generated and tested against many different criteria, including solar gain, acoustic performance and structural efficiency.'[2]

Smithsonian Institution
FOSTER + PARTNERS
Washington, DC, USA

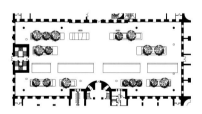

he new glazed roof over the courtyard of ʰe Smithsonian Institution building that ɔuses the National Portrait Gallery and ʰe American Art Museum evolved from ɑ design sketch of a sinuous, undulating ʳrface, which formed three continuous ɔmed areas with curved valleys in between. s built, the canopy is complex: every node, visted beam and glazing-panel shape is nique, yet all were generated from the same mple rules.

The design, which won an invitational ɔmpetition in 2004, draws many parallels ith the architects' earlier roof over the reat Court at the British Museum (p. 122). ʰere are also some significant differences. oth structures are free-form in the sense f having been arrived at through design ʳocesses other than geometrical pre- ɑtionalization. This method contrasts ith a number of other projects by the ɑme architects, in which complex, shaped

architecture was predefined as a composition of arcs or torus patches to simplify the shape definition, setting-out and process of constructing the surface from planar quadrilateral panels.

Whereas the British Museum canopy was supported on existing walls, the Smithsonian roof had to be completely free of the one sandstone and three granite walls of the historic former Patents Office, and absent from the protected views of the building from the street. The design was influenced by the choice of eight supporting column positions, and driven by acoustic and solar considerations. In the proposal, this translated to a diagonal grid of deep steel fins that twisted differentially in space to occlude light over the domed areas, while becoming normal to the glazed surface close to the columns where the structural forces were greatest. The acoustic material was inside these perforated triangular sections.

PPOSITE The impossibility of having all four ɔdes of each panel on the surface was ɔlved by placing two opposite nodes on ʰe surface and raising the other two to the ᵖane of the panel. The movement reduces

the maximum extent of deviation that occurs in areas of high curvature.

RIGHT, TOP TO BOTTOM Long section; cross-section; courtyard plan.

In the post-competition design, the beams retained their subtle, changing field-of-wheat twist across the domes and valleys, but became universally normal to the undulating surface. The solar occlusion was simplified using glass coatings, and the design emphasis shifted to giving visual access to broad tracts of sky. This reinforced the proposition of large, quadrilateral glazing panels on a diagonal grid, projected onto the flowing design surface. All eight columns are at the lowest points in the valleys between the domes and collect rainwater.

Unlike the British Museum roof, where the shape and its panellization were refined principally in response to shape and structural optimization, the design process here allowed for the 'manual' alteration of the roof shape through simple controls to explore hundreds of different versions of the form for a range of different performance issues. All of the constraints and decisions were encoded into control geometries in a computer programme by Brady Peters of Foster + Partners' Specialist Modelling Group, a programme that was changed and added to throughout the design process.[3]

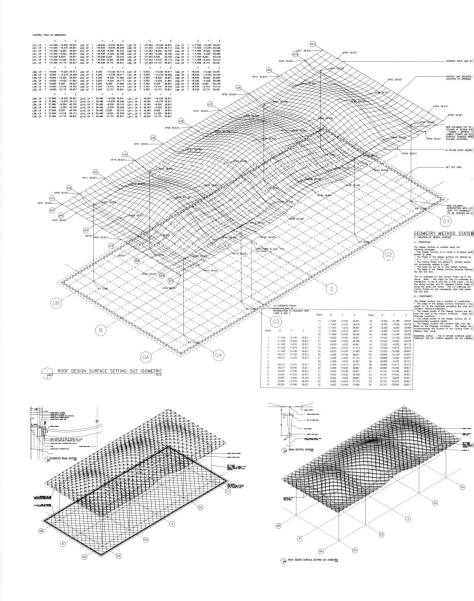

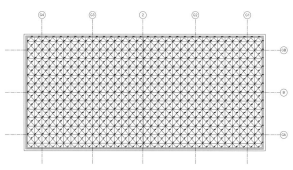

THIS PAGE The programmed model could instantly output information in a host of formats for different specializations: node and centre lines for structural analysis, and simple planar geometry for acoustic analysis. Although the fabricator worked with the architects from the early stages, they did not share the three-dimensional model. A geometry method statement was provided, and the roof was remodelled by Arnold Walz for Gartner as a contractual and checking process.

OPPOSITE Interior perspective of the roof's undulating surface.

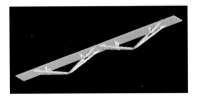

Qatar Education City Convention Centre

ARATA ISOZAKI

Doha, Qatar

The Sidra tree, a plant native to Qatar that flourishes in the country's unforgiving desert climate, forms Arata Isozaki's design for the 250m-long entrance to a new convention centre in Doha, home to the Qatar Foundation, which includes a 2,500-seat theatre, an exhibition hall and banqueting facilities. A traditional source of nourishment and medicine, the Sidra tree also symbolizes knowledge of the divine.

The exact nature of the voluptuous, tree-like shape of the building is far from arbitrary, at least structurally. It was evolved by design engineer Mutsuro Sasaki, using an optimization method known as EESO, or extended evolutionary structural optimization. For a particular set of site, material and structural loading criteria, this method achieves the best, most efficient mechanically performing shape, using the least material possible. The top of the 'tree' was constrained to remain perfectly flat.

Two support points on the ground, 100m apart, were also architectural givens. The trees were sculpted by a computational cycle of calculation and excision, with the tree forms evolving from a hypothetical block of virtual material, using structural finite-element analysis to identify and subtract the most structurally redundant areas, and then repeating the process on the residue many times over.

While the pure form adopts the structural strategy of real trees – shedding redundant material and gathering substance where it is needed to resist force – its materialization and realization outside an evolutionary biological setting becomes an intriguing challenge. In moving from the pure form to the built artifact, Büro Happold's team of specialist analysts (SMART) carried out further integrated optimization to the free-form tree structure, incorporating new constraints related to

LEFT, TOP A real Sidra tree.

LEFT The evolution of the form through EESO.

OPPOSITE Rendering of the Sidra tree entrance to the convention centre.

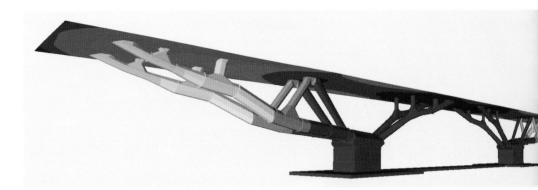

RIGHT Structural analysis.

BELOW, LEFT Relationship of the tree to the façade.

BELOW, RIGHT Movement was a concern with a huge differential between the exterior temperatures and the air-conditioned interior.

BOTTOM Computer rendering.

OPPOSITE Under construction.

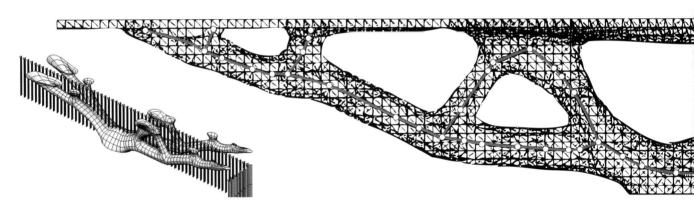

the geometry, structural stiffness and fabrication.

For the construction, the SMART team resolved the design of the complex surface into 6mm-thick superficial panels, almost all of single curvature, while maintaining the organic profile of the trees. Concealed within the trunk and branches, which are up to 7m in diameter, is a simplified core structure with an octagonal cross-section that follows the centre lines. This profile is composed of flat steel sheets. Rigorous geometrical optimization was needed to maintain the sheets of the octagonal core as close as possible to the finished panelled design surface, while maintaining their perfectly flat (rather than warped) profile over long lengths. This kept their transportation and fabrication costs within budget.

Plate thickness was also optimized to minimize the weight of the structure. Each component is unique and needed to be oriented correctly; the modelling included individual identification, tagging for fabrication, and checking for connectivity between adjacent panels. Strategically placed movement joints with gasket seals and insulation of the trees enabled the building to avoid stress caused by very high temperature gradients. The structure had to be pre-cambered by as much as half a metre, the effect of which had to be accounted for in the geometry of the model. The modelling was integrated through a central 3D modelling hub, to integrate geometry development with analysis, optimization and machined output.

• Evolutionary structural optimization (p. 257)
• Finite-element analysis (p. 257)

Melbourne Rectangular Stadium

COX ARCHITECTS

Melbourne, Australia

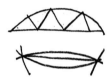

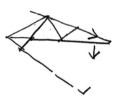

The conceptual design for Melbourne's new sports stadium was guided by a combination of environmental sustainability principles and effervescent sculptural qualities that evolved from functional and structural considerations. The new stadium joins the cluster of iconic venues that line the Yarra River to the east of the city centre, in a postcode devoted to sporting prowess and entertainment.

The roof design takes advantage of the inherent structural efficiencies of a dome to create a striking assemblage of lightweight, steel-framed geodesic bioframes that, in the final design, deploy 50 per cent less steel than a typical deep-cantilever stadium roof structure.[4] The refinement of the initial proposal, developed together by the architects and engineers Arup, is a story of 'doing the numbers' in a way that was sympathetic and responsive to the aesthetic and programmatic criteria, impacting on the detailed design.[5] With the goal of finding an optimal shape for

the roof that would both please aesthetically and perform structurally – as well as being as light as possible and divisible into easily fabricated units – flexible parametric models were set up that could vary the sweep curve of the roof, together with the curved profile of the individual domes and bay size, updating all the sub-components in the process.

Such flexible geometrical modelling was coupled with structural analysis and Arup's in-house optimization routines for assigning individual member sizes to every piece of steel in the roof structure in response to iterative analysis. Each steel member was first assigned an ideal section size, which was subsequently revised within the automated process to the nearest size conforming to manufacturing opportunities. In the analysis, the loads were updated to take into account the varying weights of the individually sized members. In this structure, there is much greater differentiation of member sizes than would be

LEFT Concept sketches.

OPPOSITE Rendered views of the stadium.

found in buildings designed through more traditional processes.

This required cautious protocols for consistency between the flexible surface model, its conversion to structural lines of force representing the steel members and their nodes of intersection, and the assignment of load cases and constraints in the structural analysis model. The transfer of information from the geometrical models to the structural analysis and optimization process, therefore, could be automated in such a way that made it possible to investigate many different design shapes and configurations in a short period of time. The team could alter the shape and observe the effects of differing curvature on the amount of steel used and the efficiency of the whole structure. The tools allowed the shape changes and the analysis to be appreciated visually through geometry and colour on screen, promoting rapid communication between the engineers and architects.

A geodesic dome is a spherical, or part spherical, shell structure, based on a network of great circles that intersect to form the stable triangular elements of a structural net. In this case, the domes were not constrained to remain spherical in refining the design for optimal aesthetic and structural criteria.

• Arup optimizer (p. 253)

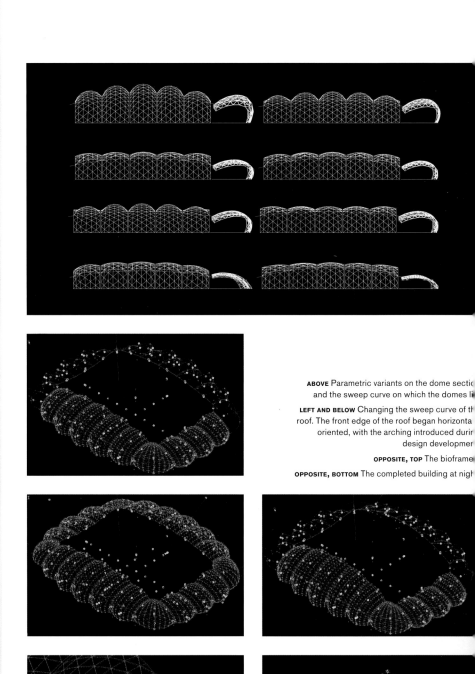

ABOVE Parametric variants on the dome sectic and the sweep curve on which the domes li

LEFT AND BELOW Changing the sweep curve of th roof. The front edge of the roof began horizonta oriented, with the arching introduced durir design developmer

OPPOSITE, TOP The bioframe

OPPOSITE, BOTTOM The completed building at nigh

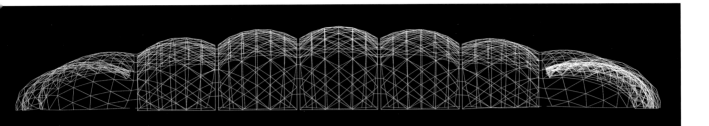

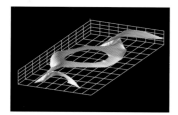

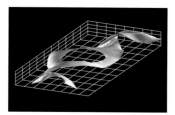

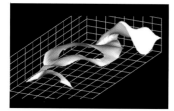

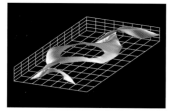

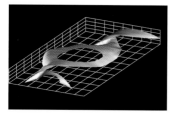

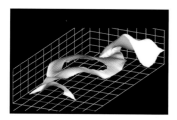

Island City Central Park

TOYO ITO

Fukuoka, Japan

The Island City Central Park project is sited on a 400-hectare island platform of flat, reclaimed land in Japan's Hakata Bay. Architect Toyo Ito's early sketches displayed an interest in complexity and fluid dynamics, which sponsored spreading wave forms for the conceptual framework of the park and its surroundings. The architecture was conceived to merge with the undulations of the larger, rippling park design, rather than to sit as autonomous objects in the landscape. This approach presented special challenges for the design of the three greenhouses, which took on a free-form, hill-like quality. Each has a different cultivation theme, with spaces for relaxation, and the roofs were planted with paths that stroll across the surface.

Finding the final shapes for the concrete shells that enclosed these areas involved a process described by engineer Mutsuro Sasaki (see also p. 130) as 'evolutionary shape design by means of sensitivity analysis'.[6] The geometry model was linked to mechanical

structural analysis modelling. Local minima for the strain energy in the structures were sought out as the shapes of the greenhouses were gradually altered in the digital model. Philosophically, this method accepted both the connection between the geometrical shape and its structural mechanical performance, and that there were many optimal structural points distributed across a landscape of possible variants of the shape. In the process of exploration, it became possible to find particular shapes that were hitherto unseen or unimagined.

The designer adjusts the design parameters and feeds them to the computer, which then searches for a theoretical solution that satisfies the mechanical conditions and given design requirements. The shape analysis takes the whole roof as the analysis area, and uses the optimization method to seek out the 'best' solutions that would enclose the maximum volume of space for the minimum use of material.

LEFT As the vertical section profiles through the building were changed, shapes were found that transmitted load by axial forces, rather than by bending movement, minimizing the strain energy.

OPPOSITE Bird's-eye view on completion.

• Evolutionary shape optimizer (p. 257)

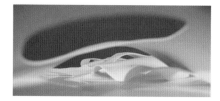

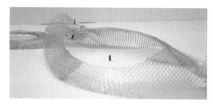

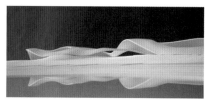

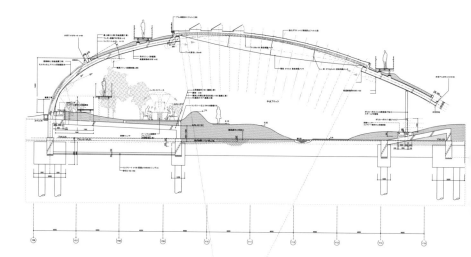

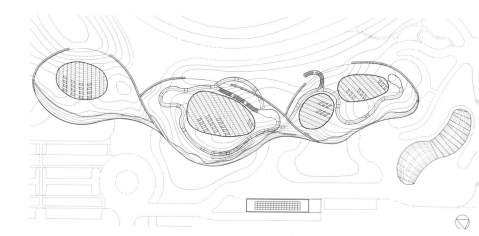

ABOVE The intention, says Sasaki, was to 'lightly wrap a huge space with an amorphous thin concrete shell, as though with a single piece of fabric'.

TOP, RIGHT Section.

ABOVE, RIGHT Plan.

RIGHT Under construction.

OPPOSITE The building's complex topography invites a multitude of perspectives to visitors.

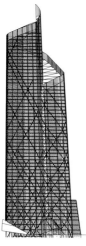

The Pinnacle
KOHN PEDERSEN FOX
London, UK

There were two mathematical tales in the design of this elegant tower, one of a crop of new high-rises planned for the City of London. The first was one of finding a sculptural form that would address the exigencies of the building's tricky site via a combination of simple geometries that were easy to communicate and set out. This was the first part of a process that the architects refer to as 'pre-rationalized design'.[7] The second was the resolution of the whole into a system of components that would achieve both elegance and a high rate of performance in terms of environmental, programmatic, structural and constructional simplicity goals, and maximum return on investment in terms of gross internal floor area (GIFA).

To reduce the building mass when viewed face-on, the structure was gradually tapered by up to 2.5°. The acute angles of the triangular plan became rounded to maintain usable interior space, and shear cones were used to unite the differentially sloping faces (which were circular arcs in plan rather than elliptical, as the plan of an inclined cone would be). The building, therefore, like the design for the Abu Dhabi airport (p. 48), can be resolved in two dimensions into simple arcs and tangential lines. The helical tap – the wrapping of the building façade like a flume curling up to a point at the apex – was the other major design move.

Over many versions, the tapering façades were resolved into regular rectilinear panels, with the mullions offset in each storey to accommodate the reducing width. The façade is composed of a single, flexible module type. There is an upright (internal) frame on the slab edge; the external frame is registered in space off the internal frame. Both panels are rectangular and of regular size all along the façade. Internal panels form the building enclosure and include opening windows, while external panels,

LEFT Physical design development models of the increasingly tapered flume form, from the point in the design process when the wrapping direction was first reversed.

OPPOSITE Computer rendering of the aerial view of The Pinnacle in the City of London.

Pressure distribution on building facade (Pa)

20.00	
18.00	
16.00	
14.00	
12.00	
10.00	
8.00	
6.00	
4.00	
2.00	
0.00	
-2.00	
-4.00	
-6.00	
-8.00	
-10.00	
-12.00	
-14.00	
-16.00	
-18.00	
-20.00	

SW wind

NE wind

Floors in NV

Floors in Mech

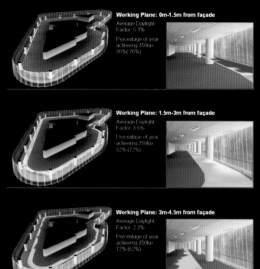

Working Plane: 0m-1.5m from façade
Average Daylight Factor 5.1%
Percentage of year achieving 350lux 86%(76%)

Working Plane: 1.5m-3m from façade
Average Daylight Factor 3.6%
Percentage of year achieving 350lux 82% (72%)

Working Plane: 3m-4.5m from façade
Average Daylight Factor 2.3%
Percentage of year achieving 350lux 72% (62%)

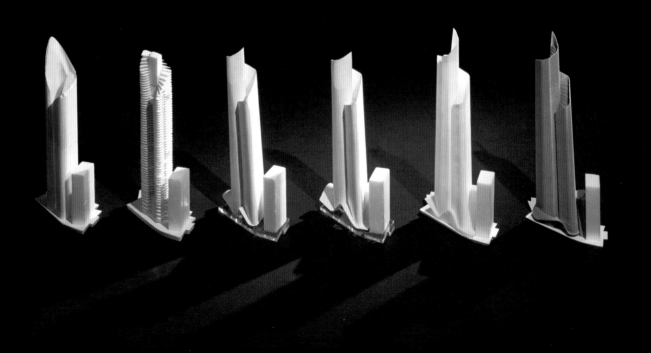

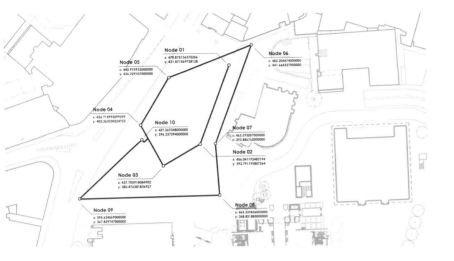

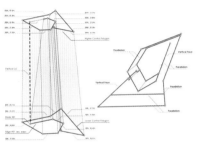

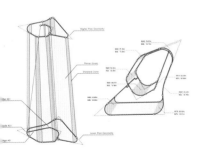

which lap in a 'snakeskin' pattern, provide weatherproofing and allow for natural ventilation, even at high level.

An optimization programme targeted the tightest packing of the external panels with the smallest opening between the lapped panels, and the best visual continuity in their orientation. The first experiment forced a constant distance between the internal and external panels, and between the external panel and maximal volume envelope. This procedure resulted in a high level of collisions between panels in the external skin, especially in areas of high curvature. The second system replaced the constant distance by a constant angle constraint between the internal and external panels, which produced some solutions in which the panels did not collide. It also resulted in a 1.23 per cent increase in GIFA as a result of the 19.05 per cent reduction in the overall cavity volume between the two skins.

The third and final version employed a heuristic, which used the gap between adjacent external panels, rather than any constant relationship between internal and external panels. It was based on imagining a person positioning each panel in relation to the preceding one, measuring a particular set of distances. Interestingly, the results from this much less constrained model were not only better in terms of clash avoidance, GIFA and cavity reduction, but also had the advantage of being non-panel specific, and allowing easy substitution of a new module with detailed variations. Significantly, it was also much more transparent to the collaborating designers and open to design intervention.

OPPOSITE, TOP Aerodynamic studies.

OPPOSITE, BELOW Sequence models showing the development of the helical tap.

TOP AND MIDDLE Control network.

ABOVE, LEFT Notional envelope.

ABOVE Controlling the shape of the top of the building: control curves for the helical clipping region.

RIGHT Three different mathematical approaches to minimizing the distance between adjacent panels in the 'snakeskin'.

BELOW, LEFT AND RIGHT 'Interference diagrams' for the horizontally and vertically adjacent panels of the outer skin of the façade.

OPPOSITE The outer layer of the façade of lapping panels, mediating the climate and allowing natural ventilation up to high level.

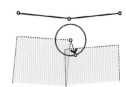

Convex configuration
Appears in the majority of cones

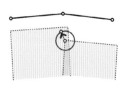

Concave configuration
Appears in the inverted cone

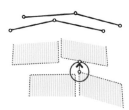

Positive shear
Appears in the bulk of the façade

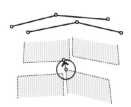

Negative shear
Appears in the top of the building where reverse winding occurs

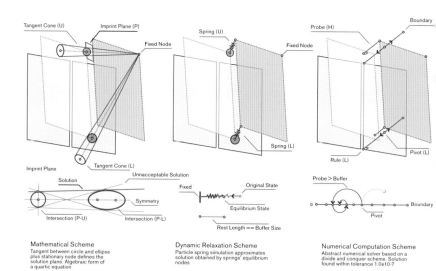

Mathematical Scheme
Tangent between circle and ellipse plus stationary node defines the solution plane. Algebraic form of a quartic equation

Dynamic Relaxation Scheme
Particle spring simulation approximates solution obtained by springs' equilibrium nodes

Numerical Computation Scheme
Abstract numerical solver based on a divide and conquer scheme. Solution found within tolerance 1.0e10-7

Al Raha Development

FOSTER + PARTNERS

Abu Dhabi, UAE

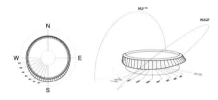

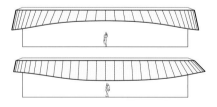

The intention of the client for this 300,000m² mixed-use waterfront development was to create an architectural icon for Abu Dhabi. In answer to the question of what an icon might be, senior partner Gerard Evenden observes that it is easy to make a shape – the practice had already mastered the art of building unusually shaped buildings as cost-effectively as conventionally shaped ones – but that shape must be *driven* to be meaningful: it must take into account the site data.[8] Every building now has to tell an environmental story; in the middle of the desert, sun and wind are the only constraints.

The story of the Al Raha beach resort is one of harnessing mathematics in order to translate the interaction of sun and wind with built fabric into numerical analysis to inform the design of the building. As with other projects in this chapter, it is a tale of two (related) models. The designers first looked for a mutable parametric description of the

building form that could morph in response to feedback about its performance when exposed to the elements. The second set of models represented the performance analysis for different variations on the building's shape: the way it heats up; the wind loads it is subjected to; and the effect of air flow in the spaces around it. Hugh Whitehead of the architects' Specialist Modelling Group speaks of 'tunable design' in relation to this process.[9] The feedback loop between the two model types is not automated: it has a subjective aesthetic arbitrator. The design team refer to a dynamic equilibrium between aesthetics and optimization that should not be polarized, even though the project is driven by environmental considerations.[10]

The proposal does not use pre-rationalization of the shape. The complex curvature is not resolved into cotangential arcs. Here, the contractor wanted the information in the form of points in

LEFT Louvre panel variation with orientation.

OPPOSITE The proposed development, viewed across the water from the southwest.

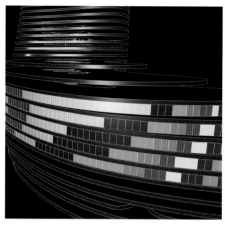
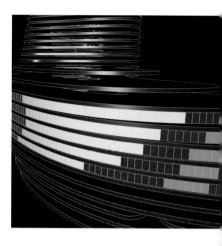

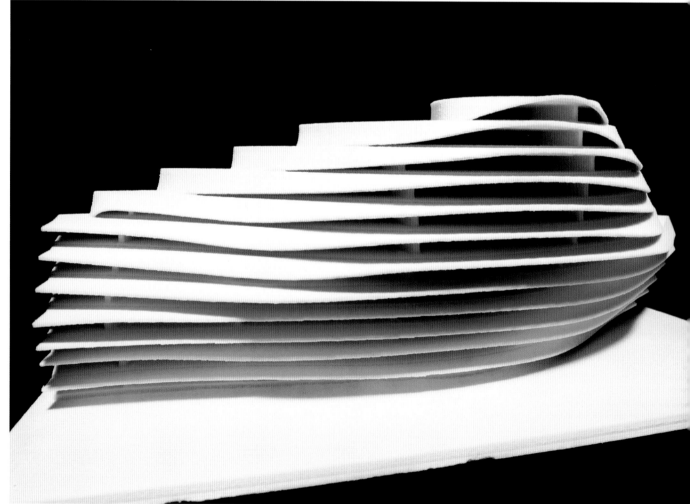

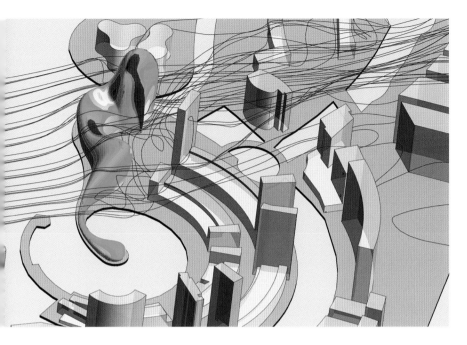

space, not to set out a series of small arcs. Details were considered at full-, half- or fifth-scale early in the design process, so that fabrication and its cost implications informed the design development from the start. This allowed the further deployment of computation to standardize panel types to a suite of approximately twenty different types that would still accommodate the complex, curving form. Working from a starting point of thousands of potential variants, limits or thresholds on the accuracy of fit required were established by closely considering the installation details for the panels, enabling partner Francis Aish of the SMG to write a programme to change the panels from their dimensions for perfect fit to conform to one of as few as twenty options that allowed for fit within the required tolerances.

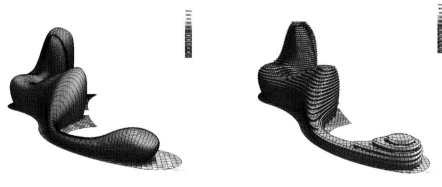

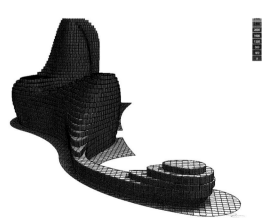

ᴏᴘ Computational fluid dynamics analysis ʏ Arup: air flows and positive and negative ʀessure.

ʙᴏᴠᴇ ᴀɴᴅ ʀɪɢʜᴛ Comparative incidence of ᴏlar radiation for smooth building profile; ᴇʀʀaced by floor levels; and protected by ᴏuvres.

ᴘᴘᴏsɪᴛᴇ, ᴛᴏᴘ Panel standardization – the ᴏlours represent panel types: (left to right) ɴlimited variation; number of types reduced ᴏ 13; further reduced to five.

ᴘᴘᴏsɪᴛᴇ, ʙᴏᴛᴛᴏᴍ The louvres.

Melbourne Recital Centre

ASHTON RAGGATT MCDOUGALL

Melbourne, Australia

Ashton Raggatt McDougall's recital centre for Melbourne is a highly purpose-specific performance space. From its inception, there was determination on the part of the client that it would share none of the flaws or ameliorations of other post-war halls. Not only would the building be perfectly tuned acoustically, but it would also have a coherent aesthetic, free from corrective reflectors or safety rails. There were two groups of people that the acousticians had to please: the audience and the musicians. Each of the 1,000 seats would be 'A'-grade, and, equally important, musicians would be attracted back to the venue by the brilliant platform (or performer) acoustic.

After a number of early explorations into more complex types of space, the traditional box was settled upon as offering the optimal acoustic. Precedents setting the standard included the Musikvereinsaal in Vienna and Wigmore Hall in London, although both vary in scale from this project. The box-type originates in the grand palace ballrooms of the past, the designs of which were driven by visual and decorative, rather than acoustic, aesthetics, but nevertheless sponsored the musical experience intended for such spaces. The stage, while allowing for the best mathematical proportions in relation to the rest of the hall, was conceived to be as seamlessly part of the room as possible, right down to the heavy revolving doors.

While there are rules of thumb governing successful acoustic design, it is a subtle art, and each design move – whether at the level of the proportions of the space, the sculpting of balconies, or the density of wall ornament – will impact on the sound. Acoustic designer Raf Orlowski visited Melbourne for regular, week-long workshops with the architects. Using a custom system developed for the project (a detailed 3D virtual model with scripts that calculated the volume of the

Section showing the pixellation in raised relief on the plywood walls and stepped ceiling for perfect platform acoustics.

space and the reverberation time, and regenerated new versions of the balconies and surface ornament), the designers were able to progressively 'tune' the space while working with the other design criteria, including seating distribution, balcony form and control-room location, in near real time.[11] The outcomes went through a more formal digital analysis process in the acoustic software Odeon; to do this, the model had to be simplified, involving a longer turnaround time. Cost dictated that most of the acoustic modelling had to be accomplished digitally, but a physical scale model was built late in the process to verify the results. Full-scale prototype textured wall panels, together with the bonded mass that gives the sound its warmth, were built and 'sounded' in the reverberation chambers at Melbourne's RMIT University.

Plywood was chosen for the interior surfaces for acoustic performance. The decoration on the walls and ceiling materialized as an undulating pattern of waves across the relief of the plywood surface – like weather, sound or the wood grain on fine instruments – selectively diffusing the higher frequency sounds. The low-frequency waves were diffused by a rectilinear pattern in deeper relief of large 'pixels', which varied in both size and depth, from 450mm² to 900mm² on the back wall, and 1,800mm x 900mm on the side walls. Four main depths of plywood were used. Attention to detail in the design of services included air conditioning with a PNC rating of 15 based on the curves of human hearing, and light dimmers with acoustic attenuators.[12]

• Acoustic optimization (p. 252)

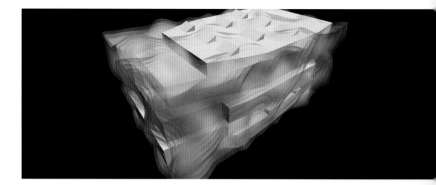

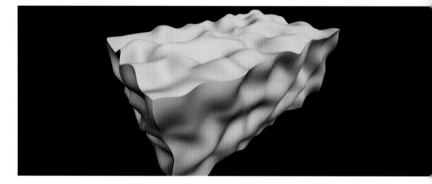

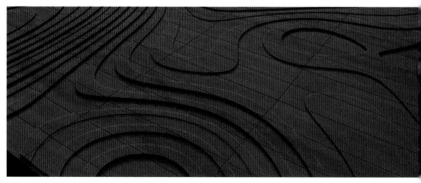

RIGHT The image that worried the clients.

BELOW View of the recital hall.

OPPOSITE, TOP Virtual sound waves collide with the box.

OPPOSITE, CENTRE Perturbations.

OPPOSITE, BOTTOM Investigations into textured relief for the wall and ceiling panels.

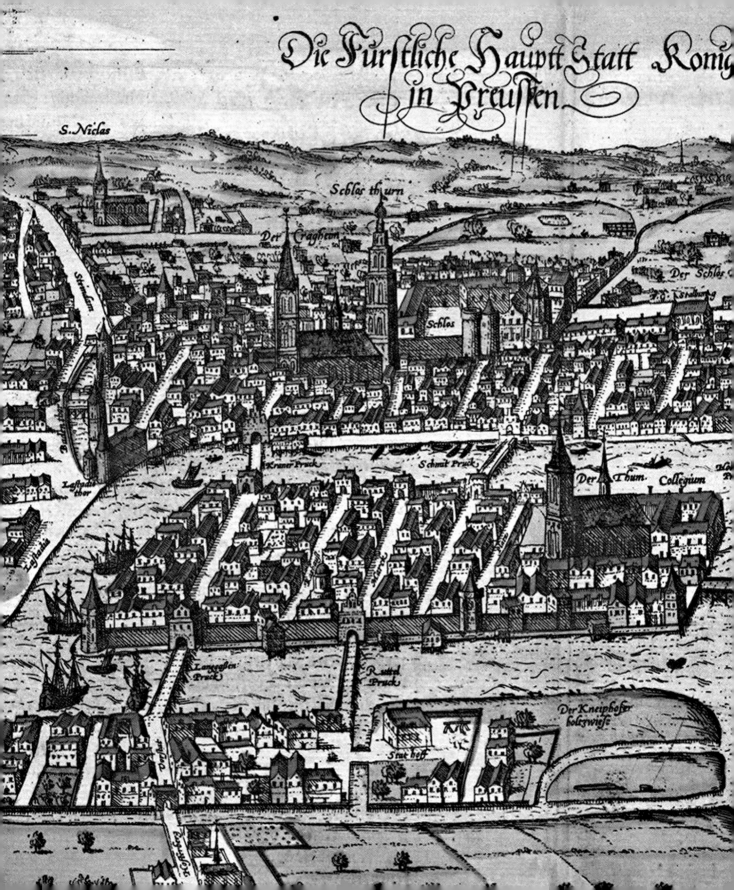

Die Fürstliche Hauptt Statt König in Preussen

S. Niclas

Schlos thurn

Der Craghteim

Der Schlos

Schlos

Stalbung

Strantein

Schmal Pruck

Kramer Pruck

Laftat thor

Der Thum

Collegium

Lastadie

Langgassen Pruck

Kuttel Pruck

Der Kneiphoffer holtzwiese

Stut heft

5 TOPOLOGY

Topology is a way of considering the Greek concept of *topos*: the place, the space, and everything that is in it. The freedom that it affords in architecture as a more generalized framework than geometry has received greater appreciation in the post-digital age. In mathematics, topology is a relatively new way of looking at the world, although as early as 1679 Gottfried Leibniz identified the need for a strictly geometrical analysis to express 'situm' (situation, or qualitative place relationship), equivalent to the role of algebra with respect to metrical relationships.[1] Thus the term 'analysis situs' was born, and remained in use until transmuting to topology in the 20th century.

Topology's conceptual birth is attributed to Leonhard Euler and a now-famous problem that he posed in 1735: was it possible to devise a continuous path that crossed each of Königsberg's seven bridges to the island in the city centre exactly once? The problem could be reduced to a diagram created by assigning a node to each river bank of departure and arrival, and creating scaleless, shapeless links to represent the bridges that spanned between them. From this simple network, it becomes immediately clear that there is no solution. A new geometry of position, therefore, became established, and its essential distinction from metrical Euclidean or Cartesian geometry understood.

The essence of architectural and urban planning is also captive in such non-geometrical diagrams, as are the relationships between component spaces or activities of buildings. This is regardless of how the building itself may solidify through the process of design and construction into a static, unchanging form that is also subject, like the city of Königsberg, to detailed geometrical description. It is possible that the organization of the early developmental world of our childhood is a similar network of connections between significant places and things, and it is only later and gradually that the absolute reference of metrical Cartesian space is superimposed on our established perception of proximities and relationships. The psychologist and philosopher Jean Piaget certainly believed this. Joseph Rykwert, in *The Idea of a Town* (1988), highlighted through his study of Rome the transition from topological and ritualistic town-making to the imposition of the geometrical grid. Nearly a hundred years earlier, Henri Poincaré gained the title 'the father of topology' after the publication of *Analysis Situ* (1895). He defined topology as the science that lets us know the qualitative properties of geometric figures, both in ordinary space and in space with more than three dimensions. These are geometric figures that can undergo such radical transformations as to lose all metric and projective characteristics, but retain their topological identity.

In 1858 astronomer and mathematician August Ferdinand Möbius described a new surface, how to create it and its properties, at a presentation to the Academy of Science in Paris. Today, this surface is known as the Möbius strip. Although the figure itself can be found in more ancient representations, including Roman mosaics, its mathematical significance at this time was to highlight a class of surfaces known collectively as non-orientable, which have an important twist in their creation. The Möbius strip is a single, continuous surface, bounded and finite in extent, but allowing infinite traversal. It was this quality of finite infinity that attracted the artist Max Bill in the 1940s, when he independently 'discovered' the surface by twisting and gluing together opposing ends of a strip of paper – just as Möbius had done – while designing a hanging sculpture.[2] In the 19th century, mathematician Felix Klein also conceptually glued together two sets of opposite edges of the strip, one set directly and one with a twist to demonstrate another well-known non-orientable surface: the Klein surface, popularly known and represented as the Klein bottle. This too can be considered an ancient archetype with ample symbolism – it is represented in a gateway of the Alhambra, for instance – as a continuous, closed surface that has neither interior nor exterior, and which mysteriously cannot be fabricated without intersecting itself. If we follow Poincaré's lead into more than three dimensions, this surface can, even more mysteriously, be embedded in four dimensions without self-intersection.

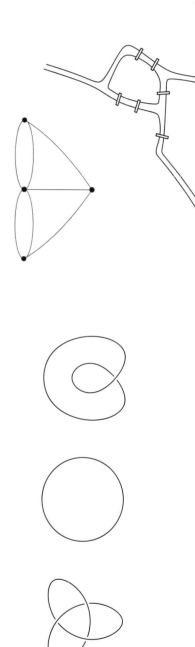

TOP Euler's topological diagram of Königsberg.

ABOVE Knot diagrams: the loop, the circle and the trefoil – all topologically equivalent.

OPPOSITE *Möbius Strip II*, by M. C. Escher.

How should we describe surfaces in topology? It is surfaces that we are largely concerned with in architectural representation; indeed, in topology itself, the sphere is generally considered to be a surface, a two-dimensional manifold embedded in three dimensions. To an insect crawling across a football, or a person walking on the surface of the Earth, there is no intrinsic distinction between a plane and the spherical surface on which they find themselves. Extrinsically, whether taking flight or setting off in a space craft, the difference soon becomes apparent. One way that it makes itself known while still on the surface is to journey a very, very long way in a straight line and then, confusingly, arrive exactly where you started. This mystery revealed itself to the main character in Edwin Abbott's novelette *Flatland: A Romance of Many Dimensions*, while the explorers Ferdinand Magellan and Juan Sebastián Elcano already understood this relationship before they set off on their own voyages of discovery. The sphere, the cube and any other shape, however complex and intricate, which could, in theory, be melded into a ball-like shape by stretching, folding, flattening, or any other plastic deformation (but without tearing or cutting), are two-dimensional manifolds of genus 0 in topology. If we change the rules and punch a hole through a ball of dough to make a doughnut, its outer surface is still a two-dimensional manifold and a continuous surface, but of genus 1. With a bit of imagination, this can be stretched into a cup with a handle, or even a sphere with a handle. The genus of a topological surface is equivalent to the total number of holes or (equivalent) handles.

From surfaces to knots: knots are too ancient and culturally ubiquitous to even begin to search for their roots. Within topology, they too have found a systematic means of description that does not require seafaring or equestrian terms. A mathematical knot is one-dimensional, as indeed any line or curve is, although it must also be immersed in two dimensions or embedded in three to be appreciated as more than an endless path along a rope. Knots have loops and crossings in their topological terminology; they have mirror images into which they cannot be transformed without cutting and rejoining.

What is it about topology and its freedom of description that has seized modern architectural production, long after the underlying ideas were in the common domain? One possible answer is the confluence of unimagined new levels of computer graphical representation with the transition of non-rational basis splines, or NURBs, from the automotive industry into other computer-aided design software. The dynamism of systems could not only be represented in truly dynamic models – models that linked external forces to form and organization, aping the unfolding understanding of natural and social systems – but their manifestations could now be understood visually. Truly visual feedback changed everything. At a simpler level, it became possible to model surfaces that could change, stretch, adopt free-

PRECEDING PAGE Königsberg, with its island and seven bridges.

OVERLEAF The Yokohama International Port Terminal, by Foreign Office Architects. Cross-section, wire-frame diagram, aerial view, interior perspective and circulation diagram (clockwise from top left; p. 160). Site plan; roof and floor plans (top and bottom; p. 161).

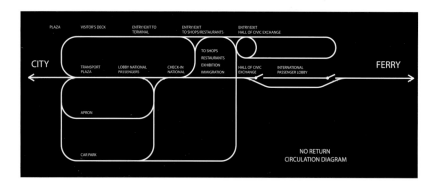

PLAZA VISITOR'S DECK ENTRY/EXIT TO TERMINAL ENTRY/EXIT TO SHOPS/RESTAURANTS ENTRY/EXIT HALL OF CIVIC EXCHANGE

CITY

TRANSPORT PLAZA LOBBY NATIONAL PASSENGERS CHECK-IN NATIONAL TO SHOPS RESTAURANTS EXHIBITION IMMIGRATION HALL OF CIVIC EXCHANGE INTERNATIONAL PASSENGER LOBBY

FERRY

APRON

CAR PARK

NO RETURN
CIRCULATION DIAGRAM

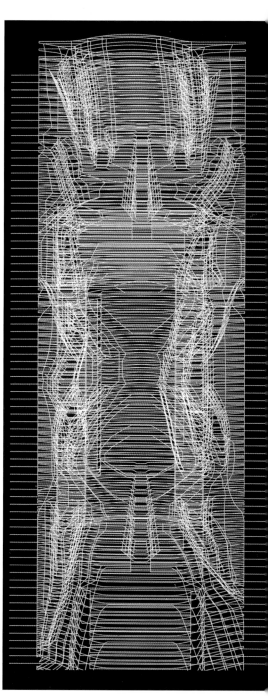

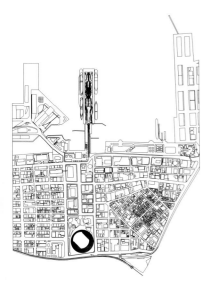

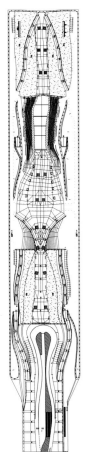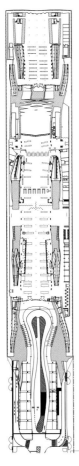

form curvature, or conform to a geometrical rationale without losing their integrity – wonderful surfaces that, plastically and geometrically at least, exceeded the behaviour of any known material surface and could be given visual material qualities at a whim.[3] Such surfaces had previously required representation in plaster as frozen moments, now they could remain alive as part of a spatial continuum of change.

The importance of architecture as process is expressed by Farshid Moussavi and Alejandro Zaera-Polo of Foreign Office Architects in the design and production of the practice's International Port Terminal (left and opposite), in Yokohama, Japan, surely one of the most arresting works of built topography and topology of recent years. 'Processes are far more interesting than ideas,' they wrote. 'What we are interested in is constructing engineering processes on different levels … these processes of temporal formation produce organizations of a far higher complexity and sophistication than instantaneous ideas.'[4]

In this project, a building grows from the circulation diagram, from the process of moving people. As with Euler's Seven Bridges of Königsberg, it is the continuity of movement that is the essential idea, the smooth connectivity; in this case, across levels and between inside and outside. Wood was chosen as the material of continuity, and in its organization across the planes of the decks is mapped in changing directions to maximize the economy of use of the material. These changing directions at the angle changes in the deck also become a navigational map, much as our innate perception of direction is thought to be derived from the topological mapping of visual data in the visual cortex. Topological description is being adopted as the means of mapping architectural intention, and with it arrives the progressive discovery of how to map this onto the frozen Euclidean moment in the physical world.

Möbius House

UN STUDIO

Het Gooi, Netherlands

This radical 590m², three-bedroom concrete-and-glass house outside Amsterdam was conceived for a young family in which to stage their diurnal, looping transition between activities on a continuous path without end. The planning, responsive to the bucolic site and daily passage of the sun, is based on a crossing, rising and falling three-dimensional path, along which the rooms and activities of the day are arranged, with the major rooms subsumed in the circulation ribbon. It leads endlessly to the periphery and back into the centre of the house in what might be diagrammed as an eternity sign, or figure of eight.[5]

In reality, the path has been deliberately planned by the architects, whose design story celebrates the power of such architectural diagrams as the Möbius strip (for which the house is popularly named),

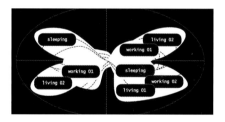

as a continuous ribbon surface that twists and joins in three dimensions to achieve its endless, single-surface continuity.[6] By supplanting traditional, more rigid terminal tree-like planning typologies, the house simultaneously embraces both the oscillating continuum of daily living and the change, over other rhythms of time, that is inherent in family and work life.

Perhaps it is also significant that in topology, the Möbius strip, unlike the unbounded, finite surface of the sphere, has a single boundary – its continuous edge. To pursue the metaphor, the house is not hermetic, but has an important edge, or periphery, where the more private spaces are to be found, and through which it interfaces with the undulating green surroundings of its site, a break point in this restless, dynamic model of domesticity.

OPPOSITE The house is located in a wooded setting.

RIGHT Concept diagrams showing the diurnal journey around the eternal looping space of the house.

- Non-orientable surfaces (p. 263)
- Topological transformations (p. 265)
- Topology models (p. 265)

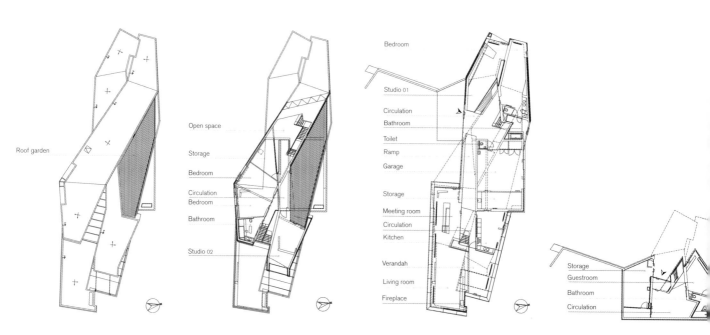

Roof garden

Open space

Storage

Bedroom

Circulation
Bedroom

Bathroom

Studio 02

Bedroom

Studio 01

Circulation

Bathroom

Toilet

Ramp

Garage

Storage

Meeting room

Circulation

Kitchen

Verandah

Living room

Fireplace

Storage
Guestroom

Bathroom

Circulation

RIGHT View along the edge of the 'strip' from the eastern living area to the meeting room.

BELOW Looking east, to the stairway.

OPPOSITE, TOP View up the east staircase.

OPPOSITE, BOTTOM Plans, basement to roof (right to left).

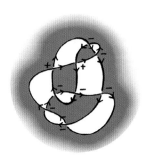

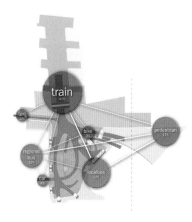

Arnhem Central

UN STUDIO

Arnhem, Netherlands

Dutch architectural firm UN Studio's new transport interchange is planned for a total capacity of 108,800 journeys per day: by bus, train, taxi, bicycle, car, and on foot. It is, by definition, and by diagram, a network of nodes and edges. In the tradition of Leonhard Euler's Seven Bridges of Königsberg, which laid the foundations of graph theory and exposed the ideas that led to topology, this problem constituted a problem of routing and connections. Euler's challenge in 1735 was to find a continuous route around the city that visited both of its islands by crossing each of the seven bridges over the River Pregel once and only once.

This idea of a continuous and coherent journey with many starting and end points is fundamental to moving people through such an interchange. In this project it is translated into another topological manifestation: the continuous non-orientable surface. In an article for *AA Files*, Patrik Schumacher

wrote: 'Guided by the notion that a landscape with holes could also be seen as a knot of planes, [UN Studio] had begun to study mathematical knots in the search for new way of understanding the station area. The diagrammatic result of this was a Klein bottle, which connects the different levels of the station area in a hermetic fashion. A figure that is as deeply ambiguous as it is comprehensive, the Klein bottle remains continuous throughout transformation from a surface to a hole and back again.'[7]

Cecil Balmond of Arup identified the same idea in the solution to another problem: the vertical and horizontal structural coherence and continuity of a building that houses a huge public transfer hall and its associated shops, bars and restaurants, along with large areas of parking structure and housing units – three programmes with disparate granularity and structural grids. 'We drew a line that

LEFT The non-orientable surface that self-intersects when embedded in three dimensions: an icon of ambiguity, continuity and connectivity.

OPPOSITE The continuous roof–wall, as expressed in the exterior of the building.

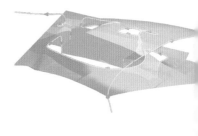

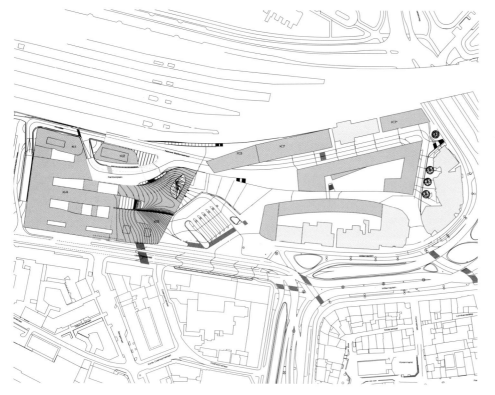

ABOVE A Seifert surface is a compact, connected, orientable surface associated with a particular knot that defines its boundary.

LEFT Site plan.

BELOW Cross-section.

OPPOSITE, TOP View of the interior, where the knot is clearly expressed in the contortions of the concrete structure: a surface whose precise shape and thinness is ready to respond to the detailed contingencies of structural optimization and programme.

OPPOSITE, BELOW Computer rendering of the terminal exterior.

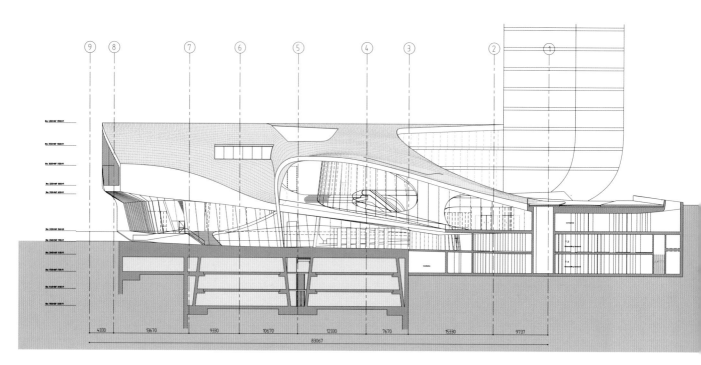

moved up from the foundations to loop and coil over space,' Balmond wrote in his book, *Informal* (2007). 'How to keep the curvature as a natural consequence of the concept? For that, a merging was needed, connecting roof and floors into one network.'[8]

The building, therefore, is a knot and a surface that is governed not as a smooth differentiable manifold, with a shape determined by measurable curvature, but as a topological diagram made matter. There is a process by which this transformation is affected, but the idea continues to inhabit the domain of connections and proximities, rather than shape and measurement. This process acquires for the building a fixed shape, measurable curvature and surface thickness; in this case, governed by repeated structural analysis and adjustment of an initial free-form surface, in-filled between the 'strings' of the knot. 'The surface produced is an optimum engineered surface, intact with the geometric definitions of its free edges,' Balmond added. 'Now the "strings" can vanish.'[9]

The surface shapes are clearly frozen flows, however, rather than surfaces derived from geometrical orderings or from material responses to structural forces. These are contrived flows that represent the design problem in a pure, idealized, geometrical space, free from gravity and the divergent influences of the physical world.

• Knot theory (p. 261)
• Topology models (p. 265)

Paramorph II
DECOI ARCHITECTS
London, UK

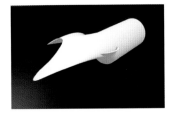

ramorph II was dECOi Architects' sponse to an invitational competition r a gateway to London's South Bank arts ntre. Approached from Waterloo Station, e major point of access to the complex as especially uncongenial and lacked any remony of arrival. Pedestrians would cross busy road and proceed through a rather tid railway underpass, before joining the kward footpath towards the performance lls. The proposed gateway was intended add a frisson to this otherwise nderwhelming experience.

The principal candidate for nprovement was the negotiation of the ilway underpass, the negative effect of hich was exacerbated by the skewed angle takes as it slices an aggressive trajectory ith respect to the tracks above, making e underpass longer than the track is wide. ather than creating a simple portal or narker for the entrance, dECOi proposed

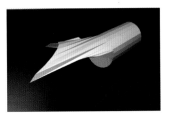

a hybrid of a funnel and tunnel, a great swirling tendril of matter, generously dimensioned at the end closest to the station, tapering and enveloping pedestrians as they progressed through to the underpass. The inspiration for this approach was the ballet, specifically William Forsythe's experimental choreography for the Frankfurt Ballet. In passing through and along this gateway, visitors to the South Bank arts complex would be undertaking their own performance.

Part of the inspiration for the design was Paramorph I, dECOi's hypothetical project, published in 1998, which explored the possibilities for the use of parametric design on architectural form-finding. As an emerging and novel architectural construct tied to digital design practice, the 'paramorph' was defined as an object with consistent topology but variable topography. In other words, the shape and volume of

OPPOSITE Computer rendering of the entrance passage.

RIGHT Parametric changes to form.

a form would be decided by a declared set of parameters; if any or several of the parameters were changed, a change would necessarily then be made to the object. For the first time in digital practice, the designer could 'steer' the form towards meeting a set of objectives, whether defined by performance or aesthetics. Given the vagueness of the proposal for the gateway – it was conceived more as a gesture than as an artifact – the paramorph approach allowed the design gesture to relax into designed form.

The original sketch was interrogated for more tangible spatial information, which, when extracted as data, would become the parameters with which the serial deformations of the paramorph would be driven. What was originally conceived as a tube with dimensions governed by a series of deformable rings, which allowed for local variability in the separation of the inner and outer surfaces, could be progressively morphed into a form that closely approximated the early sketches simply by altering the values ascribed to the parameters. An additional advantage was the chance to play out several constructional and structural scenarios at once. At each iteration of the paramorph's development, a free-form NURBs surface, ruled surfaces between the deformed 'rings', and a triangulated faceted surface could be developed simultaneously, offering different cost scenarios.

In the end, Paramorph II was not the selected entry, but the architects further developed the paramorph approach with a proposed extension to a residential tower block, coincidentally also located in London's South Bank.

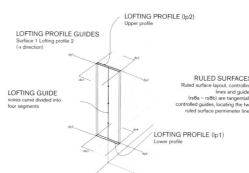

LOFTING PROFILE GUIDES
Surface 1 Lofting profile 2
(-x direction)

LOFTING GUIDE
NURBS curve divided into
four segments

LOFTING PROFILE (lp2)
Upper profile

LOFTING PROFILE (lp1)
Lower profile

RULED SURFACES
Ruled surface layout, controlling
lines and guides
(rs8a – rs8b) are tangentially
controlled guides, locating the two
ruled surface perimeter lines

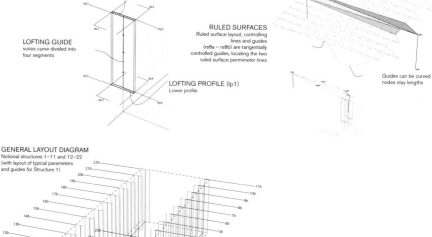

RULED SURFACE @ EACH SEGMENT
There are three ruled surfaces that define both the horizontal
and vertical surfaces of each segment

Guides can be curved by alte
nodes stay lengths

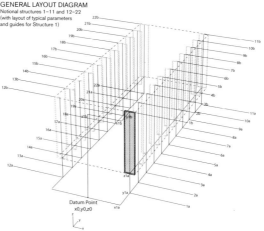

GENERAL LAYOUT DIAGRAM
Notional structures 1–11 and 12–22
(with layout of typical parameters
and guides for Structure 1)

Datum Point
x0,y0,z0

TOP Model of Paramorph II at th
2000 Venice Biennal

ABOVE AND LEFT Paramorph
parameters explaine

OPPOSITE, TOP Paramorph
16 stages of parametrical
induced contortion

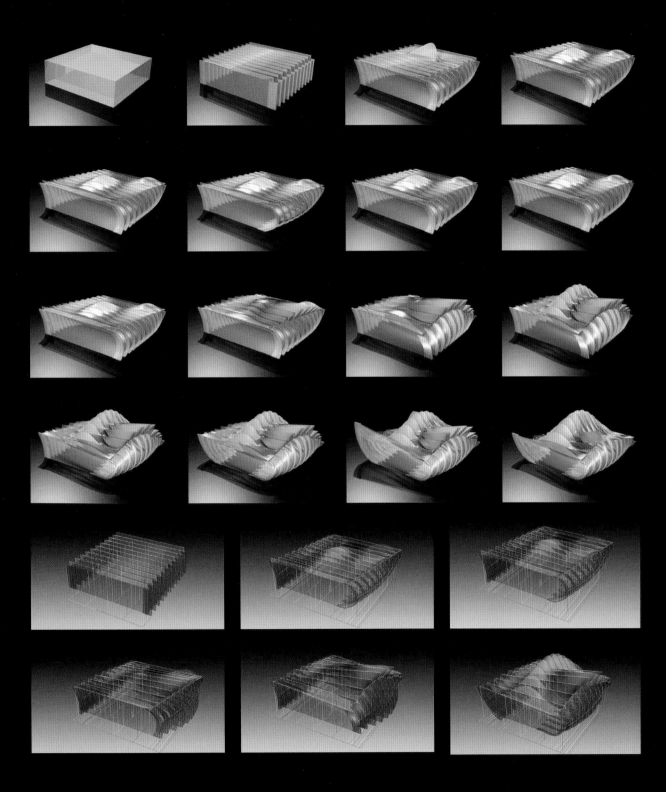

Cape Schanck House

PAUL MORGAN ARCHITECTS
Mornington Peninsula, Victoria, Australia

This weekend house is located near to the rugged coastline of the Southern Ocean. Although somewhat protected by a grove of native tea trees, it is nevertheless subject to strong prevailing winds, which, together with the direction of light stimulus, affect the trees' growth patterns. In this project, explain the architects, 'the analysis of dynamic forces (wind energy, wind turbulence and phototropism)' have been used to inform the modelling of the building envelope, almost to streamline its profile.[10]

At the presentation of the RAIA Robin Boyd Award for Residential Buildings in 2007, it was said that the resultant shaping provides a drag coefficient bettered only by a CX Citroën! The idea underlying the design is one of surface continuity and topology, with the form sculpted by the wind flows interpreted through the application of fluid dynamics analysis software. Like the surrounding tea trees, the fabric of the house deforms elegantly to the sunlight and out of the wind, and gathers water into its continuous

surface to stabilize the internal temperature, optimizing the comfort derived from the site and minimizing the house's use of external energy and water sources.

'Within the living room, the ceiling wraps down to an internal water tank,' note the architects. 'The tank cools the ambient air temperature of the living room during summer, supplies rain water, and structurally carries the roof load. Wind-scoops on the south elevation also act as a passive thermal device. These scoops trap cooling winds during summer, while providing shade from the hot afternoon sun.'

The house works hard to marry beauty and environmental propaganda, and to speak eloquently to students, design organizations and the public, as well as to other architects. By locating the water tank as the centrepiece of the house, the issue of water use and its conservation – so acutely critical in the local community and progressively more so worldwide – is brought to the fore.[11]

View from the street.

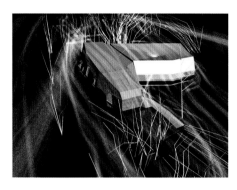

OPPOSITE, TOP LEFT Wind-flow analysis during design development.

OPPOSITE, CENTRE LEFT 'Wind rose' at the location of the house site.

OPPOSITE, RIGHT Diagram of the contours of prevailing winds.

OPPOSITE, BOTTOM The living room, featuring bulb tank.

RIGHT Under construction, becoming smooth and continuous.

BELOW The entrance and front decking.

Blowhouse: Life Support Unit

PAUL MORGAN ARCHITECTS

Mornington Peninsula, Victoria, Australia

owhouse was conceived as part of the ▪atforms for Living' component of ▪e exhibition, *Out of the Square: Beach ▪chitecture on the Mornington Peninsula*, ▪ld at the Mornington Peninsula Regional ▪allery. Five architects were asked to submit ▪signs for 'coastal houses of the future', ▪hich would demonstrate new ways of living ▪ided by the principles of sustainability, ▪novation and design.

Of this project, the architects have ▪ritten: 'Climate change has affected ▪ustralia's environment so dramatically ▪at the interior desert now meets the ▪utheastern coastline. Average temperatures ▪ve increased, the sea level has risen, and ▪infall has dropped. Many animal and plant species are by now extinct. The island continent is in terminal drought.

'In this context, the challenge is how to survive the environment. Our speculative design for the Blowhouse is a "life support unit". As with other future dwellings, our approach is one of "terraforming", or the creation of a survivable micro-ecology, an example being the structures built to create a life-supporting atmosphere in the film *Aliens*. The site is adjacent to the Blowhole, a promontory to the west of Flinders on the south coast. The design principle of the bioengineered Blowhouse is to create an energy-neutral life support unit that utilizes the environment's kinetic potential, forming a kind of lung – a structure that breathes.'[12]

OVERLEAF:

▪PPOSITE Site renders.

▪GHT The semi-rigid exoskeleton.

LEFT, ABOVE Wind and pressure studies.

LEFT, BELOW Operational diagram.

RIGHT Interior view.

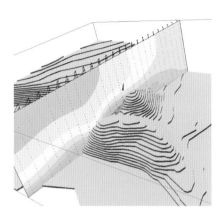

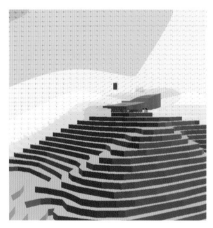

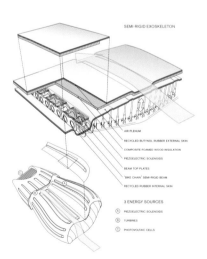

SEMI-RIGID EXOSKELETON

AIR PLENUM
RECYCLED BUTYNOL RUBBER EXTERNAL SKIN
COMPOSITE FOAMED WOOD INSULATION
PIEZOELECTRIC SOLENOIDS
BEAM TOP PLATES
'BIKE CHAIN' SEMI-RIGID BEAM
RECYCLED RUBBER INTERNAL SKIN

3 ENERGY SOURCES

Ⓐ PIEZOELECTRIC SOLENOIDS
Ⓑ TURBINES
Ⓒ PHOTOVOLTAIC CELLS

Slavin House

GREG LYNN
Venice, California, USA

Slavin House is architect Greg Lynn's own home in Venice, California, and follows in the lineage of a series of projects, including the Embryological House, which are more concerned with the relationships and hierarchy of part to whole in architecture than his earlier work. Lynn has pulled back from an earlier focus on using digital tools to explore animate form and smooth, time-based morphologies. Despite this returning of form to the architectural language of hierarchy and scale, there remains an enduring interest in the variation of the topologically homologous form over discrete but infinitesimal intervals of variation, whether viewed as spatial or temporal.

Here, the smooth, seamless form is a structural truss of two continuous, curved, welded and hollow steel tubes that are braided and looped through one another. The house was modelled as a series of cotangential arcs and linear segments that,

regardless of their changing length and curvature/radius, remain contiguous and tangential in the process of change. The basket structure supports and contains, sets up solids and voids, and unites the spaces of the two floors of the house. Like the Embryological House, the Slavin House is organized around a topological family of morphs: a series of voids (light wells), which vary in shape, size and form. Each is a particular instance of a single, uniting parametric blueprint.

'Most architects want to understand the Embryological House experiment as a search for an ideal house,' Lynn has said, 'as if the whole collection of houses was a conceit to then select the best one. They are all equivalent. I love them all equally as if they were my children. The design problem was not the house but the series, the entire infinitesimally extensive and intensive group.'[13]

Model.

• Homology (p. 260)
• Topological transformations (p. 265)

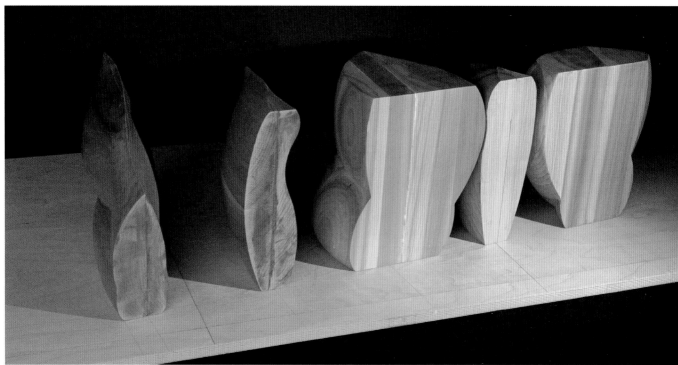

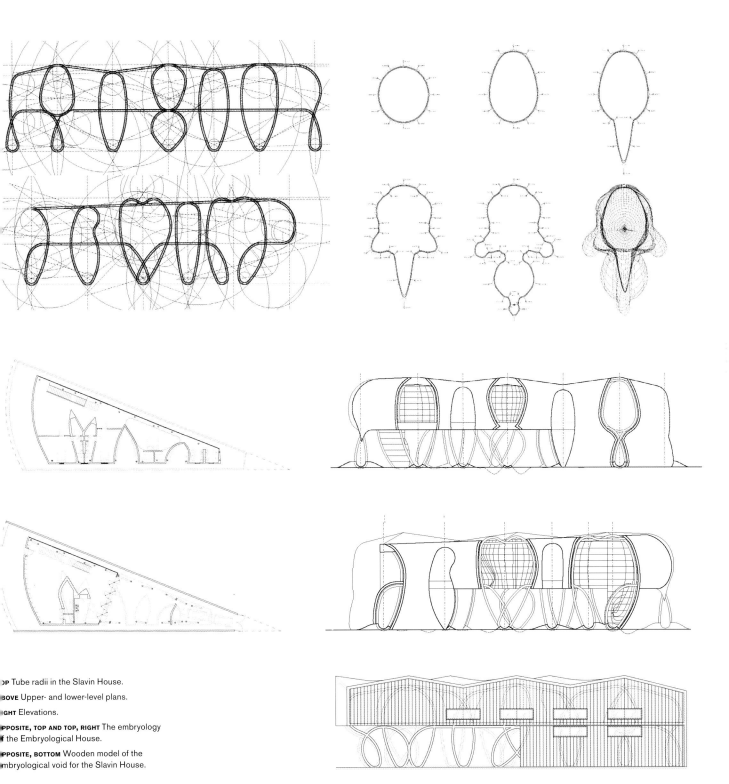

OP Tube radii in the Slavin House.

ABOVE Upper- and lower-level plans.

RIGHT Elevations.

OPPOSITE, TOP AND TOP, RIGHT The embryology of the Embryological House.

OPPOSITE, BOTTOM Wooden model of the embryological void for the Slavin House.

Klein Bottle House

MCBRIDE CHARLES RYAN

Mornington Peninsula, Victoria, Australia

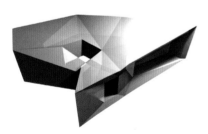

The site of this award-winning holiday home on the Mornington Peninsula, like Cape Schanck House (p. 174) and Blowhouse (p. 178) by Paul Morgan Architects, set among the windswept tea trees so characteristic of the area, became somewhat of a topological adventure. Architect Rob McBride has described how the team began with a spiral shape, but as work continued upon the topography, a new shape – the Klein bottle – emerged. The so-called Klein bottle, or Klein surface, is a continuous, non-orientable surface that intersects itself when immersed in three dimensions. More significantly, it has one continuous, two-sided surface.[14]

This lack of distinction between the internal and external gave expression to the designers' intentions and organized the house into all sorts of spaces, gathered around a central area, thus creating a new type of family home in which everyone has proximity to each other. The organization was also seen as a journey and metaphorical shell, its experiential qualities driving the form ahead of the mathematics. The mathematical model tied together all of these intentions. The spiral had a beginning, an end, and an openness in between; when the start was collapsed with the end, the topology of a Klein bottle emerged. Once this was recognized, it could be explored and further exploited by knowingly pushing the connection in the design models. Spatially, this was an original place to be. Movement through the house is without a strong sense of direction; infinity is implied in the looping continuity between parts, the endless cycle in the Klein bottle.

An early origami model of a Klein bottle, notes fellow architect Debbie Ryan, conformed with intriguing sympathy to the architectural impulse to site the house with regard to the best views, wind protection, and optimal use of the topography to

LEFT Evolution of form: the opening in the façade is like the neck of a bottle, while the self-intersection of the surface occurs just below the courtyard, next to the entrace.

OPPOSITE The consistent language of folding is visible throughout the building's surfaces.

minimize excavation. As the term 'bottle' is probably an inaccurate translation of Felix Klein's use of the German word *Flashe* (surface), as opposed to *Flasche* (bottle), the Klein bottle's familiar smooth, voluptuous and glassy incarnations have no particular significance for the mathematically defined surface. The origami version offered a way of actually building the building, realizing a continuous surface from planes using the available technologies. It was also seen as possessing an echo of the original 'fibro' beach houses of the area. In early models, the entire house was white, but the origami model offered a way to introduce colour. One side of the paper was white, the other black: the yin and yang. This idea was not applied rigorously, but in a painterly way: white to indicate the entrance; black where the house is close to the tea trees; and red for the platform, the metaphorical 'ship in a bottle'.

Within the site, the house is located right on the cusp where the land becomes very steep. It negotiates the topography. Topologically defined forms like the Klein surface, as McBride has observed, can be infinitely distorted to suit topography and programme, creating a new model and opening up a whole new area of architectural exploration.

• Immersion (p. 260)
• Non-orientable surfaces (p. 263)
• Topology models (p. 265)

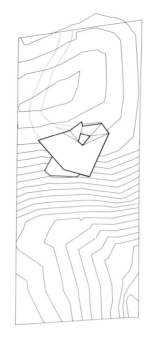

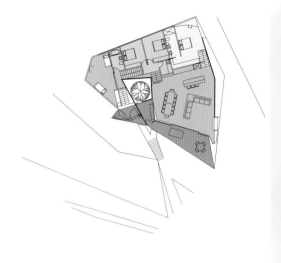

LEFT AND ABOVE, RIGHT Plans.
BELOW Sections.
OPPOSITE, TOP Models reveal the arrangement of the interior spaces and roofscape.

OPPOSITE, BOTTOM The Klein Bottle House nestled among the tea trees.

OVERLEAF The complex geometries unfold from the exterior entrance (below, left), through the interior passageway (above, left), and into the main living area (right).

1. Rumpus room 2. Stairway 3. En suite
4. Master bedroom 5. North deck

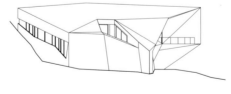

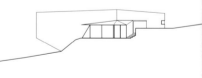

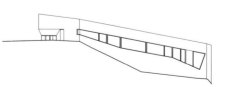

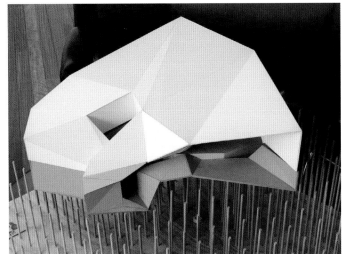

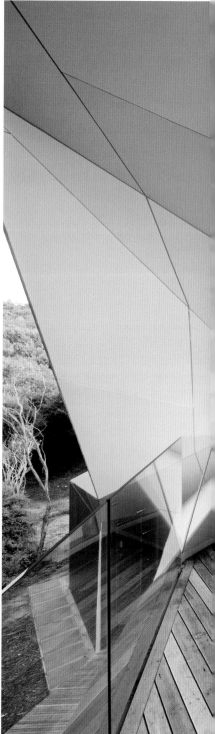

Möbius Bridge
HAKES ASSOCIATES
Bristol, UK

is competition-winning design for a
[foo]tbridge across the River Avon that was
[str]ucturally independent of the river banks
[an]d unthreatening to the historic fabric (on
[on]e side are the ruins of a Norman castle,
[an]d on the other is an old brewery building)
[s]o had to be a structurally hermetic form,
[at l]east with regard to lateral forces. This
[wa]s achieved with the simplest and best-
[kn]own non-orientable surface: the Möbius
[ba]nd, created in topology by attaching two
[op]posite ends of a rectangular surface and
[sw]itching their orientation to create a twist,
[ge]nerating a continuous, one-sided surface.[15]

The resulting form is an elegant gestural
[cu]rve, a twisted asymmetrical figure of eight,
[wh]ich appears to float above the river. The
[de]ck is braced by a minimal crossing point
[w]here the curve that sweeps up from the
[riv]er to become the compression arch meets
[th]e deck. The bridge is passively prestressed
[by] the arch on one side being set higher
[th]an intended and allowed to drop under

gravity, thus increasing tension, torsion and
strength. The shape was refined through
a series of paper models, which informed
the designers' approach to optimizing the
structure. The Möbius surface achieves
torsional stiffness, notes architect Julian
Hakes, and gives the right orientation of the
arch for the cables to the deck.[16]

The assembled bridge was designed to
be floated from the Netherlands on barges,
under the Clifton Suspension Bridge in
stately procession to take up its position.
Once in situ, it will be anchored to steel piles
that will appear as small pebble islands. As
a final touch to accentuate the paradoxical
nature of the one-sided Möbius band, the
designers have envisioned a hanging human
figure, walking on the underside of the arch
– an Anthony Gormley sculpture, perhaps.
This is all part of the holistic approach to
structural and formal design espoused by
Hakes Associates – in this case, the damping
for the bridge to kill unwelcome oscillation.

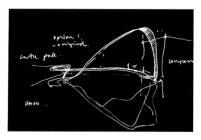

• Non-orientable surfaces (p. 263)
• Topology models (p. 265)

OPPOSITE 3D contextual visualization.
RIGHT Early conceptual models.

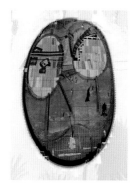

Villa Nurbs
CLOUD 9 ARCHITECTURE
Girona, Spain

'Uncompromising' would be the word to best describe the architects' approach to inserting this villa into a coastal 'suburban' village in Catalonia's Empuriabrava marina. Located in the Empordà Valley, Villa Nurbs makes no concession to the folksy yet faux conventionality of the surrounding homes, other than sharing their defensive postures as private enclosed residences. For all its relaxed seaside appeal, the region has been developed as a tawdry suburb comprised of weekend retreats and second homes. Cloud 9's project, commonly likened to a landed UFO, addresses this artificiality head on. It is unashamedly alien.

The house is a blob: its main areas are supported one level above ground by two flaring concrete columns, one containing the entrance vestibule and staircase, and the other guest accommodation and a home office. The columns dissolve into the first-floor slab, much of which is cantilevered beyond these two supporting structures. Running along the sides of the slab are two crescent-shaped covered areas that enclose a private courtyard and swimming pool, which has a glass bottom that allows natural light to filter through the water into the column enclosures below. One of the crescents contains the living spaces; the other, the bedrooms.

The blobbiness of the whole is no mere gesture; rather, it is comprehensively followed through to the last. There are no walls as such dividing the space, and the roof and ceiling form a matrix of Ethylene-tetrafluoroethylene (ETFE) pillows, which first appeared at the Eden Project in Cornwall, and more recently in PTW Architects' Water Cube for the 2008 Beijing Olympics (p. 86). But whereas these pillows were restricted in function as highly insulating transparent elements, at Villa Nurbs a performative quality has been

LEFT Aerial views of the project under construction.

OPPOSITE The structure's curvilinearity stands out in its urban context.

introduced by allowing the pillows to control the degree of solar penetration, simply by varying the degree of inflation. This was achieved by screenprinting an image on one wall of the pillow, with its negative on the opposite wall. When the pillows are highly inflated, more sunlight can find a path through them than when they are deflated (when the positive and negative images align more closely, effectively occluding more of the sun's entry than when inflated).

It is the project's name – Villa Nurbs – that reveals its main conceit. It is as if a CAD project has been directly translated from computer-generated non-uniform rational B-spline surfaces (NURBs) directly to built object, which is of course what has happened – hence the description of the house in its suburban context as 'uncompromising'. If the direct translation of the voluptuous, curved surfaces comes across as self-conscious savoir faire, perhaps the most tongue-in-cheek giveaway is the manner in which the concrete supports and lower level have been constructed. As with a student using foam core board for a school project, cut at the contour levels to make those oddly terraced landscape models, the concrete supports for Villa Nurbs have been cleverly contour-crafted in exactly the same manner, to brilliant effect.

• NURBs (p. 263)

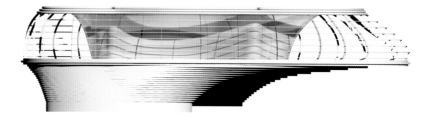

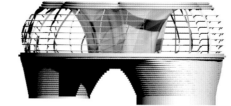

ABOVE AND LEFT Side and end elevatio

BELOW The building under constructi

OPPOSITE, LEFT Continuous surface un
constructi

OPPOSITE, RIGHT View of the ETFE pillow
climate-responsive means to modify inter
temperature and daylight penetrati

ABOVE Detail of the roof 'pillows', showing ducts that regulate solar penetration by inflation and deflation.

ABOVE, LEFT Attached to a network of tension cables anchored to the façade, the tiles can block sunlight, rain and strong winds, but can also be permeated by a cool breeze.

LEFT Contour model.

OPPOSITE The structure's geometry is heightened through illumination at night.

National Museum of Australia

ASHTON RAGGATT MCDOUGALL

Canberra, Australia

The title of a monograph devoted to the National Museum of Australia, *Tangled Destinies*, reflects the tangled inseparability of histories from different cultural perspectives, and the impossibility of simplifying the relationship between them, which dominates the museum's conceptual design. The geometry of threads that entwine in a series of knots is one of a range of devices in the highly wrought assembly of cultural allusions, architectural motifs and visual puns that tell Australian history – not as a consensual national story but as many stories interwoven together.[17] This tangle of threads becomes the central organizing device for the distribution of the buildings, the internal and external spaces, and the journey through the exhibitions.

There is a second twist in the mathematical/geometrical telling of the Australian story in this building, and that is the significance given to what is not there.

As a pathway taken by visitors through the museum, the thread becomes a huge, virtual, twisted extrusion of a regular pentagon. This five-sided figure is generally only seen where the thread cuts through the building envelope as it enters the interior. The thread is experienced as space, but not seen except in the residual built fabric after its knotted tangle has been subtracted from the museum's mass.

'We wanted to deeply problematize the idea of a single singularity, of an intersection,' notes Howard Raggatt, who summarizes the design of the museum's main hall in terms reminiscent of Dr Seuss: the 'knot in a box'.[18] For Raggatt, the verbal pun of 'not' and 'knot' refers to earlier work: his own thesis (*This is Not Architecture*) and the practice's competition entry for Melbourne's Federation Square (p. 58), in which a knot is subtracted from a sphere. The architects' competition entry for the

Entry ribbon.

National Museum of Australia carried the slogan: 'This is *not* yet a design.' Raggatt says of the project, 'This is a knot and no one can read it as a knot. Anti-space is the thing.'

For all the wit and quips in the present building, the story of Australia is seen as an impossible journey and the museum is seen as a puzzle, a very partial fragment of a story. It is really, says Raggatt, about 'death, longing, waiting and anguish'; it has been suggested that the use of the number five in the building's geometry is an allusion to the stigmata of Christ.[19] Where the knotted thread crosses the bounding box and its virtual presence materializes, roof lights take on the actual rather than subtracted form of the thread as it passes through the top of the box. During the design process, their number was reduced from eight to six, and the knotted thread had to be retied to reduce the number of intersections. Similarly, the warped surface of the twisted pentagonal section thread could not be reproduced in glass, and the knot must be untwisted to achieve flat, glazed surfaces.

Neither mathematics nor the digital process were starting points for the conceptual design of this building; it was only through the use of computation that these convoluted representations of meaning could adopt their knotted topology and assert their negative presence in the spatial sequence of the museum.

• Knot theory (p. 261)

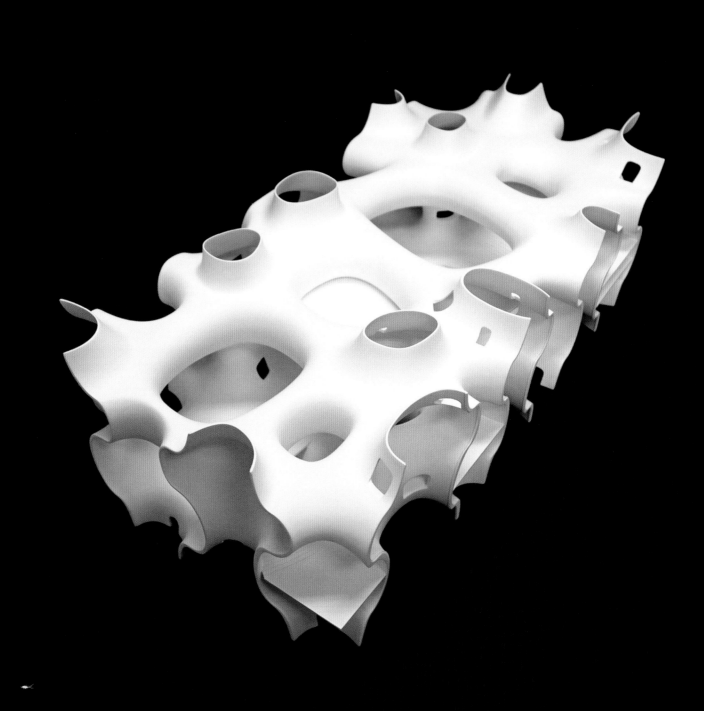

Metropolitan Opera House
TOYO ITO
Taichung, Taiwan

[T]yo Ito's opera house for the city of Taichung [is a] rectangular box containing a continuous [su]rface, developed from the idea of a loose, [flo]wing grid of continuous and infinite [sp]aces, interrupted by a bounding box. This [loo]se grid is fluid enough to deform and [ac]commodate the differentiated spaces of [th]e building. The opera house exhibits the [arc]hitect's recent interest in more continuous [sp]aces, as seen in such projects as the Tama [Ar]t University Library in Hachioji City and [c]rematorium in Kakamigahara, both in [Ja]pan. This smoothness is not just an aesthetic [de]cision; it also ensures structural efficiency.

The surface form is powerfully suggestive [of] families of mathematical surfaces that [ar]e seen in other contexts. Minimal triply [p]eriodic surfaces similarly create infinite [c]ontinuous gridded spaces, which can be [sh]own through the use of contrasting colour [to] extend forever separated, interlocked [o]n either side of a continuous surface.

Such hyperbolic surfaces offer useful representations of curvature in condensed matter at atomic and molecular scale.[20] Ito's opera-house design similarly starts from a structural and spatial idea of a continuous surface or shell of linked catenoids. The catenoid is the only minimal surface that is also a surface of revolution, and as a swept catenary curve, it is also a structurally significant surface.

Ito calls this open structure the 'sound cave', a continuous horizontal and vertical network of linked spaces to promote encounters between different arts and artists, interior and exterior. Sited within a park in a dense, urban high-rise area, the fluid cellular interior extends to make connections to the outside via sectional cuts through the surface made by the bounding box of the building. The regular cellular structure is deformed and distorted to accommodate the building's diverse spatial and functional requirements:

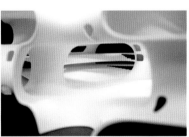

[O]PPOSITE Study model.

[RI]GHT Interior detail perspectives [fr]om study model.

the Grand Theatre; the Playhouse; and the Black Box, an experimental and intimate stage, connected to a rooftop terrace. The Metropolitan Opera House also houses an art workshop, art market, foyers, restaurants and parking. The stretching and morphing of the surface to house the variety of scales and types of space mean that the resulting surface is not everywhere funicular or catenary in shape, and that the shell will have out-of-surface forces under gravity load. This is accommodated by having a double surface. Each cement shell is everywhere equal in thickness, but the spacing between the two surface layers varies to accommodate the varying deviation of out-of-plane forces.

To develop a digital model of the surface as one continuous entity, a smoothing subdivision algorithm, programmed by Arup's Advanced Geometry Unit using Rhino 3D software as the visualization interface, was used. This was first developed by the AGU for the continuous roof and walls of Arnhem Central (p. 166), and interpolates between neighbouring vertices in the surface mesh to even out curvature in the surface. Those vertices coinciding with the exterior box remain on the box, and are only allowed to perform a 2D smoothing of the curve of the opening on the façade. The wire-frame for the edge curves of the doubly curved surface and the corner points is then sufficient for the structural software to generate a so-called Coons patch, which is translated into information that can be executed instantly in a finite-element package for structural analysis.[21]

• Knot theory (p. 261)

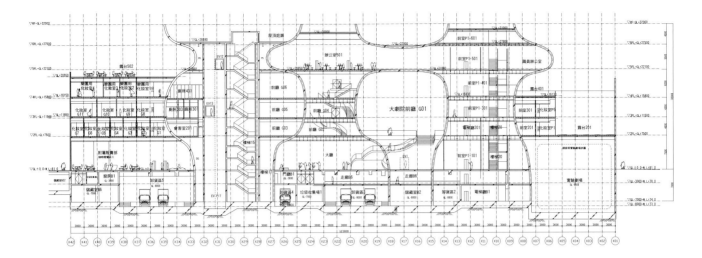

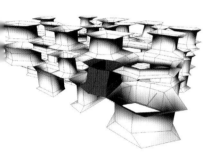

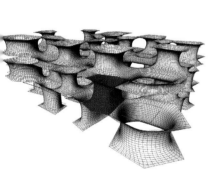

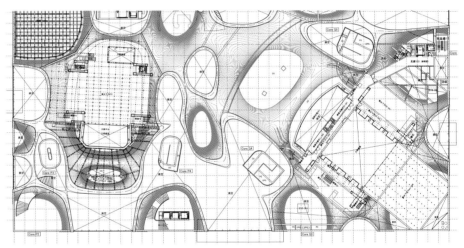

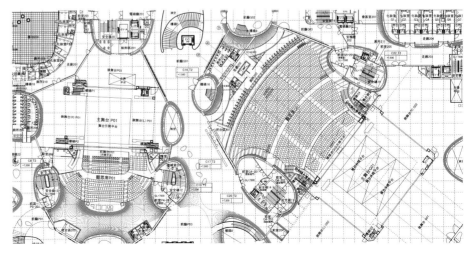

OPPOSITE, TOP Study model.

OPPOSITE, BOTTOM View from the park.

TOP Section.

ABOVE Catenoid, crude and smoothed.

RIGHT Plans.

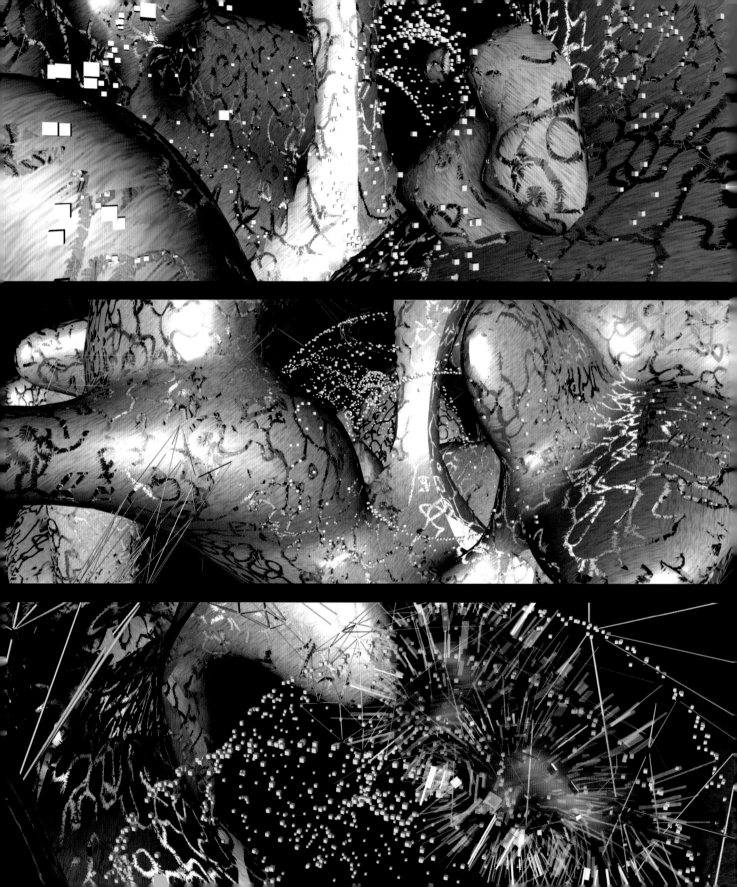

6 DATASCAPES AND MULTI-DIMENSIONALITY

'Datascape' is an ill-defined word for an important idea: the translation of abstract patterns that are inherent in all sorts of datasets and information flows into visual, spatial and temporal spaces and events. 'Data' has its etymological roots in things that are given, while 'scape' is an abbreviation of 'landscape', a painterly word that came into the English language from the Dutch at the end of the 16th century, along with an interest in capturing in paint their own rapidly changing countryside. Just as those earlier artists developed techniques for rendering the visual (and with it other resonances of place) in luminous landscape paintings, modern-day designers of datascapes investigate means of rendering the given within sensually enlivening and cogitatively accessible scapes of their own.

This often includes representing what cannot be seen, such as the visual representation of shifting ambient conditions (atmospheric changes, for example). What distinguishes these mediascapes from the virtual worlds of, say, digital gaming is their imminent relationship to a referenced world outside. Generally there is a near real-time mapping between the represented and the representation. Moreover, not all datascapes are virtual; many re-represent the data in the physical world. As the projects in this chapter illustrate, 'datascapes' encompass a broad spectrum of design activity.

Although we tend now to associate 'data' with numbers to represent things, designers are often engaged in a double translation. Events and phenomena in the physical or virtual world are first translated into digitally digestible numerical data, which is processed to generate accessible visual and/or visceral representations through a second translation, which itself recreates events and phenomena, either in virtual worlds or enacted in a choreographed space in the physical world. These are highly designed, representational, spatial worlds, and are a relatively recent design domain for architects, designers and artists. The focus is the design of environments for the interaction of their human participants. By contrast, the design process may be highly engaged in mechanisms and procedures data translation.

Datascapes follow the realization of the power of algorithms, in the context of digital computation as procedures for tirelessly processing extensive inputs and making connections. The purpose may be art and revelation; it may be research: data-mining for significant patterns through an intuitive interface. Or it may be to explore architecture that is as sensitive and kinetically responsive as we are. What binds these ideas is the bringing of information into our world, in a colourful, sound-filled, visually changing form to which we can apply our innate pattern-finding and spatial intelligence. Since it is difference, and our perception of that difference, that creates information, these might more appositely be called 'informationscapes'. But these are potentially revelatory spaces, rather than controlled ones. Their design is concerned with mapping and translation, bringing out difference in ways that it can be read. Datascapes are dynamic places in which spatial representation extends to more than the three static Cartesian dimensions, where change and, at the very least, a fourth temporal dimension are engaged in a time-based spatial representation. In the physical world of human perception, there is no static, homogenous three-dimensional space. Heraclitus, in the 6th century BC, pointed out that it was not possible to step twice into the same river: everything is in a state of constant change, or flux.[1] In 1908, Henri Poincaré grappled philosophically with our changing physical frame of reference as we move and act in the world. Using the reference to our own bodies to constantly re-establish the cardinal axes, we are able, through our own subjective movement, to distinguish between changing form and changing position in other 'objects'.[2]

In architectural representation, the three static dimensions have traditionally been the basis for an abstracted and transcendent understanding of space. The building of architecture extends Cartesian certainty into our perceptual environment, providing literal representation of the orthogonal reference planes and response to our gravitational relationship with the Earth. It is the spatial frame of reference for urbanized culture.[3] Its representation has traditionally been through orthogonal slices or projections onto a two-dimensional plane. In architecture, the third dimension is tacitly present in the

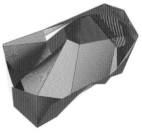

PRECEDING PAGE 'Construct', part of the 2001 Symbiosis series developed for the Melbourne International Film Festival by Metraform. The continuously changing, emergent forms cut through the body of the observer, wearing 3D glasses, to create strange, kinaesthetic impacts.

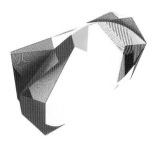

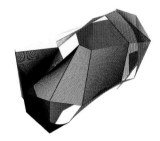

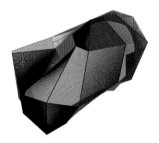

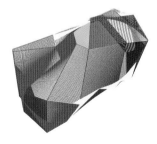

ABOVE AND OPPOSITE Studies for the skin panelling and light effects at the Hotel Prestige Forest.

sequence of parallel sections or in perspective projection. Time sequences are there in the turning of pages, or in flat layers of cartographic information. The advent of film and other devices that employ sequential frames brought time, at least in its linear manifestation, into visual representation: a literal mapping, rather than mere inference, found in painting, sculpture and architecture. Mechanical engineering brings this into the tactile realm, but again the actions of the machine have traditionally been preplanned and sequenced with varying opportunities for real-time human control and input.

What if architecture, or designed spatial environments in general, also ceased to be the static backdrop for action in the world, and started to respond and participate more actively in the play? This has happened tacitly in the increasing servicing and mechanization of our built environments, but what if the space-defining fabric played a more active role in spatial representation and human interaction in space? Digital computation has greatly extended the scope for the programmed linking of events to spatial configuration. It offers representation of an event-based understanding of time and space, free from the constraints of a pre-choreographed linear sequence.[4] Movement and change in virtually represented and physical space can now be linked to other, unlimited changing forces in the world. To represent a system using a database and programmed links between objects and phenomena within it as a possibility for designing multi-dimensional spaces is clear. But our ability to link this to a dynamically changing physical or virtually inhabitable space that we can read intuitively is less certain. We are accustomed to reading abstracted symbolic associations between phenomena in the world and their representation in two-dimensional graphical displays, or static three-dimensional models.

In the world of virtual networks, the continuity and homogeneity of the concept of Newtonian space is substantially dissolved. Experiments in perceptual psychology that exploit visual illusion, such as the Ames room (a room that appears cubic from a monocular peephole, but is in fact trapezoidal with a sloping floor and ceiling, with the result that occupants appear to shrink and grow dramatically as they move from one end of the room to the other), also alert us to the shifting subjectivity of the ground we occupy. The abstract mathematical notion of higher dimensional space leaves us uncertain as to the relationship between our bodily experience of space and its metrics. The matter of using our spatial intelligence, honed in the physical domain and abstracted to the three geometrical dimensions of familiar conceptualization, to engage more directly with this contemporary place-based or event-based space has intrigued and challenged architects since their adoption of digital computation. Digital networking invites us to live in a space that is more closely aligned with mathematical idea of multi-dimensional space. (Roger Penrose noted that a space that has five variable parameters is a five-dimensional space, extensible to any number of dimensions,[5] but Henri Lefebvre dismissed the notion as a conceit of mathematicians and nothing to do with space itself.[6])

The projects discussed in this chapter range from those that engage a multi-dimensional model for the process of design to those for which the design outcome is a fully interactive dynamic environment in space, virtual or physical. While making a number of aspects of the site use and infrastructure explicit, Karres en Brands' programmed model for the De Draai Extension (p. 214) has room to generate both new housing configurations and intriguing bits of serendipity, including erratic road systems that would have been unlikely to be conceived by human agency, but which both optimize the housing layout for the given criteria and enliven the experience of dwelling. The unbuilt Streaming House (p. 222), by Australian firm Minifie Nixon, explores the process of medical imaging. Just as a brain scanner extracts from the organic continuum of the body a series of slices that yield information concealed from the external eye, the architects have deconstructed formal Modernist ordering and reassembled it as a totally new space. Design practice dECOi's experimental Aegis Hyposurface (p. 226) reaches for an architecture that is as supple, responsive and kinetic as ourselves, using digital simulation to build a shimmering wall that creates images through movement, taking its cues from any number of real-time or pre-programmed stimulae.

Servo's Spoorg (p. 230) is a spatial installation that is sensitive to light. In this case, the assembly of 'cellular organisms' is brought to life through ambient environmental change, engaging in an interactive relationship with the place and between cells to generate emergent patterns of response that evolve across the network of individual cells. The Digital Water Pavilion (p. 248) by Carlo Ratti Associati introduces a curtain of water that responds to visitors' presence and parts to let them through, while Hyperbody's Muscle ReConfigured (p. 242) and Interactive Wall (p. 246) are all about physical responsiveness and the conversation with their human counterparts. And the Hotel Prestige Forest (p. 234), in Barcelona, by Cloud 9 Architecture seems to respond thoughtfully to its climate, twinkling leaf by twinkling leaf.

The New York Stock Exchange Project by Asymptote, the architects of the Yas Hotel in Abu Dhabi (p. 238), is a leader in this area of exploration. It is a virtual-reality trading floor, displayed on an array of flat-screen monitors for the nyse command centre, also designed by the practice. Through graphical displays of real-time information, it enables staff to oversee events and activities all over the trading floor.

Asymptote's virtual New York Stock Exchange.

DJIA
DJIA
S&P 500
NYSE VOL.

NYS

5

ME TO BUY

78.9

29.3

523.6

2R	T	2R	S	2J			20	20	OZ	2L		N	2L		LZ		2J	K	2J	
RD		HB								BKB	HMC		ORI	HMC			RIR		KOF	
FCH		YIH					LB			MTW	ICS		PDI	ICS			RIR		SQM	
RTI		INT					LS	DTF		CTL	LTT		NXR	LTT			IO		DES	
CMB		CMB					RIL	TYW		MHI	MUO		REG	MUO			GML		BAS	
								GIS		BRR	GFD		YES				CIC		AME	
CMB		MJA						PGR		NYD	MCT		UVN				FLH		CXW	
CMB		FJA									NGL		ONA				VPI		EVI	
SNV		PHY									NYB		NUF				RIR		CBD	
RBD		HTD									NMG		ZF				CXE			
VMT		FCH									PCN		OXY				TCT			
OEI		ICN									HBT		OXY				COP			
CMB		MPV									MXG		NSS				LCI			
CMB																	TMM			
																	SQF			

CHANGTOTAL VOLUME V

T	S	RZ	R
8 7 6 5 4 3 2 1 0			

2R

DOW XON DOW WSH DOW UTX DOW U

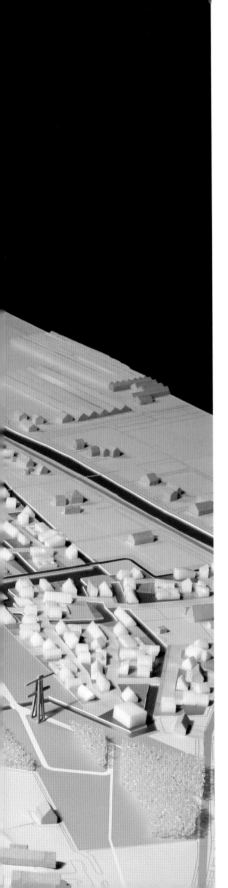

De Draai Extension
KARRES EN BRANDS
Heerhugowaard, Netherlands

Bart Brands and Marco Broekman of Karres en Brands give expression to their fascination with the beauty of the unexpected through the use of software as a design tool. At Heerhugowaard, the firm's collaboration with the Swiss Federal Institute of Technology (ETZH) for the masterplanning of De Draai, an estate of 2,700 new houses, provided ample scope to explore how the multi-dimensionality of a computational system that internalized generative procedures could begin to create multiple 'unexpected' housing layouts. The designers could then design with criteria and parameters, rather than directly seeking their own solutions, and the system was complex enough to compute and generate suggestive surprises.

Brands and Broekman have said that because unexpected influences can look like terrible mistakes, it is tempting to dismiss them as 'accidents'; in fact, such accidents can be a gift to the designer. Generally they are the result of changing political ideas, economic influences or technical developments: an increase in the density of programme; the discovery of polluted soils; a stubborn plot owner who doesn't want to sell; a politician who suddenly wants to make a personal statement by changing the premises of the plan. While these accidents can pop up from the outside, it is also possible to 'design' them, planting them in the plan as a minor but high-precision landmine.

For the present design, a framework was made that could be distorted by such unforeseen events. In order to distribute and site the desired programme for the new houses, the designers used special software that enabled them to create 'test-plot' layouts for the entire area. This 'parcellation' software, developed by ETZH, reacted to the differentiated framework and developed unexpected housing layouts, without compromising either efficiency or

The model indicates the diversity of lot types and the unexpected housing layouts generated.

programmatic parameters. This involved the simultaneous processing of data, the complexities of which would normally make excessive demands on the designer.

Clearly the solutions that the software generated were not ready-made urban designs. The computer does not replace the creative process, but organizes complex interdependencies that can help develop and test scenarios that cannot be made manually, or would require considerable investments of time. Through this process, spatial, programmatic and economic parameters and their effects become more transparent for planners, owners and developers, and can be adjusted during the process to meet new demands.

• Algorithm (p. 252)
• Multi-dimensional spaces (p. 262)
• System dynamics (p. 265)

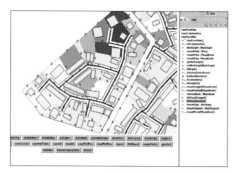

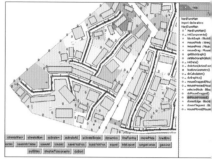

ABOVE, LEFT Accidents like erratic roading, which can occur within the logic of the parameters set up in the software, are exploited to create site-specific solutions.

ABOVE, RIGHT Infrastructure, topography and programme are analyzed in terms of their own characteristics and consequences. While no hierarchies of scale are applied, each scale is capable of exercising influence on the eventual plan.

RIGHT Every phase of construction should reflect the programme, and thus consist of various types, one beside the other. Each type has its own plot, creating an organic model in a variety of densities, but always with a village-like looseness.

OPPOSITE, LEFT Principal road network; water network; institutional buildings; housing.

OPPOSITE, RIGHT The site plan in context.

freshHtwoOexpo

NOX ARCHITECTS

Zeeland, Netherlands

The design for this pavilion, part of an interactive installation for WaterLand Neeltje Jans, located in Zeeland, a southwestern region of the Netherlands, was based on the metastable aggregation of architecture and information. The form is shaped by the fluid deformation of fourteen ellipses, spaced out over a length of more than 65m. Inside the building, which has no horizontal floors or external relation to the horizon, walking becomes related to falling. The deformation of the object extends to the constant metamorphosis of the environment, which responds interactively to visitors via a variety of sensors that register the constant reshaping of the human body (action).

Edit Sp(l)ine, the interactive installation, does not 'contain' an exhibition in the classic sense, nor does it contain a classic architectural programme. In addition to non-interactive events such as ice, rain, spraying mist, water on the floors, and an enormous well inside the building, sensors connect various visitor actions to displays of the fluidity of water. Light sensors for crowds, pulling sensors for groups, and touch sensors for individuals create the Wave, the Blob and the Ripple in real-time projections and sound manipulation, and the interference of these patterns in the 'sp(l)ine', the pathway through the exhibition, with its 190 blue lamps.

An array of sensors is coupled to multiple distributed processors, which produce interference in the continuous processing of a virtual real-time model of water. Sensed changes in the environment produce changes in the virtual water system, images and sounds, which are projected into the interior space of the pavilion. This dynamic interaction is augmented by destabilizing the static environment; an exploration of topology in the structure of the building extends not only to the curving walls and roof, but also to the never-horizontal floor.

• Multi-dimensional spaces (p. 262)

Edit Sp(l)ine: the interactive water experience.

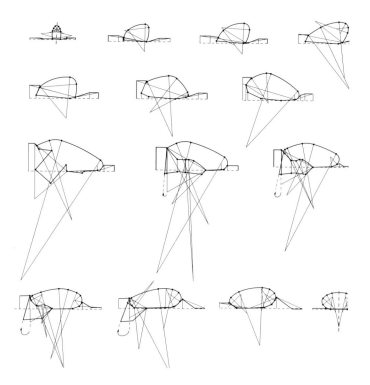

ABOVE Diagram of the deforming elliptical sections, generating the building.

ABOVE, RIGHT Exterior.

BELOW Digital model.

OPPOSITE, BOTTOM Edit Sp(l)ine.

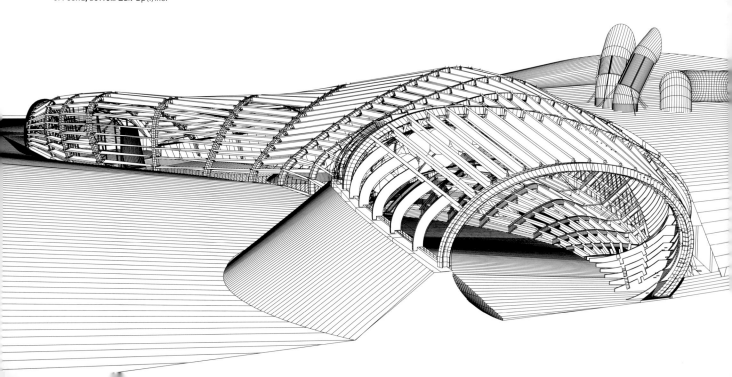

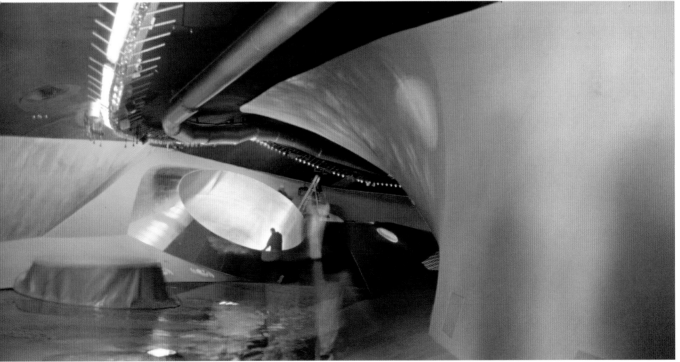

Streaming House

MINIFIE NIXON
Melbourne, Australia

...eaming House is an experiment in 'found ...hnique'; in this sense, it is a project used ...pick up processes from quite different ...ntexts than architectural design, and to ...vestigate how they can be used creatively ...generate architecture. Digital processes ...e, despite an early rhetoric of infinite ...lirious virtual masculinity, bound by ... strictures of the algorithm, which ...nders each method finite and particular. ...chniques have a degree of autonomy; they ...e not bound to a particular end. Solving a ...mplex problem rarely occurs by applying ...e technique that accurately recreates ...d solves all dimensions of the problem ...imetically. Rather, different methods are ...pically organized by a heuristic to provide ...e most useful outcome in a given situation.

The project redeploys a technique ...veloped to create certain kinds of ... medical images. Computer-aided ...mography, or CAT scans, work by integrating individual density readings of successive beams of x-rays. They produce a 3D grid of discrete numbers representing tissue density throughout the body. To isolate discrete organs and structures, a surface is generated at the threshold of a particular density. Such isosurfaces thread continuously through the regular density matrix, always producing closed volumes. The algorithm used here was developed by Graham Treece at Cambridge University. A video stream is an identical data structure to that produced by a CAT scanner, and so can be subject to a similar isosurface technique to isolate structures, this time within the image stream. In its operation, the isosurface technique makes no distinction between time and the third spatial dimension.

Streaming House is the sum of the progress of the architectural pilgrim through Mies van der Rohe's Barcelona Pavilion of 1929. Enthralled in the play

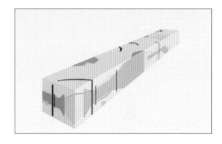

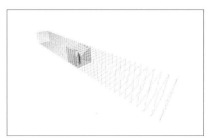

of elements, this particular pilgrim traverses a loop, returning to the start point, and continues round again. This entrapment is something of a purgatorial experience. The pilgrim negotiates a path past furniture, negotiates the mirroring of glass, water and figure, the dematerialized marker points of the columns, and the over-materialized sliding planes of the walls, accruing an understanding of Mies's technique of revealing Cartesian space.

The present building captures this experiential accrual as a set of volumes. Columns stretch and become walls. Ceilings and floors buckle as walls approach and recede. Furniture is transformed from being a gesture of inhabitation, but scars pristine onyx walls and marble floor. The sky is no longer a sign of absent spatial stuff, but is brought into the house as a volume, clogging all residual gaps (and so needs to be actively committed). Each point on a surface describes the inflection of a boundary within the pavilion. Streaming House is an integral of the original Miesian function.[7]

• Algorithm (p. 252)
• Multi-dimensional spaces (p. 262)

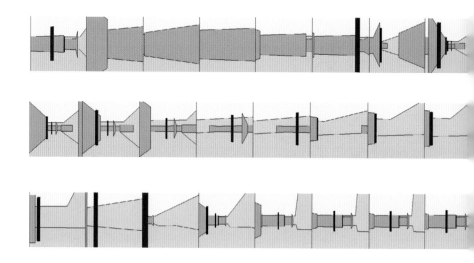

ABOVE Image frames.
BELOW Render of the house.
OPPOSITE, TOP Process diagram.
OPPOSITE, BOTTOM Perspective render.

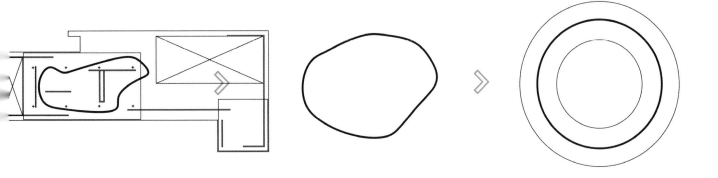

Aegis Hyposurface

DECOI ARCHITECTS
Birmingham, UK

To mark the renovation of the Birmingham Hippodrome, a number of artists and architects were invited to submit proposals for an art installation that would take the form of a large wall surface, soaring 5m above the heads of the passing pedestrians below. Although visitors today will find the wall no more than a highly prominent sign board, originally the competition called for an artwork that would interactively reflect upon the building's exterior interpretations of the activities within. The then Paris-based practice dECOi won the competition with Mark Goulthorpe's proposal that the wall surface itself should be the interactive medium, rather than simply placing an art object upon it – thus spawning the world's first interactively displaced architectural surface of grand dimension.

The winning idea was a far simpler statement to make than its subsequent resolution. In order to articulate a convincing scheme, a multimedia presentation was key. Essentially a 4D proposal, the principal component was an animation of the wall. The animation demonstrated responses to stimuli as diverse as a passerby's footsteps, registered as real-time plop, plop effects on the surface above; a stream of cyclists, who engendered a more complicated effect; and the applause from an audience, manifested as a series of mad fibrillations ebbing and surging in sync with the sound volume from inside the auditorium.

From the start this turned out to be more than a multimedia problem: what exactly is a 4D movement effect on a surface? The practice realized that mathematicians would need to be consulted in order to direct appropriate algorithms to the computer programmers, who were assisting in the production of the multimedia animation, and later the wall surface once built. In fact, there were far fewer types of effects available than might first be imagined: circular waves might radiate from a point, or roll longitudinally or vertically across the surface; sprites might dart across, leaving a wake behind them; or a point disturbance might spiral away from the centre. What emerged was a new designer construct: choreography. While the mathematician and the programmer could make an effect as an effect, a narrative overlay was required that placed the designer in the centre, for it is the combination of effects and idiosyncrasies that ultimately enrich the dialogue as the essential difference between screensaver and artwork.

The project was prototyped and shown first at the 2000 Venice Biennale, and as a large, fully interactive unit, 10m wide and 3m in height, which enthralled audiences at the 2001 CeBIT show in Hanover. While the piece ultimately never made it to its proposed Birmingham site, the project continues to be developed at MIT in Boston. Over the ensuing decade, the mathematical basis for the designed effects continues to evolve, enriching the narrative.

THIS PAGE Research and development of prototype.

OPPOSITE Public demonstration at the 2001 CeBIT show in Hanover.

aAbB

abc

aAbBcCcCCc

abcABC

Spoorg

SERVO

Los Angeles, California, USA

Spoorg is a responsive, photosensor/sonic installation, originally commissioned for the Gen(h)ome exhibition at the MAK Center for Art and Architecture in Los Angeles and later installed at the International Biennial of Contemporary Art in Seville.

'Spoorg', or semi-porous operable organism, takes its name from a primitive, usually unicellular, often environmentally resistant, dormant or reproductive body produced by plants and some micro-organisms. These micro-organisms are capable of developing after fusion with another spore, producing a new individual that is, in some cases, unlike the parent. In the context of this project, each spoorg cell is embedded with local intelligence, enabling it to communicate with other, adjacent spoorgs. The spoorg aggregate is locally in fluctuation, but also produces larger scale atmospheric effects in the specific region in which it is located.

The Spoorg system is a cellular system that interfaces with the interior and exterior of glass-building skins. It is essentially a demonstration project, exploring the potentially productive effects of integrating contemporary material, geometric, sonic, and photo-sensing technologies. The intelligence of the system is distributed (as opposed to being centralized), and based on wireless radio communication. Spoorg reacts to both local and regional environmental changes of light, and responds by generating various forms of ambient sonic output. The behaviour of each spoorg individually, and of the network of spoorgs collectively, evolves over time through the modulation of sound textures, based on a series of algorithmic rules.

Each spoorg cell is comprised of a thin plastic shell, manufactured through sintering and vacuum-casting, with hollow regions for embedding local infrastructure,

LEFT Catalogue of spoorg cell combinations and configurations.

OPPOSITE The semi-porous operable organism, seen against a natural setting.

such as micro-controllers, photosensors, small-scale speaker elements, and wireless radio communications technology for local communication between the cells.

The spoorg system allows the cultivation and decoration of domestic space by distributing and expanding shading and sound into a cellular, semi-porous membrane. Through this form of cultivation, new behavioural patterns emerge. A lack of cultivation will result in a certain decay of the spoorg system's performance. The difference between decay and growth renders the domestic space with subtle changes of atmospheric moods. Varying states of transparency emerge as the spoorg interfaces with natural lighting. Shifts in the density and pace of ambient sound become apparent through the spoorgs' modulations of frequency. Sensitivity in the spoorg cells can be programmed and adapted for specific forms of monitoring and interacting with the environment.

Spoorg cells can operate both individually and collectively, producing aggregates through stacking and clustering, as well as through cell division, fusion or nesting with other cells to create new individuals that are unlike the parent cells. The electronic infrastructure operates with a similar logic. Each unit is responsive to local sensory input and produces sound individually. The sonic behavioural patterns can further fuse with others via input from neighbouring cells through wireless communication. The aggregation of cells allows for different distributions and densities of electronic infrastructure, affecting the system's performative qualities.

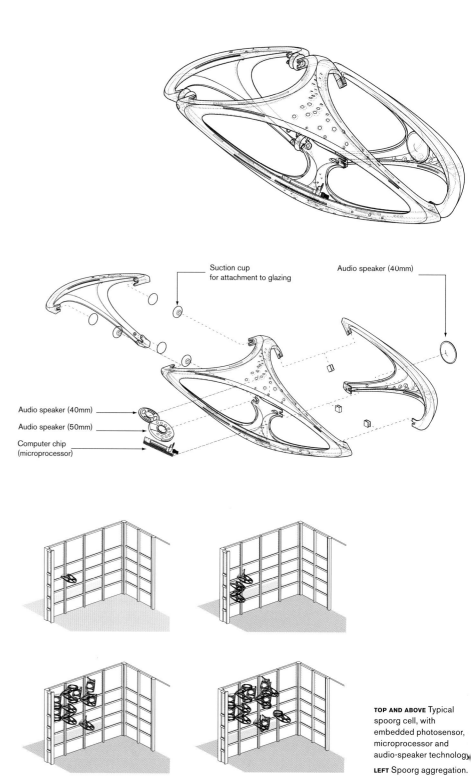

Suction cup for attachment to glazing

Audio speaker (40mm)

Audio speaker (40mm)

Audio speaker (50mm)

Computer chip (microprocessor)

TOP AND ABOVE Typical spoorg cell, with embedded photosensor, microprocessor and audio-speaker technology.

LEFT Spoorg aggregation.

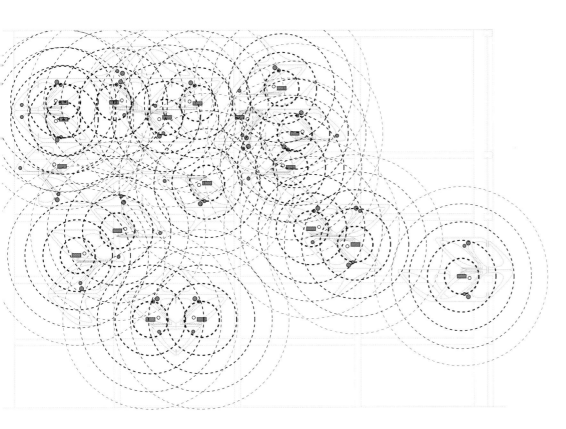

LEFT Diagram of radio frequency and sonic distribution patterns.

BELOW, LEFT Exploded axometric.

BELOW, RIGHT Diagram of the inter-cell wireless communication network.

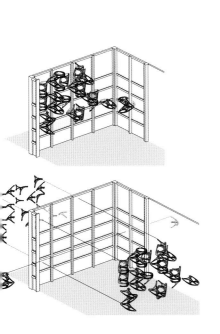

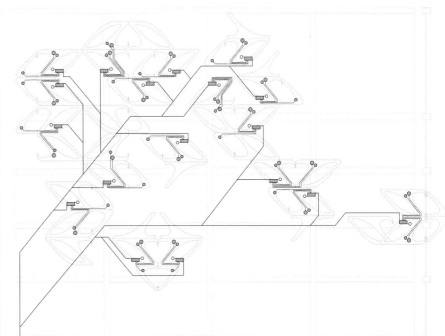

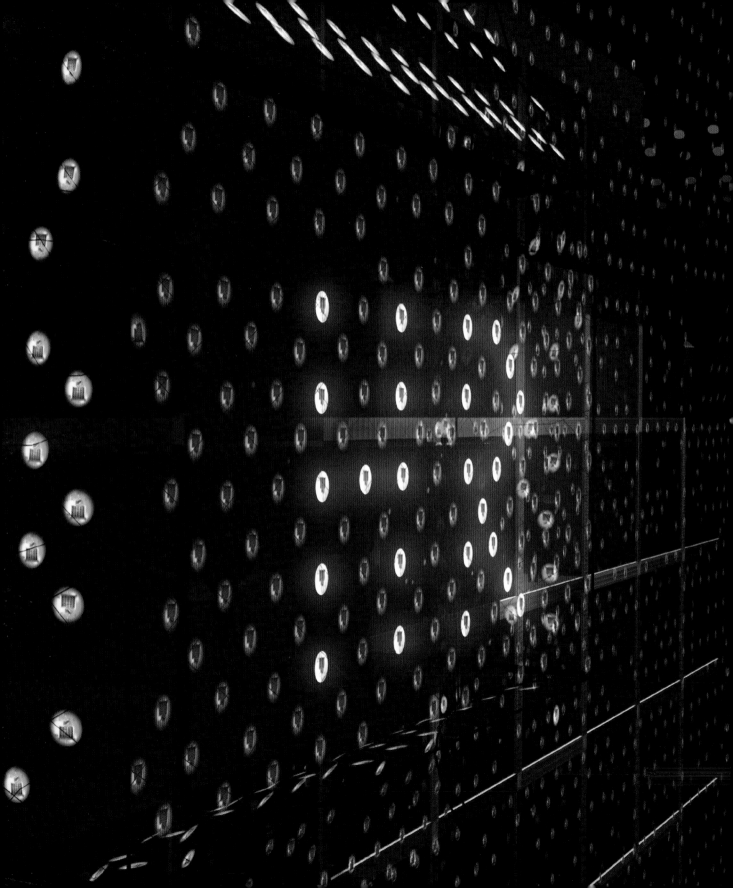

Hotel Prestige Forest
CLOUD 9 ARCHITECTURE
Barcelona, Spain

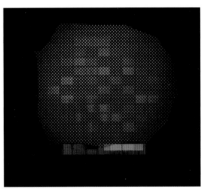

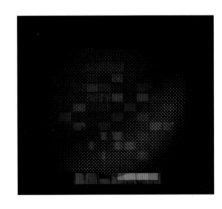

[T]o those who know Barcelona well, the highly [in]dustrialized l'Hospitalet neighbourhood [w]ould seem an unlikely setting for a four-[st]ar hotel. The area is set to change, however, [an]d as part of the urban renewal Cloud 9 [ar]chitecture have proposed a conspicuously [at]ypical, ten-storey 'urban forest': 'your room [is] a tree', says architect Enric Ruiz-Geli. The [gu]est-rooms, with their fair-faced concrete [w]alls and standard glazed façades, are not so [di]fferent from those of a typical hotel. The [ro]om configuration, however, hints at more [ca]re than usual in offering guests a sense of [th]e individual, as each guest-room differs [th]rough a clever combination of furniture, [w]indow and entry door placements.

The building mass is referred to by [R]uiz-Geli and his colleagues as 'compact', [an]d as such would appear somewhat [u]nprepossessing for a hotel were it not for its [ap]plied 'skin', a stainless-steel tensegrity mesh [d]raped over the entire building. The armature supports 5,000 artificial 'leaves', sealed disks, 25cm-wide, that contain a photovoltaic cell, a battery, a tiny CPU and a three-colour light-emitting diode (LED). Together yet independently from each other, each 'leaf' absorbs energy and converts it during the day into stored power, which, controlled by the CPU, powers the LED at night. Depending on how much light is absorbed, the CPU calculates the response as a colour: the colour of the hotel at night in the summer, for example, will be different than in winter. The building could in fact be a carefully gradated series of colours throughout the year, only repeating with the reappearance of each season. More sophisticated still, the building acts as a thermometer, replaying the earlier heat of the midsummer sun during the warm, balmy evening that follows.

This approach to interactivity appears to be highly constrained; the individual solar-powered illuminations are not connected to each other, but the effect is highly appealing all the same. Eschewing any temptation to network the individual cells as a centrally controlled performance device, the skin takes its lessons directly from nature and is refreshingly uncontrived. Each leaf is independent from its companions, yet interacts similarly through a shared set of environmental circumstances. The electronics, therefore, are as simple as possible. There are relatively few wires to get crossed, and few components to fail.

Functioning as a skin, the leaves offer 15 per cent shade to the building and reduce the air-conditioning load appreciably. The sense of nature artificially referenced through the digital forest canopy is echoed more literally elsewhere in the building. Several artists have been invited to contribute, most notably landscape architect and installation artist Vito Acconci, who proposed a vegetable garden for the ground-floor interior, which would extend through the lobby to the land outside the hotel.

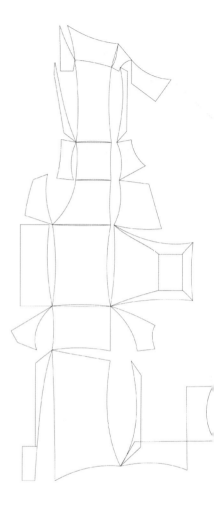

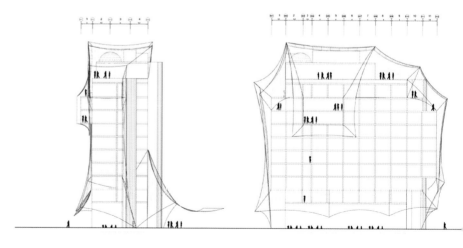

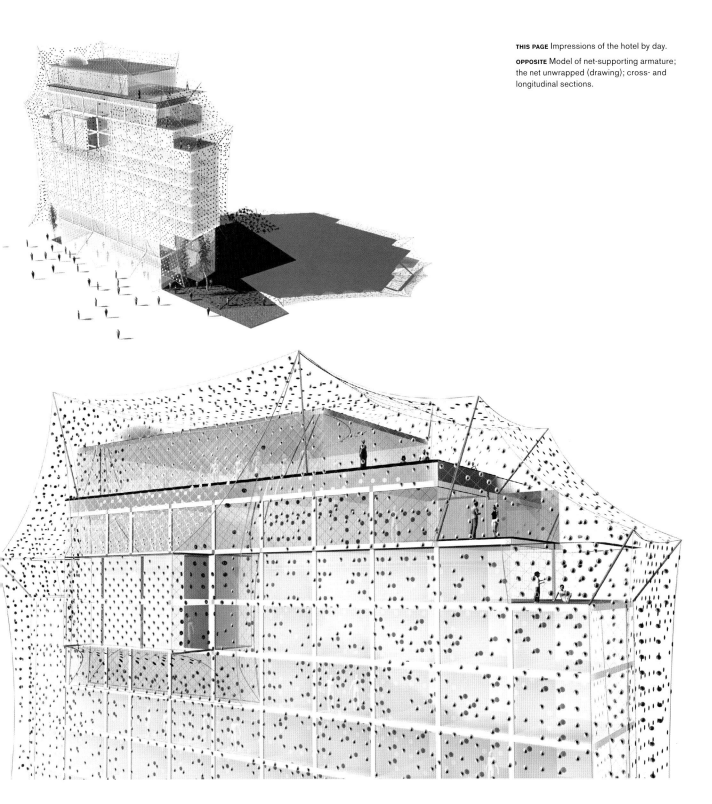

THIS PAGE Impressions of the hotel by day.

OPPOSITE Model of net-supporting armature; the net unwrapped (drawing); cross- and longitudinal sections.

Yas Hotel

ASYMPTOTE

Abu Dhabi, UAE

The 500-room, 85,000m² Yas Hotel is the centrepiece, along with the new Formula 1 race circuit, of the ambitious Yas Island complex, and was designed to be a significant landmark destination for Abu Dhabi and the United Arab Emirates at large. Having been awarded the commission to design the building and environs of the complex, Hani Rashid and Lise Anne Couture of Asymptote envisioned an architectural landmark that would embody key influences and inspirations, ranging from the aesthetics and forms associated with speed, movement and spectacle to the artistry and geometries that form the basis of the ancient craft traditions of Islam.

Of architectural and engineering significance is the focal point of the design, a 217m expanse of sweeping, curvilinear forms, constructed of steel and 5,800 pivoting, diamond-shaped glass panels. This 'grid-shell' component creates an atmospheric veil that contains two hotel towers and a link bridge,

constructed as a monocoque sculpted steel object that crosses the race circuit. The grid-shell visually connects and fuses the entire complex together, while producing optical effects and spectral reflections that play against the surrounding sea, sky and desert landscape. The building 'performs' as both an environmentally responsive solution and as an architecture of spectacle and event. The jewel-like composition responds visually and tectonically to its environment to create a distinct and powerful sense of place, as well as a breathtaking backdrop to the Grand Prix and other events.

The building's design, says Rashid, is 'a perfect union and harmonious interplay between elegance and spectacle. The search here was inspired by what one could call the "art" and poetics of motor racing . . . coupled with the making of a place that celebrates Abu Dhabi as a cultural and technological tour de force.'

The building three-dimensionalizes the curving geometry of the Formula 1 race course that it straddles.

FAR LEFT Steel grid of the operable façade under construction.

LEFT Relationship to the water.

BELOW The façades lit up at night.

OPPOSITE Interior view of the operable façade under construction.

Muscle ReConfigured + Interactive Wall

HYPERBODY RESEARCH GROUP

Delft, Netherlands

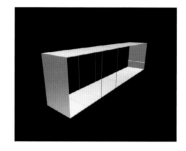

MUSCLE RECONFIGURED

[St]artled visitors arriving at the entrance to [th]e Non-Standard Architecture exhibition at [Pa]ris's Centre Georges Pompidou in 2003 were [co]nfronted with a fribulating air-filled blue [bl]adder the size of a room. Captured within a [tes]sellated network of seventy-two pneumatic ['m]uscles', made by Festo, and under constant [lo]w pressure, this rubber creature was the [fir]st-ever interactively adaptable space to [re]configure itself in real time. Its reactivity [to] human presence was more sluggish [th]an highly animated, but a relationship [ne]vertheless quickly developed between an [en]gaged public and Muscle, the name given [to] the installation created by architectural [fir]m Oosterhuis Lénárd and Hyperbody, the [re]search base led by Kas Oosterhuis at the [De]lft University of Technology.

Proximity-awareness signals from [se]nsors fed data into a CPU for calculation [an]d interpretation, allowing the pneumatic [m]uscles to contract or expand in coordinated

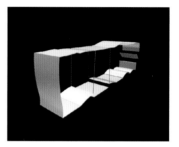

unison. Rather than any spastic convulsions, the most disconcerting aspect was the sense of life Muscle conveyed through these rhythmic exertions. It wasn't just changing human proximities that caused a reaction, but also a human interactive augmentation, whereby a direct engagement was facilitated by sliders on a computer interface. While the sliders represented an opportunity for overt control, this control was overridden by a covert resilience to such conscious interference, manifested by Muscle crawling back to an earlier state in quiet defiance.

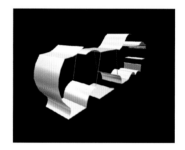

A follow-on to the Muscle project was Muscle ReConfigured, created by Hyperbody in 2004. Some direct lessons were drawn from the earlier prototype, including that of an interactive spatial volume, which leads to an interactive environment with a reconfigurable floor, wall and ceiling. To make this transition, the actuation system was brought over from Muscle, but the surfaces themselves were

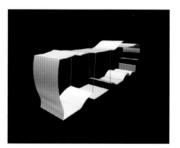

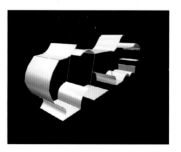

OPPOSITE The structure's 'muscles' are made [of] aluminium.

RIGHT Section through space, showing the progressive contortions to floor, ceiling and walls.

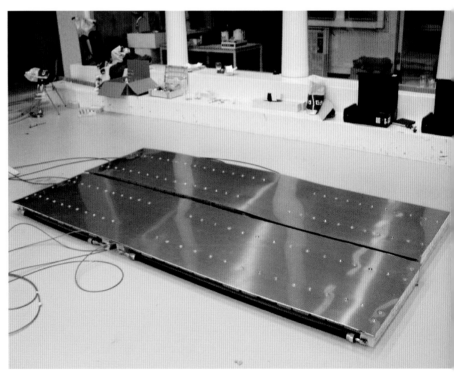

ABOVE AND RIGHT The prototype in active and resting states.

OPPOSITE, TOP The original Muscle project, at the Pompidou in 2003.

OPPOSITE, BOTTOM Working prototype section of Muscle ReConfigured.

entirely rethought. Individual panels were made of Hylite, a sandwich of a plastic core encased between two thin aluminium layers, resulting in a very lightweight but resilient material. From forming a conventional rectilinear box, the enclosing surfaces were able to transform into sensuously curved sections through the contraction of the pneumatic muscles. A flat floor surface could ripple into a comfortable seat, for example. Vertical walls could warp to envelop the occupants in comforting concave niches, while ceilings could morph with skylights to emerge as sheets that curved differentially away from each other.

As with the earlier Muscle, an interactive relationship developed between occupant and artifact. It would be too easy to make Muscle ReConfigured simply a reactive environment, responding to consciously motivated human intervention. Such control was possible through local sensors with which the space-morphing could be steered. Other sensors, however, picked up signals from separate activities, remote to the occupants and leading to a different set of instructions to the pneumatic muscles. The designers configured the relationship between the different sets of sensors, the software used to parse the resulting data (Virtools), and the actuation network so that over time the space and the occupants would develop a familiarity with the interactive environment – a form of self-learning leading to mutual benefit. Having set out to make an organic structure that was intended to be both 'intimidating and perplexing', and despite being a prototype for an environment slightly out of control, the designers wanted a friendliness to emerge all the same.

INTERACTIVE WALL

The designers' Interactive Wall is just what its name suggests: a wall capable of interacting with its environment. When in repose, the seven individual 1.2m-wide and 3.6m-high vertical panels stand erect, tapering up from 300mm-thick bases to a feathered edge along their tops. The project is a prototype for a wall that picks up signals from various sensors, responding with movement, light and sound. Using hidden pneumatic 'muscles' that contract in length when pressurized, the panels can sway backwards and forwards at will. The panel surfaces are encrusted with LEDs, which are controlled by an electronic nervous system that also drives the local sound emission.

The project was motivated by the quest for an interactive architecture that responded to emerging demands for programmable, 'multi-mediated', flexible and customizable environmental conditions for the digital age, and was 'emotive, responsive, and interactive' with its participants. To be 'interactive' is significantly different from simply being reactive to surroundings, a distinction that identifies Interactive Wall as a piece of design, rather than merely a remarkable feat of engineering. Interactivity impels a spatial conversation between participants, both human and mechanical; it is not just an 'I move, therefore the wall moves' outcome. To say that the wall has a life of its own would also diminish the relationship it has with its correspondents. Human participants are drawn into an adapted emotional state through engagement with the wall, which is what makes the project especially ambitious.

ABOVE Interacting with the Interactive Wall.

LEFT Placement of Servo drive piston units and speaker in structure.

BELOW The Fin Ray bending, as applied in the Interactive Wall.

OPPOSITE, LEFT Layers of interactivity.

OPPOSITE, RIGHT The Interactive Wall.

The project sets out to do more than enrich an existing situation; emerging sensor technology has been used to offer an entirely new spatial experience for participants. There are no precedents for this experience as the essential combination of sensor technology and real-time computation and actuation (pneumatic, motorized, magnetic, etc.) is only now emerging as a technical possibility. What makes Interactive Wall more than an art installation is the fact that we learn from the human–machine dialogue that the project encourages. The quest for an emotive interaction might appear to be conceit were it not for the fact that for the first time humans will be corresponding spatially with a machine; we might assume that this novelty alone is bound to induce an emotional response. Those emotions might be picked up by the sensors and be interpreted by Interactive Wall in a self-learning way, which will in itself charge the event emotionally.

The conversation can be three-way, between the wall itself and participants on either side of it. A potential game emerges with the wall favouring a participant on one side of the wall by providing a safe enveloping arc, while repelling the participant on the other side through the opposite gesture. The wall can also engender states of nervousness, as well as describing its own: lights get brighter and flash more frantically as increasingly agitated states are induced.

Digital Water Pavilion

CARLO RATTI ASSOCIATI

Zaragoza, Spain

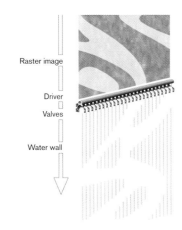

Raster image

Driver

Valves

Water wall

he Digital Water Pavilion, originally sited
the entrance to Expo 2008 in Zaragoza,
oused a tourist office, an information point,
exhibition space and upper-level terraces
verlooking the entire venue. Long after the
hibition has closed, it remains as a tourist
traction and showcase of the city's 'Milla
igital' (digital mile) urban renovation
oject. The pavilion walls are formed of
gitally controlled 'water curtains', with
nbedded sensors that signal the approach
visitors and create openings in the water to
low them to pass. (The technology is similar
that of an ink-jet printer.) The surface is
escribed as a one-bit-deep, 100m x 4m digital
splay that continuously scrolls downward.

The pavilion has just one main solid
ement: a movable roof, a high-tech, 400mm-
ick structure, engineered by Arup and built
Siemens, supported on twelve hydraulic
ainless-steel pistons that allow for variation
the height. The roof is normally 4m above

ground level, but can be lowered to 2.5m if
strong winds threaten to disperse the droplets
of water. It can also be flattened onto the
ground, at which point the whole building
disappears. In addition to the pistons, the
structure contains 3,000 solenoid valves,
several dozen pumps, and a digital control
system based on open-source software. The
architects ask visitors to the pavilion to
imagine a building made completely of water,
with liquid curtains that can be programmed
to display images or messages, as well as
to sense approaching objects. The desired
effect is like a curtain of falling water with
gaps at specific points, a pattern of pixels
created from air and water instead of from
illuminated points on a screen.

Expos have always been ideal venues
in which to promote innovation in
architecture, and several buildings that have
now achieved iconic status, from the Joseph
Paxton-designed Crystal Palace for the Great

PPOSITE The reconfigurable façade, made
water.

RIGHT, TOP The valves system functioning.

RIGHT, BOTTOM Pattern on the digital water
curtain.

Exhibition 1851, held in London's Hyde Park, to Mies van der Rohe's Barcelona Pavilion of 1929, to, more recently, the pavilion designed by MVRDV for Expo 2000 in Hanover, were originally created for international exhibitions. The present building serves as a manifesto for digital, responsive architecture; the question for the designers was how to create architecture that was also extremely fluid and reconfigurable. The resulting structure aims to stand as a possible answer to that endeavour: it is fluid in the most literal sense of the word, but also fluid in terms of being reconfigurable and responsive.

In the 1990s, digital technology led to fantasies about distant virtual worlds, observes architect Carlo Ratti. The dream of digital architecture has always been to create reconfigurable, responsive buildings. It is not always easy to achieve such effects when dealing with concrete, bricks and mortar, but becomes possible with water, a dynamic and fluid element that, when digitally controlled, can appear and disappear. 'The future of architecture might really deal with digitally augmented environments,' says Ratti, 'where bits and atoms seamlessly merge.'

• Algorithm (p. 252)

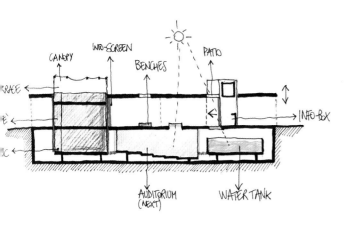

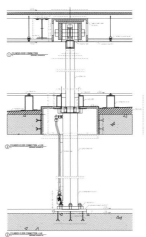

FAR LEFT Sketch.

LEFT Hydraulic piston section.

BELOW The movable roof in the down position.

OPPOSITE, TOP Pattern on the digital water curtain.

OPPOSITE, BOTTOM The lighting infobox.

GLOSSARY

Acoustic optimization

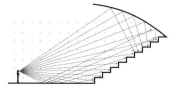
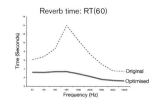

Acoustic optimization is a very qualitative process, despite the contribution of measurement and quantitative analysis. Two positions in a room may give equivalent measures, but still sound different subjectively. A performance space needs to be designed with several different acoustics in mind, from the seating acoustic (which varies significantly from point to point in the space), to the platform acoustic for the performers, to the recording and broadcasting acoustic. Sound experience is also highly subjective, and will not necessarily reflect even the most accurate measurements taken when the listener is in the built space. The three principal measurements are clarity, reverberation and loudness. Clarity depends on the length of early time delay; the ear collects the sound received in approximately the first 80 milliseconds and reinforces the initial sound. Reverberation received outside this time starts to be detected as loss of clarity. As sound travels 1m in roughly 3 milliseconds, there are critical dimensions of halls that determine the arrival of the first reflection.

Algorithm

```
to square :size
repeat 4 [forward :size right 90]
end

to flower :counter
if :counter > 100 [stop]
rotateZ :counter * 0.1
square | sin (:counter) |
flower :counter + 1
end

flower 0
```

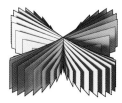

An algorithm is a very specific set of instructions for carrying out a procedure that generally includes an instruction to stop. It may be long or very short. The word is almost certainly a Latin corruption of Al-Khwārizm, the name of a Persian mathematician who wrote a treatise on calculation in 825 AD. The idea of an algorithm or programme as a formal procedure predates the existence of electronic computers, but to use a computer always means to activate an algorithmic procedure that transforms input to output. In architecture, this means formalizing the design process as a set of procedures and specific instructions. These may be opaque to the designer through the interface of a CAD programme, in which a library of generic geometrical objects, relationships, attributes as potential inputs, and their visual representation as outputs is already encoded. They are more visible to the designer who programmes or scripts to control the software inputs and customize the outputs.

...mmann tiling

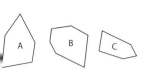

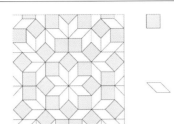

...nateur mathematician Robert Ammann ...946–94) independently discovered five ...s of aperiodic tiles, later published in ...anko Grünbaum and G. C. Shephard's *...lings and Patterns* (1986); proofs ...r four of which were subsequently ...blished in collaboration with the ...me authors. In a letter written in 1975, ...nmann revealed his discovery of an ...eriodic set of two tiles and a foursome ...'golden rhombohedra', which formed ...eriodic tilings in three dimensions. The ...st-known Ammann tile set combines ...lim rhombus with a square tile. One ...the interesting phenomena exhibited

in this tiling, in common with Penrose Rhombus tiling, is called Ammann bars. Certain patterns of line segments on the tiles result in straight lines of infinite length that run through the tiling. Intriguingly, these lines are parallel and the separation of neighbouring lines consists of one of two dimensions. If the unit dimension is assigned to the smaller of these, the second is the Golden Section number Phi. If the numbers 1 and 0 are assigned to these two dimensions, their sequence, the consecutive separations of the parallel Ammann bars, is found to correspond to the Golden String.

Aperiodic tiling

There are some sets of tile shapes that in combination tile the plane completely only in tilings, or tiling patterns, that cannot be mapped onto themselves by translation. This contrasts with well-known periodic tiling, such as at the Alhambra in Spain, where numerous symmetries can be discovered and the whole tiling shifted by a repeating amount to map it onto itself. A lattice of square tiles may be considered the simplest periodic tiling. Aperiodicity is a property of the set of tiles themselves. An aperiodic set of tiles is distinguished from a set of tiles that admits an aperiodic tiling (of

which there are many) by admitting only aperiodic tilings. Roger Penrose's tiles are the best-known example. Other names associated with the discovery of aperiodic tilings are Robert Berger, Donald Knuth, Raphael Robinson and Robert Ammann. They were first known as non-Wang tiles in response to a conjecture by Hao Wang in 1961 that the tiling of the plane by a set of tiles is decidable only if at least one periodic solution exists.

...rup optimizer

...r both the Water Cube (p. 86) and the ...elbourne Rectangular Stadium (p. 134), ...a Arup in-house application was used to ...dividually size the members in the steel ...ructures. In contrast to the traditional ...ginccring method of deriving member ...zes for stressed elements from tables ...nd charts, it allowed iterative evaluation ...f the most appropriate member size ...r each structural element individually. ...he optimizer works on the very simple ...rinciple of constraint satisfaction, ...hich carries out design-strength checks ...r each individual member in a group. ...ne constraint is active when a series of

checks is being carried out. The system is very input-sensitive; it is important to select appropriate starting values for the member sizes to avoid finding local, rather than global, minima. It takes approximately 30 minutes to calculate the whole structure by considering the case of each individual member in turn.

Catenary models

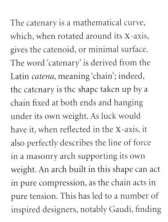

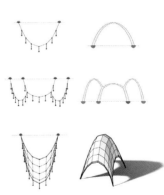

The catenary is a mathematical curve, which, when rotated around its x-axis, gives the catenoid, or minimal surface. The word 'catenary' is derived from the Latin *catena*, meaning 'chain'; indeed, the catenary is the shape taken up by a chain fixed at both ends and hanging under its own weight. As luck would have it, when reflected in the x-axis, it also perfectly describes the line of force in a masonry arch supporting its own weight. An arch built in this shape can act in pure compression, as the chain acts in pure tension. This has led to a number of inspired designers, notably Gaudí, finding

the shape for their masonry structures from hanging or funicular models. The parabola is a close approximation to the catenary. (Galileo believed it to be the shape of the hanging chain.) It has a simpler formula and is easily constructed by finding points equidistant from a point and a line.

Cellular automaton

In 1970, John Horton Conway devised the Game of Life, a zero-player game. It is an evolutionary process that depends only on its initial state with no further input from humans. The universe of the game is an unlimited orthogonal grid of square cells, each of which can exhibit one of two possible states at any time: dead or alive. Each cell interacts with its eight vertically, horizontally and diagonally neighbouring cells. The rules are as follows:

- Any live cell with fewer than two live neighbours dies, as if caused by under-population.

- Any live cell with more than three live neighbours dies, as if by overcrowding.

- Any live cell with two or three live neighbours lives, unchanged, to the next generation.

- Any tile with exactly three live neighbours cells will be populated with a living cell.

Chaos theory

Chaotic systems have a number of general characteristics. They are non-linear; deterministic (rather than probabilistic; each event is determined by what went before, although the events may appear random); sensitive to initial conditions; and exhibit sustained irregularity, order in disorder. Chaotic systems are also characterized by patterns that may appear similar, but never precisely repeat. The modern understanding of chaos is largely attributable to the work of Edward N. Lorenz. In the 1960s he created a simplified computer model that represented the air flows that caused weather. It was a recursive system with a number of variables, and could be left to run overnight. While attempting to repeat a particular cycle, Lorenz discovered the significance of small changes to starting values (an issue with his system had caused a small change to the number of decimal places given to a particular starting value). Over many iterations, this resulted in a dramatically different state of the system.

Complexity theory

Hypercube Graph Q₄

Complexity theory is the study of complex systems, or any system that is considered fundamentally complex. While there is no one universal definition of a complex system, complexity theory is rooted in chaos theory, but may not be deterministic in that it may not be possible, even theoretically, to determine the state of a system from its initial conditions and subsequent events. One key idea in complexity theory is that of a rich, diverse system that results from small, simple components or responds to simple, local rules of combination, but results in non-simple interaction overall.

Complexity is integral to many different disciplines. In architecture, buildings themselves can be viewed as complex systems. Complexity theory is a tool for analyzing cites; the use of computation to model architecture in a systemic, relational or generative way results in models that exhibit the characteristics of complexity.

Computability

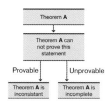

No theorem or machine is consistent and complete

The question of what can be computed predates the existence of the modern electronic computer. In the 1930s, a collection of the best mathematical minds independently turned to the question of what it means to be computable, and came up with different definitions: Alonzo Church's λ-calculus, Kurt Gödel's recursive functions and Alan Turing's abstract machines are three examples. The models all turned out to be equivalent in that what was computable in one was also computable in the others. In 1931 Gödel caused a mathematical earthquake by proving his incompleteness theorem, which showed that all consistent axiomatizations of number theory contained propositions that were undecidable. Leaving aside the philosophical chasm this created, the practical implications were that it is a good idea not to set computers tasks where the output sought is a determination on something that is undecidable, in which case the programme will never halt, or semi-decidable, in which case it will halt only if there is positive result, but will run for ever if no positive is found.

ontrol theory

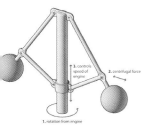

ntrol theory began life as a formal
nch of engineering and mathematics
h the invention and study of the
ernor on steam engines (the feedback
ice that rises, causing the valve to
se, and falls as the pressure drops in
ponse, keeping the system operating
hin a workable range). An application
control theory was one of the more
rtling aspects of the Wright brothers
ing to the air and being able to control
plane. It deals with the behaviour of
namic systems. Architectural models,
well as our highly serviced flexible
ldings, have now entered the sphere

of dynamic systems. This is, therefore,
a theoretical stream that has had some
direct relevance to the growth and
development of digital working.

Curvature

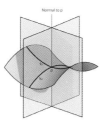

Curvature is a huge topic that has
occupied the minds of many great
mathematicians: Christiaan Huygens,
Gottfried Leibniz, Sir Isaac Newton, Carl
Friedrich Gauss, Nikolai Lobachevsky,
János Bolyai, Henri Poincaré and David
Hilbert, to name a few. It is essentially
the amount by which a curve or a surface
deviates from being straight or flat,
respectively. The simplest case is that of a
curve in the plane. Its curvature may vary
at every point along the curve, but may be
quantified at each point as the inverse of
the radius of the circle that most closely
fits the curve locally at that point. A

circle is a figure with constant curvature;
a small circle has high curvature and a
larger one has less extreme curvature,
hence the inverse relationship to radius.
Gaussian curvature is an intrinsic measure
of surface curvature, the product of the
two principal curvatures of the surface
at a point. Convex surfaces like spheres
have positive curvature, saddle surfaces
like hyperboloids have negative curvature,
and planes have zero local and global
curvature. Curves have only extrinsic
curvature; intrinsically they are linear, and
only have curvature when embedded in a
Euclidean plane or R3.

anzer packing

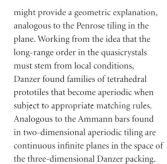

e convex and discrete geometrician
lwig Danzer (b. 1928) was one of the
t to study seriously the challenging
thematical problems of aperiodic tiling
response to the discovery in 1984 of
asicrystals (the name given to alloys
covered by Dan Shechtman with a
vel kind of structure, intermediate
ween crystalline and amorphous).
ey exhibit long-range orientational
ler, but no translational symmetry.
e-fold, and even icosahedral (twenty-
ed regular polyhedron), symmetry
observed leading to the conjecture
t the so-called 'golden rhombohedra'

might provide a geometric explanation,
analogous to the Penrose tiling in the
plane. Working from the idea that the
long-range order in the quasicrystals
must stem from local conditions,
Danzer found families of tetrahedral
prototiles that become aperiodic when
subject to appropriate matching rules.
Analogous to the Ammann bars found
in two-dimensional aperiodic tiling are
continuous infinite planes in the space of
the three-dimensional Danzer packing.

Developable surfaces

A developable surface is a surface that
has zero Gaussian curvature at every
point. This could be a plane, but it could
also be a cylinder, a cone, or any of the
many other curved or folded shapes
one can make from a flat sheet that is
dimensionally stable and cannot stretch,
but can be cut and glued. All developable
surfaces are ruled surfaces – one of their
principal curvatures at every point is a
straight line in the surface. Consider the
cylinder: the curvature at each point is the
product of the positive curvature of the
circular section and the zero curvature of
the straight line of the circle's extension in

the third dimension. Developable surfaces
are very significant in architectural design,
affording a wide range of shapes that can
be fabricated from flat sheet material, and
flat materials that will accommodate only
limited single curvature.

Dynamic relaxation

 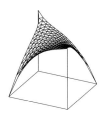 

Dynamic relaxation is a method of computational modelling for the form-finding of cable and fabric structures. In the example of the roof for the British Museum's Great Court (p. 122), this method had to be used to find the structural subdivision of the complex, curved dome into glazed facets. It assumes that all the mass is concentrated at the structural nodes. The system oscillates about the equilibrium position under the influence of loads. The iterative process is achieved by simulating a pseudo-dynamic process in time. At each iteration, the geometry (node position) is updated,

using Newton's second law, where force is equal to the product of mass and acceleration. This is doubly integrated to give a relation between speed, geometry and residual force. Gradually the forces acting on each individual node are equilibrated. Finally, the friction component tangential to the surface at each of the structural nodes via imaginary strings to its four nearest neighbours converges at zero.

Elliptical geometry

  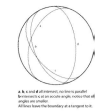

a, b, c and d all intersect, no line is parallel
b intersects c at an accute angle, notice that all angles are smaller.
All lines leave the boundary at a tangent to it.

Elliptical geometry, also known as Riemannian or spherical geometry, is a non-Euclidean geometry. It contradicts Euclid's parallel postulate, in which given a line L and a point P outside that line, there is exactly one line that passes through P that is parallel to L. In elliptical geometry, there are exactly zero lines that pass through P parallel to L. Imagine the lines of elliptical geometry as the great arcs or lines of longitude on the near spherical Earth. They all intersect at the poles. Imagine a triangle inscribed on the same globe between the cities of London, Berlin and Madrid. In contrast to

a triangle created in the Euclidean plane the sum of the angles subtended by the lines of the triangle between the three cities would be greater than 180°. The importance of non-Euclidean geometry in architectural representation has increased with the increasing facility that digital computation offers for modelling the non-planar.

Embedding

Embedding is taking an object and placing it in a space so that its topological qualities are preserved. In the case of graphs, this is maintaining connectivity. A simple graph can be embedded onto a sphere without any crossings. A more complex graph will produce crossings on a sphere so needs a hole to maintain connectivity. The number of holes or handles the graph needs to be embedded into a space relates to its genus.

Emergence

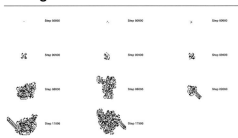

In mathematics, emergent properties are those that are global, topological properties of the whole, rather than the properties of the component parts. In architecture, emergence is thought of similarly, though less rigorously, as spontaneous order appearing within a system that cannot necessarily be inferred or predicted from the simple components of the system and their basic relations, but has resulted from their interaction. Contrast this with top–down ordering. In nature, the ant colony is often cited as the archetypal example of emergent behaviour and form. The queen does

not give direct orders. Instead, each ant reacts individually and spontaneously to chemical scents, in turn leaving scents for the other ants. This is effectively a recursive behaviour that results in order patterns of movement, construction, searching and disposal at a macro-level. It results in the recognizable typology of the termite mound, and even solves such geometrical problems as finding the site furthest from all the entry points to the nest or search zones of constant radius from the colony.

...volutionary shape optimizer

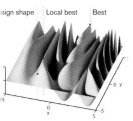

olutionary shape design by means
sensitivity analysis is the exercise of
ning to understand how local and
re global shape changes affect the
chanical performance of the structure
erms of its efficiency and low-strain
rgy. The strain energy is generally
nimized when most of the loads are
nsmitted axially in the structural
mbers, and there is very little bending.
lobal minimum may represent the
st structurally efficient shape, but
er local minima may represent very
d solutions that are much closer to
design shape and to meeting all the

other design criteria. Sensitivity analysis is
the study of how variation (uncertainty)
in the output of a mathematical model
can be apportioned, qualitatively or
quantitatively, to different sources in the
input of a model. The aim is to identify
the relative weighting of sources of
uncertainty. This understanding of the
response to changes in its inputs is often
obscured in mathematical models, but
it is important in making correct and
meaningful use of the model.

Evolutionary structural optimization

Evolutionary structural optimization was
originally proposed in 1992 by Mike Xie
and Grant Steven. It is a recursive iterative
routine that uses finite-element analysis to
discover the von Mises stress or strain
energy in each element in a structure. A
starting 'cube' of virtual finite elements is
given some real material properties, say
those of stone, steel or concrete, and some
loads and constraints are applied: gravity,
support points, etc. After analysis, the
elements recording stress below a certain
threshold, say the least stressed 1 per cent,
are removed. The analysis and removal of
the lowest stressed elements is then

repeated on the residual form recursively
many times over (50 to 100 in this
example). This method will optimize a
structural form to use the least material
The software was developed by Xie and
his researchers to evolve tension-only
structures, such as steel cable structures or
compression-only structures like masonry,
and a combination of the two. They have
also developed bidirectional ESO or
BESO, whereby elements are both
subtracted and added during the
evolution of the form. This is poetically
close to such processes observed in nature
as bone growth.

...nite-element analysis

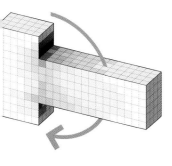

ite elements are like tiny cubic blocks
t make up the whole. They can be very
all, their size a balance between the
inyness or pixellation of the form at
resolution and the computing time,
ich increases very steeply with the
uction of element size. Each element
mpacted by the forces transferred from
immediate neighbours, and this type of
lysis uses these forces.

Fixed-point theorem

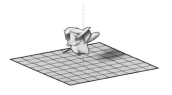 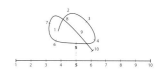

L. E. J. Brouwer (1881–1966) allegedly
arrived at his theorem of topology while
stirring sugar into a cup of coffee and
observing that there was a least one point
on the liquid's surface without motion. It
was used in calculating the trajectory to
the moon, assuming that there would be
at least one path by which the spacecraft
would comply with Newton's laws of
motion; a 10-dimensional problem was
solved to find its fixed point. The theorem
proves that if a continuous function is
mapped into another shape, there will be
at least one point that is common between
the two functions, provided that the new

function is within the domain of the old
and is continuous. Two other examples:
- Take two sheets of paper of equal
  size, one lying directly on top of the
  other. If the top sheet is crumpled
  up and placed on top of the other
  sheet, there must be at least one
  point on the top sheet that is
  directly above the corresponding
  point on the bottom sheet.
- Take a map of the city where you
  are and lay it on the floor. At least
  one point on the map will tell the
  location of the corresponding point
  below it on the floor.

Fluid dynamics

Fluid dynamics is a sub-discipline of fluid mechanics that deals with fluid flow – the natural science of liquids and gases. It is a practical science that developed from the observation of the behaviour of the flow measurements of fluids and gases. The difficulty of scale means that the fact that liquids and gases are made up of discrete molecules that move and collide with one another and other objects is ignored – they are treated as a continuum that varies continuously from one point to another. Each particle used in smoothed hydrodynamics, the digital simulation of fluid behaviour, represents many air molecules and has more sophisticated behaviour than that of molecules in the kinetic theory. Each is aware of its neighbours and behaves in order to model macro-effects such as viscosity and pressure. In architecture, particularly in design development, the calculated pressures and wind speeds from digital modellers may not be accurate except to within a very large factor, but the relative effects are useful for form-finding in determining 'better' and 'worse' shapes with regard to air flow.

Four-dimensional space

1D - x axis   2D - xy axis   3D - xyz axis   4D - $wxyz$ axis

Mathematicians use four-dimensional Euclidean space (that is, space with four spatial dimensions or mutually orthogonal directions of movement) to study four-dimensional polytropes. In the chapter devoted to Topology, we have seen that the Klein surface, while it can be created conceptually by joining the edges of a flat sheet, cannot be embedded in three dimensions, but can in four. In four dimensions, the surface does not intersect itself. Imagine stretching a zero-dimensional point into a one-dimensional line, and the same line stretched into a two-dimensional square, with a third stretch in a third dimension, and we ha[ve] a cube. By stretching the cube once mo[re] in the same way in a fourth dimension, [we] arrive at the tesseract, which has a three-dimensional cell equivalent to the two-dimensional faces of the cube. (This is quite distinct from Hermann Minkows[ki's] four-dimensional geometry of spacetim[e] in which the fourth dimension represe[nts] time, but the space is not metrical or Euclidean.)

Fractals

'Many important spatial patterns of Nature are either irregular or fragmented to such an extreme degree that Euclid… is hardly of any help in describing their form,' wrote Benoît Mandelbrot in 1976. Mandelbrot coined the term 'fractal', or 'fractal set', to collect together examples of a mathematical idea and apply it to the description of such natural phenomena as clouds and coastlines. The term is derived from the Latin *fractus*, meaning irregular or fragmented. A central concept in this new geometry is that of the fractal or Hausdorff-Besicovitch, dimension. This gives an indication of how completely a particular fractal appears to fill space as the microscope zooms in to finer and finer scales. Another key concept in fractal geometry is self-similarity, the same shapes and patterns to be found at successively smaller scales. There are two main approaches to generating a fractal structure: growing it recursively from a unit structure, or constructing divisions in the successively smaller units of the subdivided starting shape, such as Sierpiński's triangle (1915).

Functional analysis

Original function
$y = f(x) = \cos[x] + 0.7 \cdot \cos[1.6 \cdot x]$

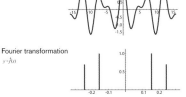

Fourier transformation
$y = \hat{f}(x)$

First derivative
$y = f'(x) = -\sin[x] - 1.12 \cdot \sin[1.6 \cdot x]$

Functional analysis is a branch of mathematics that studies vector spaces and the operators upon them. It deals with functions whose argument is a function, and is concerned with transformations of functions, for example the Fourier transform and the study of differential and integral equations.

Functional surfaces

For mathematicians, visualizing functions may be a useful aid to understanding the characteristics, singularities and periodicity of a function. In architecture, functions are a useful and potentially precise and economical way of designing, modifying or communicating the shape of a profile or surface. We have seen projects in which the height of each point on the surface, its Z coordinate, is a function of its position in the X and Y directions. Architects and mathematicians have worked from well-known functions, and have iteratively edited the algebra to refine and sculpt quite specific complex shapes. As a function expresses dependence between two quantities, functions can also be used to create quantitative dependencies between shape and spatial organizational characteristics of the architecture on the one hand, and external inputs such as incidence of sunlight or imposed gravity and wind loads. Functions are also used to try and digitally emulate the shape and behaviour of physical materials.

Game theory

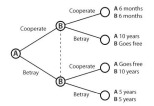

	B Cooperate	B Betray
A Cooperate	A 6 months B 6 months	A 10 years B Goes free
A Betray	A Goes free B 10 years	A 5 years B 5 years

Game theory attempts to capture mathematically the outcomes of combinations of choices of individual 'players' in a strategic game situation, where the outcomes to one are affected by the choices of others. This is generally done in the form of a payoff matrix, or a tree with bifurcations for each choice and different possible outcomes from each choice based on the choice of others. The tree is known as the extensive form of the game. Individuals' choices are treated as simultaneous and uninformed by the moves of other players. In some games, there is a clear path visible to both players that gives the best overall return to both parties, regardless of the choice of the other. In others, according the minimax theorem, there is a mixed strategy based on a set of probabilities for each player; if they play rationally, weighting their actions according to these probabilities, they will receive exactly the same average return. This is relevant to multi-player urban design decision-making and virtual world equivalents.

Graph theory

In mathematics, the study of graphs to represent relations between certain objects, which are represented as a collection of vertices, or nodes, and a collection of edges that connect pairs of nodes. Graphs may be undirected, in which case there is no distinction made between the two nodes connected by an edge, or the edges may be directed from one node to another. The essential quality being represented is connectedness; they are scaleless and non-metrical. The discipline was born in 1736 when Leonhard Euler published his paper on the Seven Bridges of Königsberg and demonstrated a route around the city that crossed each bridge exactly once. Apart from the direct mapping to spatial organization, in architecture graphs are a useful way of relating building services and systems, understanding complex construction processes, viewing dependencies and/or constraints in digital geometrical models, and understanding the flow of data and generation of information in systems.

Hill climbing

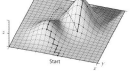

Hill climbing is a generic name for a technique in computer science that searches locally and progressively for better solutions to a function until it can find no further improvement, at which point it stops. There is no guarantee that the programme will find the optimum solution, and it is susceptible to getting stuck at a local maximum. Hill climbing has been used in architecture to search for 'best fit' geometrical and structural solutions in a constrained design context.

Homology

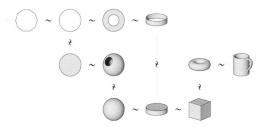

Homology is a concept found in many branches of algebra and topology. It was first used in the topological sense by Henri Poincaré, and is now used to mean a homology group or abelian group, a set of elements and an operation. Some of the best-known examples of topological homologous objects are the cube, which is equivalent to the sphere, and the coffee cup, which is equivalent to a torus.

Hyperbolic geometry

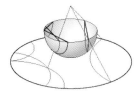

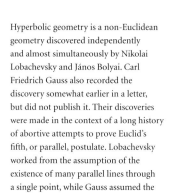

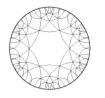

Hyperbolic geometry is a non-Euclidean geometry discovered independently and almost simultaneously by Nikolai Lobachevsky and János Bolyai. Carl Friedrich Gauss also recorded the discovery somewhat earlier in a letter, but did not publish it. Their discoveries were made in the context of a long history of abortive attempts to prove Euclid's fifth, or parallel, postulate. Lobachevsky worked from the assumption of the existence of many parallel lines through a single point, while Gauss assumed the sum of the internal angles of a triangle to be less than 180°. These assumptions led both men to the discovery of the hyperbolic plane. There are four models of the *n*-dimensional hyperbolic space, of which the most familiar from art is probably the Poincaré (or conformal) dis model, in which it is represented in the interior of a circle with lines represented by arcs orthogonal to the boundary and diameters of the boundary circle.

Immersion

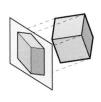

The three-dimensional representation of the Klein surface more commonly known as the Klein bottle is the best-known illustration of the immersion of a higher dimensional surface in three dimensions. It cannot be represented without self-intersection; that is, it cannot be embedded in three dimensions. There are many other examples of surfaces of this kind, such as the Boys surface and other representations of the real projective plane. The diagrams illustrate the concept of embedding by showing network diagrams that can and cannot be embedded in surfaces of different genus.

Inversion

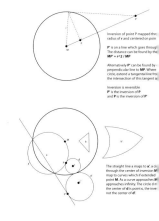

Inversion is a mapping of points to their corresponding inverse points. It is another geometry discovered in the 19th century that transforms figures in ways not familiar from Euclidean transformations. In the plane, it is commonly the mapping of the points within a circle to the points outside a circle. The mapping is governed by the equation $\mathbf{MP.MQ} = \mathbf{R}^2$ where $\mathbf{P}$ is the original point, and $\mathbf{Q}$ its inverse, $\mathbf{M}$ the centre of the circle and $\mathbf{R}$ its radius. The centre of the circle is a special point that maps to infinity. Points close the centre of the circle map to the outer reaches of space, while those close to the perimeter map to points close to the perimeter on the outside. Points on the circle itself map to themselves. In three dimensions, point within a sphere may be mapped to points outside. And in fact, it is possible to apply the same mapping method with a two- or three-dimensional figure of variable radius, of any shape.

Kelvin conjecture

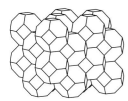
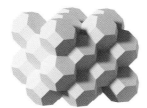

ir William Thomson (later Lord Kelvin) (1824–1907) tackled the problem of the ideal ordered foam structure in 1887, when he was already in his sixties. His career publications then numbered over 600, and covered subjects as diverse as telegraphy and electrical technology to the second law of thermodynamics, giving his name to a unit of temperature. His reasons for investigations into the ordering of foam were driven by wider speculations, but arrived at a useful answer to the question: 'What partitioning of space into equal volumes minimizes their surface area?' His answer was accepted for over a century. The unit cell described by Kelvin for this foam of uniform bubbles was a form of truncated octahedron, to which Kelvin gave the longer name of tetradecahedron. It was one of the thirteen Archimedean solids. This solution, informed by Kelvin's knowledge of crystallography, survived as the packing model that gives the best solution until 1993, when Robert Phelan and Denis Weaire reopened the search.

Knot theory

We have been tying knots since prehistoric times, but their theoretical description only entered mathematics through Gauss's work in the 19th century. In mathematics, a knot is a topological embedding of a circle in three-dimensional Euclidean space (R3), but it is generally represented by a two-dimensional diagram in which the crossings are represented. One knot may have several two-dimensional diagrams.

- *Knotequivalence*: Is one knot topologically related to the other knot? It is if you can make the knot without cutting the other one.
- *Knot addition*: Knots can be added together by cutting the two knots and splicing the ends together without introducing any new crossings.
- *Prime knots*: A prime knot is one that cannot be created through the addition of two other knots.

Lindenmayer systems

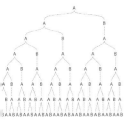

L-systems are named after the biologist and botanist Aristid Lindenmayer (1925–99), who studied the growth patterns of multicellular organisms, including algae and bacteria, to develop L-systems as a formal description of their development. Later it was extended to higher plants and complex branching structures. Lindenmayer's original L-system for modelling the growth of algae:

Variables : A B

Start : A

Rules : (A → AB), (B → A), which produce:

n = 0 : A
n = 1 : AB
n = 2 : ABA
n = 3 : ABAAB
n = 4 : ABAABABA
n = 5 : ABAABABAABAAB
n = 6 : ABAABABAABAABABAABABA
n = 7 : ABAABABAABAABABAABABAABAABABAABAAB

The number of letters in each successive line increases according to the Fibonacci sequence. L-systems follow recursive rules and result in fractal-like forms that exhibit self-similarity. They have been applied in the generation of artificial life.

Minimal surfaces

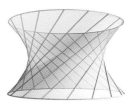

The technical definition of a minimal surface is a surface of zero mean curvature (such as a plane). Other well-known examples that have equal opposite overall curvature are the catenoid (formed by sweeping a catenary curve around an axis); the helicoid (swept out by a simultaneously rotating and translating line); the Enneper surface; and the more recently discovered Costa-Hoffman-Meeks surface, but there are many more. The investigation into minimal surfaces began with the work of Joseph-Louis Lagrange (1736–1813), when he posed the question of whether there existed for every arbitrarily complicated boundary curve one surface of least area. Soap-films on a deformable wire-frame boundary proved a wonderful medium in which to investigate this question. Minimal surfaces include, but are not limited to, surfaces of minimal area. The sphere, although it represents the minimum surface area for a given volume, is not a minimal surface according to the mathematical definition.

Multi-dimensional spaces

The dimension of a space is the minimum number of coordinates needed to specify every point within it. In a parametric model, a dimension can be ascribed to every variable parameter, and thus the model becomes a many-dimensional space of considerable complexity. This is the case in many of the digital architectural models described in this book. Parts of the model can move and change in so many different ways that the scope of possible change cannot be represented in two or three dimensions. In animation and film, time is represented as a fourth dimension, but is limited

to a single linear sequence and hence only adds one additional dimension to a three-dimensional scene or model. A circle is one-dimensional, even though it is embedded in two dimensions – it can be described by a single polar coordinate angle. This is called its intrinsic (as opposed to extrinsic) dimension.

Multi-objective optimization

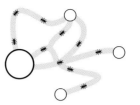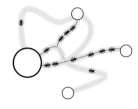

Architects are generalists. Architectural design is concerned with bringing things together and with synthesis. One area of design research that is very pertinent in this respect is multi-objective optimization, in which optimal values for two or more conflicting objectives are looked for (maximizing the penetration of sunlight into a building in the winter, and passively regulating the internal temperature in the summer, for example). The striking foraging patterns of ants, apart from being a top exemplar of geometrical and organizational emergence, also provide an empirical

testing ground for the mathematics of multi-objective optimization. It seems that the ants have optimized the amount and combinations of types of food they can gather relative to the energy expended, despite the fact that different food categories require different foraging patterns.

Non-Euclidean geometry

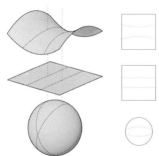

The Greek mathematician Euclid (fl. 300 BC) was the first scholar to develop a systematic exposition of planar and solid geometry in his treatise *Elements*. It proves many theorems based, in the planar case, on five basic assumed axioms. Of these, the fifth, or parallel, postulate always had a different status from the first four, which covered the existence of a straight line between two points, the infinite extension of straight lines, the description of a circle by any centre and radius, and the equality of right angles. With the publication of hyperbolic and Riemannian geometry, which demonstrated multiple parallel

lines through a point and triangles with angular sums less than 180°, and no parallel lines and triangles summing greater than 180° respectively, it was proved that not all geometry conformed to Euclid's *Elements*. Bernhard Riemann's *On the Foundations of Geometry* (1868) and Felix Klein's Erlangen programme of 1872 established the idea of many geometries, not all Euclidean.

Non-linearity

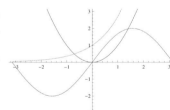

Non-linear systems are those for which output does not change proportionally to input, and effect is not proportional to cause. In mathematics, non-linear equations cannot be mapped as straight lines, and may or may not be solvable. They are characterized algebraically by including at least one exponential of a variable greater than 1, e.g. an x^2 or x^3. One of the characteristics may be large, abrupt and unexpected changes or fluctuations. The motion of a pendulum is one of the best-known problems, and a significant contributor to a mathematical understanding of non-linear systems.

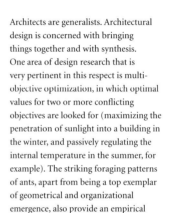

on-orientable surfaces

n example of a non-orientable surface is e Möbius strip: one continuous surface th one continuous edge. A surface is ientable if a consistent choice of surface rmal can be made at every point that ows the right-hand rule to be used to fine the 'clockwise' direction of loops in e surface. If we choose a surface normal rection at a point on the Möbius strip d create a coordinate system based on is normal as the Z-axis, then slide it ound the surface, it can pass through e same point in the surface again, but th the Z-axis oriented to a surface rmal exactly opposite to the original

direction. In other words, a surface in the Euclidean space R3 is orientable if a two-dimensional figure cannot be moved around the surface and back to where it started so that it looks like its own mirror image. Otherwise the surface is non-orientable. The diagram on the right shows the effect of moving the letter R across a three-dimensional surface (a cylinder and a Möbius strip); the diagram on the left shows how the surfaces are constructed, by joining a to a and b to b, and how the R becomes inverted. The cylinder, therefore, is orientable and the Möbius strip non-orientable.

NURBS

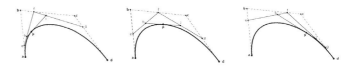

Non-uniform rational basis splines (NURBs) are curves and surfaces that began development in the 1950s to introduce precision to the description of free-form surfaces such as ships' hulls and car bodies that were otherwise referenced from one-off models. Pierre Bézier, an engineer at Renault, and Paul de Casteljau at Citroën worked simultaneously on this problem. In computer graphics, splines with control points off the curve are today recognized as Bézier splines. They moved from the CAD packages of car makers to become ubiquitous in computer-aided design, manufacturing and engineering.

A NURBs curve is defined by its order, a set of weighted control points and a knot vector. NURBs usefully provide a single mathematical form that can be used for both mathematically defined and free-form shapes, and are economically stored in numerous industry standard formats. They have arguably had a significant influence on architectural aesthetics, particularly during the period of steep uptake of digital CAD in the discipline and practice.

areto optimization

solution where no element of the lution can be significantly improved thout negatively affecting the other ments (circles in triangles, for ample). A solution can be considered timal if none of the circles can grow thout shrinking the others. Named er Vilfredo Pareto (1848–1923), an onomist, sociologist and philosopher o was fascinated by the inequality of come distribution in the population, reto optimization is a measure of iciency. The significance for architecture that it is possible to identify an optimal nge of solutions in the middle of

the graph where all variables perform relatively well, but a slight shift will improve one at the expense of another. An example might be the trade-off between natural light and thermal performance as the percentage of external glazing is varied. An outcome of a game is Pareto optimal if no other outcome makes every player at least as well off and at least one player strictly better off. That is, a Pareto optimal outcome cannot be improved upon without hurting at least one player. A Nash equilibrium is often not Pareto optimal, implying that the players' payoffs can all be increased.

Penrose tiling

In a 1974 paper, Roger Penrose proposed, among other things, an aperiodic tiling that took its inspiration from the work of Johannes Kepler, who had explored tilings built around pentagons in his book *Harmonices Mundi*. Tiling the plane with pentagons leaves gaps, and Penrose proposed to fill these gaps with three other shapes: a star, a boat and a diamond. By publishing his tile set with an accompanying set of rules about their matching and adjacency, he ensured that their tiling was aperiodic. Penrose was not the first to prove the existence of aperiodic tilings. In 1964, Robert Berger produced

an aperiodic set of 104 different tiles, and in 1971 Raphael Robinson simplified his proof and found a set of just six tiles. Penrose went on to find two other sets of aperiodic tiles that used just two tiles, one consisting of a kite and a dart and the second of just two rhombuses with sides of similar length but different angles. Although there is no translational symmetry – 'aperiodic' means that the pattern cannot be shifted and mapped onto itself – any bounded region, no matter how large, will be repeated an infinite number of times within the tiling.

Reachability

Undirected

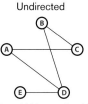

E is reachable from **A** via the path **A D E**
A is reachable from **E** via the path **E D A**

Directed

E is reachable from **A** via the path **A C B D E**
A is not reachable from **E**

Modelling in architecture and spatial design often involves using object-oriented software and programming that does not allow circular references. If the position of a door is dependent on the position of the wall surface, for instance, it is not possible conversely to alter the wall position by moving the door, meaning that the links between objects in the model are the edges and nodes of a directed graph (objects linked by edges in the graph represented by arrows in one direction only). This leads to a strongly hierarchical tree-like map of dependencies, all flowing in the same direction. In graph theory, reachability is the notion of being able to get from one vertex in a directed graph to some other vertex (or not). Reachability in undirected graphs is trivial; just find the connected components in the graph.

Recursion

One of the most important concepts in complexity is recursion, a method of defining functions in which the function being defined is applied within its own definition. Within a procedure, therefore, one of the steps is to run the whole procedure again; another way of saying this is that the output of once applying the function becomes the input of the next iteration. The Fibonacci number sequence is well-known mathematical example of recursion, where n = (n-1) + (n-2), or the current term is the sum of the two previous terms in the sequence, each of which is the sum of two before it.

Ruled surfaces

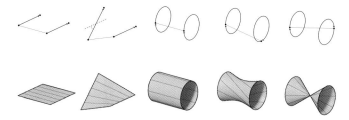

Ruled surfaces are a class of surface that can be generated by sweeping or revolving a straight line in space. This includes the plane, cylinder, cone, and any number of irregular surfaces. Some ruled surfaces are doubly curved, including the hyperbolic paraboloid (saddle-shape) and the hyperboloid of one sheet (cooling tower). The rulings provide a rational basis for the production of curved form; this was exploited by Gaudí both in model-making and in cutting stone along linear rulings between marked points of stone templates. The helicoid created by sweeping a revolving line along a linear axis is the only ruled minimal surface apart from the plane. There are only three types of surface that contain two families of rulings, where each point on the surface has two distinct straight lines that lie in the surface intersecting at that point: the hyperbolic paraboloid, the hyperboloid of one sheet, and the plane (pictured).

Series and sequences

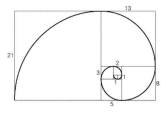
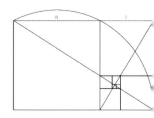

In mathematics, a series is generally the sum of all the terms in an infinite sequence. A mathematical sequence is an ordered list of objects (or events), which may be infinite. It is like a set, but unlike a set; the order in which the terms appear matters, and the same term may appear multiple times in the ordering. The Fibonacci sequence (0, 1, 1, 2, 3, 5, 8, 13, 21, 34, 55, 89 …) is a well-known example of a mathematical sequence, in which each term is the sum of the preceding two terms. It can be interpreted geometrically, and is commonly found influencing architecture, particularly in its relationship to the Golden Ratio. The ratio of adjacent terms in the sequence (for instance, ⅔, ⅗, ⅝, ⁸⁄₁₃, ¹³⁄₂₁, ²¹⁄₃₄) tend in an oscillation that goes first above and then below the value towards the value of the Golden Ratio.

Singularity theory

...ystems are not the same everywhere. ...raphs of smooth functions frequently ...ave a number of critical points. These ...re maxima (where the value of the ...unction starts to fall as the value of X ...ncreases), minima (where the value starts ...o rise), and points of inflection (where ...e local gradient – or rate of change – of ...e curve stops increasing and starts to ...ecrease). As the function parameters ...re changed, some of these points prove ...egenerate', or cease to be defined, and ...e fundamental shape of the graph ...hanges. In mathematics, the point is the ...egenerate form of the circle as its radius tends to zero, the circle the degenerate form of the ellipse as the length of its axes converge. Within real systems, such as the stock exchange or the local eco-system, these represent points near which there is disproportionate change in the overall state of the system relative to a small change in one or more of the variables. Another useful visualization is to imagine a tiny insect walking over a piece of paper that has been crumpled in the hand. The creature will encounter at least three different states: smooth areas; points on creases like cliff tops; and points where a pleat is just starting.

System dynamics

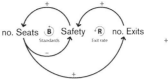 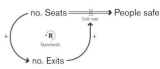

System dynamics is the study of the behaviour of complex systems over time. It takes into account that changes in the parts of system impact elsewhere, so a change in A may result in a change in B that in turn affects A. For instance, the cost estimate for a building exceeds the budget, so the programme is reconsidered and the building redesigned to reduce the overall volume. This results in a building with a higher cost per square metre, which in turn has implications for the budget. By building relational and simulation models, it is possible to observe the dynamics of the system when changes are made, to explore 'what if' scenarios. If the number of seats in a theatre are increased, how will this impact the number and position of fire exits, air handling, space needed front of house, etc? In architecture, such models that encompass multiple aspects of the building design, procurement and management are still in their infancy.

Topological transformations

...he transformation of one object to ...nother, without cutting or splicing, ...aintains its topological identity. ...he object can be stretched because ...istances and volumes are not important ...n topological transformation. The ...ost famous example is the pretzel ...ransformation, shown in the diagram ...bove, which demonstrates how a ...andcuff-shaped object attached to a ...ing can be taken off the ring by using ...opological transformations.

Topology models

Topology has been known as rubber-sheet geometry. Each of the geometries illustrated – the cylinder, the Möbius band, the torus and the Klein bottle surface – can also be represented as a flat sheet that has been stretched and had its edges joined or glued together. Two of the figures (the cylinder and the torus) are orientable, or have their edges glued together in the same orientation. The remaining two (the Möbius band and the Klein bottle) are non-orientable, or have their edges glued together in opposing orientation with a twist in the sheet. The cylinder and the Möbius band have only two opposite edges joined, while the torus and the Klein bottle have both sets of opposite edges joined. There is another important non-orientable surface: the projective plane, the final development following the Klein bottle surface, in which both pairs of edges are joined in opposing orientation. The projective plane is familiar in geometry, represented in the two-dimensional canvases of artists using constructed perspective in their works. It has also been represented immersed in three dimensions.

Toroid patch

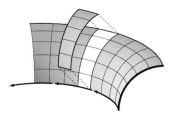

A torus is described variously as the product of two circles, or the revolution of a circle around an axis in the same plane, or a doughnut. Sweeping a circular arc along a circular arc path is a useful way in architecture of generating a surface that is variable in terms of its shape and curvature; not immediately visually identifiable in the manner of a spherical surface, but simple to describe and construct as it has a circular section in two orthogonal directions.

Voronoi diagram

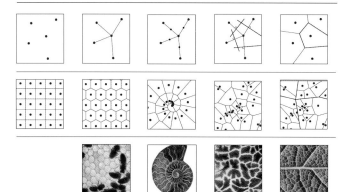

At its simplest, a Voronoi diagram is the division of a space into contiguous neighbouring cells. The cells relate to a set of points (Voronoi sites) in that space. Each point has an associated cell consisting of all the points closer to that site than to any other. The Voronoi diagram, named after mathematician Georgy Voronoi (1868–1908), is also known as a Dirichlet tessellation after

Lejeune Dirichlet (1805–59), who used two- and three-dimensional Voronoi diagrams in his study of quadratics. Voronoi diagrams have many applications: mapping in the spatial sciences, for example, and relating diverse social and political organization. They also have a long history of informal application that predates Voronoi's formal work in 1908 to define the general n-dimensional case.

Vierendeel truss

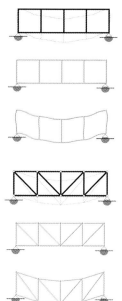

The Vierendeel truss is one in which the members are not triangulated; the openings in the truss are polygonal, but not triangular. The frame has fixed joints that are capable of transferring and resisting bending moments. This contrasts with more commonly used trusses that are assumed to have pin joints with no bending moments at the jointed ends. The Vierendeel truss is named after engineer Arthur Vierendeel (1852–1940), who developed the design in 1896, and is sometimes referred to as a strong-joint, weak-member elastic structure.

Weaire-Phelan model

Robert Phelan began his research at Trinity College Dublin in 1993 to explore the Kelvin problem and variations on the theme, using Ken Brakke's surface evolver programme. Phelan joined a group with a background in solid state and materials science, who already had some hunches about what types of structures might compete with Kelvin's conjecture that were already manifest in nature. Phelan started with the covalent bonding structure of clathrates compounds, in which the bonds can be envisaged as foam cells. Most of the rings of bonds on the sides of the cages are five-fold, creating

pentagonal faces. It is a regular assembly of two types of irregular polyhedral cells with twelve and fourteen faces, respectively, combined in the ratio or 2:6 in a repeating unit of eight polyhedra. It turned out to have a cell surface area for volume that was 0.3 per cent less than the venerable conjecture of Kelvin.

THEMATICS AND DESIGN

Auguste Comte, *Système de politique positive*, 4 vols (1851–54).

Daniel Pedoe, *Geometry and the Liberal Arts* (Harmondsworth, England, 1976).

James R. Smart, *Modern Geometries* (Pacific Grove, California, 1973).

Pedoe, 16.

Sanford Kwinter, afterword, in Benjamin Aranda and Chris Lasch, *Pamphlet Architecture 27: Tooling* (New York, 2005), 92.

Ibid.

Ingeborg M. Rocker, 'When Code Matters', in 'Programming Cultures: Art and Architecture in the Age of Software', special issue, *AD Profile 182* 76:4 (July/August 2006): 16–25.

Michael Speaks, 'Design Intelligence: Part 1: Introduction', in *A+U* 387:12 (December 2002): 10–18.

Robin Evans, *The Projective Cast: Architecture and its Three Geometries* (Cambridge, Massachusetts, 1995).

Michael J. Ostwald, *Multi-Directional Appropriations of Theory Between Architecture and Sciences of Complexity: An Analysis of Motives and Efficacy*, PhD dissertation, University of Newcastle, New South Wales, 1998.

Gilles Deleuze, *Spinoza* (Paris, 1981).

Speaks.

Evans, 323.

Theo van Doesburg, 'Towards a Plastic Architecture', in *De Stijl* 12:6/7 (1924).

Lionel March, 'Architecture and Mathematics Since 1960', in Kim Williams and José Francisco Rodrigues, eds, *Nexus IV: Architecture and Mathematics* (Turin, 2002), 7–33.

MATHEMATICAL SURFACES AND SERIALITY

Dennis Shelden, keynote address, 'Advances in Architectural Geometry' conference, Vienna University of Technology, 15 September 2008.

Gerd Fischer, ed., *Mathematische Modelle*, 2 vols. (Braunschweig/Wiesbaden, 1986).

Stephen Hyde, et al., *The Language of Shape: The Role of Curvature in Condensed Matter: Physics, Chemistry and Biology* (Amsterdam, 1997).

Gregory Bateson, *Mind and Nature: A Necessary Unity* (London, 1979).

Naomi Stead, 'Australian Wildlife Health Centre', in *Architecture Australia* 95:2 (March/April 2006): 80–87.

Ibid.

Interview with Jonathan Parr, Foster + Partners, 18 December 2008.

Hugh Whitehead and Brady Peters, 'Geometry Form and Complexity', in David Littlefield, *Space Craft: Developments in Architectural Computing* (London, 2008).

Martin Manning, et al., 'Beijing Airport Terminal 3', in *Steel Construction* 2:1 (2009): 1–8.

George L. Legendre, *Mathematical Form: John Pickering and the Architecture of the Inversion Principle* (London, 2006).

Marius Leutenegger, *Aesthetic of Disappearance*, vol. 10 (2005/2006), 48–57.

Christoph Ingenhoven, *Main Station Stuttgart – Zero Energy Station*, Global Holcim Awards, project booklet.

Michael Webb, 'An Animated Affair', in *Architecture* 92:10 (October 2003): 66–71.

Interview with Dennis Shelden, 28 January 2009.

Shelden, keynote address, 'Advances in Architectural Geometry' conference.

16. Kohn Pedersen Fox, *Mathematics and Parametric Design in the New Abu Dhabi Terminal Airport: Marcel Jean's Utopia and Jacques Lacan's Diagrams*, unpublished manuscript.

17. Ibid.

2. CHAOS, COMPLEXITY, EMERGENCE

1. Michael Hensel, Achim Menges and Michael Weinstock, 'Emergence: Morphogenetic Design Strategies', special issue, *Architectural Design* 74:3 (May/June 2004).

2. Michael Batty, *Cities and Complexity: Understanding Cities with Cellular Automata, Agent-Based Models and Fractals* (Cambridge, Massachusetts, 2005).

3. Benoît Mandelbrot, *The Fractal Geometry of Nature* (San Francisco, 1983).

4. Nikos A. Salingaros, 'Architecture, Patterns and Mathematics', in *Nexus Network Journal* 1:1/2 (June 1999): 75–86.

5. Michael Hensel, 'Computing Self-Organization: Environmentally Sensitive Growth Modelling', in 'Techniques and Technologies in Morphogenetic Design', special issue, *AD Profile 180* 76:2 (March/April 2006): 12–17.

6. Although chaotic systems are deterministic and follow causal rules, the rules of a programmed chaotic system might engage chance and therefore introduce probability or stochastic process.

7. Donald Bates and Peter Davidson, 'Editorial', in 'Architecture After Geometry', special issue, *AD Profile 127* 67:5/6 (May/June 1997): 7–11.

8. Donald Bates, 'Surface Strategies', in *Architectural Review Australia* 90 (October 2004): 106–10.

9. Donald Bates, in *Architectural Review* 219:1307 (January 2006): 38–39.

10. Charles Jencks, 'The New Paradigm in Architecture', in *Architectural Record* 191:6 (June 2003): 108–19.

11. Ateliers Jean Nouvel, design statement, 2008.

12. Shrikant Sharma and Al Fisher, SMART group, Büro Happold, *Louvre Abu Dhabi: Integrated Optimization for Structural and Environmental Performance*, unpublished manuscript.

13. John H. Holland, *Emergence: From Chaos to Order* (New York, 1999), 3.

14. Steven Johnson, *Emergence: The Connected Lives of Ants, Brains, Cities and Software* (New York, 2001), 18.

15. Pia Ednie-Brown, 'All-Over, Over-All: Biothing and Emergent Composition', in 'Programming Cultures: Art and Architecture in the Age of Software', special issue, *AD Profile 182* 76:4 (July/August 2006): 72–81.

16. Pia Ednie-Brown and Alisa Andrasek, 'A Self-Engineering Creature-Culture', in 'Collective Intelligence in Design', special issue, *AD Profile 183* 76:5 (September/October 2006): 18–25.

3. PACKING AND TILING

1. Ludwig Danzer, 'Three-Dimensional Analogs of the Planar Penrose Tilings and Quasicrystals', in *Discrete Mathematics* 76:1 (1989): 1–7.

2. Parkview International and Arup AGU, 'The Auditorium, Work Stage 2 Design Report', vol. 1, *The Foyer & Crystal* (2006).

3. Interview with Francis Archer, Arup AGU, 13 February 2009.

4. Jonas Risen, 'Kelvin's Conjecture: The Sustainability of Optimization and Integration', 2007 (greenlineblog.com).

5. Tristram Carfrae, 'Engineering the Water Cube', in *Architecture Australia* 95:4 (July/August 2006): 103–5.

6. Stuart Bull and Steve Downing, 'Beijing Water Cube: The IT Challenge', in 'Information Technology', special issue, *Structural Engineer* 82:13 (July 2004): 23–26.

7. Xueyi Fu, et al., 'Beijing Olympic National Swimming Centre: Structural Design', in 'Beijing Olympics 2008', special issue, *Structural Engineer* 85:22 (November 2007): 27–33.

8. Heneghan Peng and Francis Archer, Arup AGU, unpublished project descriptions.

9. Interview with Francis Archer, Arup AGU, 13 February 2009.

10. Interview with Howard Raggatt, Ashton Raggatt McDougall, 26 February 2009.

11. Brent Allpress, 'Digital Interface', in *Monument* 56 (August/September 2003): 40–47.

12. Minifie Nixon website (minifienixon.com).

4. OPTIMIZATION

1. Chris J. K. Williams, *Definition of Geometry as Built*, part I, unpublished manuscript.

2. Paul Shepherd, *Exploration of Alternative Scheme Using Subdivision Surfaces*, unpublished manuscript.

3. Interview with Brady Peters, SMG, Foster + Partners, 18 February 2009.

4. 'Melbourne Rectangular Stadium', in *Australian Stadiums* (austadiums.com), 23 May 2007.

5. Unpublished interview with Graham French, Cox Architects, and John Legge Wilkinson, Arup, Melbourne, by Dominik Holzer, 25 February 2008.

6. 'I project, Fukuoka, Japan 2002–2005', in 'Toyo Ito: Under Construction', special issue, *A+U* 5:404 (May 2004): 26–43.

7. Kohn Pederson Fox, *Pinnacle Geometric Mechanisms*, unpublished manuscript.

8. Interview with Gerard Evenden, senior partner, Foster + Partners.

9. Interview with Hugh Whitehead, partner and director of SMG, Foster + Partners.

10. Interview with Gerard Evenden; Xavier De Kestelier, associate partner, SMG; Emanuele Mattutini, associate partner and project leader; Christopher Junkin, associate partner and principal parametric modeller; Francis Aish, partner, SMG and programming specialist, Foster + Partners, 18 December 2008.

11. Interview with Peter Holmes, acoustic designer, Royal Melbourne Institute of Technology, 8 May 2009.

12. Interview with Jonathan Cowle, Ashton Raggatt McDougall, 21 July 2009.

5. TOPOLOGY

1. Jean-Michel Kantor, 'A Tale of Bridges: Topology and Architecture', in *Nexus Network Journal* 7:2 (November 2005): 13–21.

2. Michele Emmer, *From Flatland to Hypersurfaces* (Basel, 2003), 67–93.

3. Giuseppa Di Cristina, ed., *Architecture and Science* (London, 2001), 6.

4. Alberto Ferre, et al., *The Yokohama Project: Foreign Office Architects* (Barcelona, 2002), 35.

5. Joseph Giovannini, in *Architecture* 88:3 (March 1999): 96.

6. Connie van Cleef, 'Radical Domesticity: The Möbius House's Reflection of Modern Living', in *Architectural Review* 206:1231 (September 1999): 47.

7. Patrik Schumacher, 'Deep Plan', in *AA Files* 38 (1999): 23–25.

8. Cecil Balmond, *Informal* (New York, 2007), 349, 352.

9. Ibid., 363.

10. Paul Morgan Architects website (paulmorganarchitects.com).

11. From the transcript of the 2007 RAIA Robin Boyd Award for Residential Buildings, awarded to Paul Morgan Architects for Cape Schanck House.

12. Paul Morgan Architects website (paulmorganarchitects.com).

13. Ingeborg M. Rocker, 'Calculus-Based Form: An Interview with Greg Lynn', in 'Programming Cultures: Art and Architecture in the Age of Software', special issue, *AD Profile 182* 76:4 (July/August 2006): 88–95.

14. Interview with Rob McBride and Drew Williamson, McBride Charles Ryan.

15. Kirsten Hannema, 'Möbius Bridge, Bristol', in 'New European Architecture', special issue, *A10* (November/December 2005).

16. Interview with Julian Hakes, Hakes Associates, September 2008.

17. John Macarthur, 'Australian Baroque: Geometry and Meaning at the National Museum of Australia', in *Architecture Australia* 90:2 (March/April 2001): 48–61.

18. Interview with Howard Raggatt, Ashton Raggatt McDougall, 26 February 2009.

19. Macarthur, 48–61.

20. Hyde, et al.

21. Michael Meredith and Mutsuro Sasaki, *From Control to Design: Parametric/Algorithmic Architecture* (Barcelona, 2008), 54–59.

DATASCAPES AND MULTI-DIMENSIONALITY

1. Morris Kline, *Mathematics and the Search for Knowledge* (New York, 1986).

2. Henri Poincaré, *Science et méthode* (Paris, 1908).

3. Bruce Chatwin, *The Songlines* (Franklin, Pennsylvania, 1986).

4. Alfred North Whitehead, *The Concept of Nature* (Cambridge, England, 1920).

5. Roger Penrose, *The Road to Reality: A Complete Guide to the Laws of the Universe* (London, 2004).

6. Henri Lefebvre, *The Production of Space* (Oxford, 1991).

7. Paul Minifie, 'Streaming House', in *Architectural Review Australia* 90 (March 2002): 78–80

BIBLIOGRAPHY

Brent Allpress, 'Digital Interface', in *Monument* 56 (August/September 2003): 40–47.

Robert Ammann, et al., 'Aperiodic Tiles', in *Discrete and Computational Geometry* (New York, 1992).

Benjamin Aranda and Chris Lasch, *Pamphlet Architecture 27: Tooling* (New York, 2005).

Benjamin Aranda, Chris Lasch and Daniel Bosia, 'Grotto', in Irene Hwang, et al., eds, *Verb Natures* (Barcelona, 2007).

Ashton Raggatt McDougall, 'Storey Hall', in *Architectural Design* 67:9/10 (September/October 1997): 40.

Tomaso Aste and Denis Weaire, *The Pursuit of Perfect Packaging*, 2nd ed. (London, 2008).

Cecil Balmond, *Informal* (New York, 2002).

Michael Barron, *Auditorium Acoustics and Architectural Design* (London, 1993).

Donald Bates, in *Architectural Review* 219:1307 (January 2006): 38–39.

———, 'Surface Strategies', in *Architectural Review Australia* 90 (October 2004): 106–10.

Donald Bates and Peter Davidson, 'Editorial', in 'Architecture After Geometry', special issue, *AD Profile 127* 67:5/6 (May/June 1997): 7–11.

Gregory Bateson, *Mind and Nature: A Necessary Unity* (London, 1979).

Michael Batty, *Cities and Complexity: Understanding Cities with Cellular Automata, Agent-Based Models and Fractals* (Cambridge, Massachusetts, 2005).

Mirco Becker and Stylianos Dritsas, 'Research and Design in Shifting from Analog to Digital', in *Expanding Bodies: Art, Cities, Environment*, Proceedings of the 27th Annual Conference of the Association for Computer-Aided Design in Architecture, Halifax, Nova Scotia, 1–7 October 2007.

Leo L. Beranek, *Music, Acoustics and Architecture* (New York, 1962).

Stuart Bull and Steve Downing, 'Beijing Water Cube: The IT Challenge', in 'Information Technology', special issue, *Structural Engineer* 82:13 (July 2004): 23–26.

Jane Burry, et al., 'Dynamical Structural Modelling: A Collaborative Design Exploration', in *International Journal of Architectural Computing* 3:1 (2005): 27–42.

Tristram Carfrae, 'Engineering the Water Cube', in *Architecture Australia* 95:4 (July/August 2006): 103–5.

Renos Charitou, et al., 'The Bishopsgate Tower Case Study', in *International Journal of Architectural Computing* 5:1 (2007): 62–81

Bruce Chatwin, *The Songlines* (Franklin, Pennsylvania, 1986).

David Clark, 'Weird Beauty', in *Architectural Record* 188:11 (November 2000): 106–11.

Auguste Comte, *Système de politique positive*, 4 vols. (1851–54).

Ludwig Danzer, 'Three-Dimensional Analogs of the Planar Penrose Tilings and Quasicrystals', in *Discrete Mathematics* 76:1 (1989): 1–7.

Norman Day, 'Storey Hall', in *Architecture Australia* 85 (January/February 1996): 34–41.

Gilles Deleuze, *Spinoza* (Paris, 1981).

Giuseppa Di Cristina, ed., *Architecture and Science* (London, 2001).

Pia Ednie-Brown, 'All-Over, Over-All: Biothing and Emergent Composition', in 'Programming Cultures: Art and Architecture in the Age of Software', special issue, *AD Profile 182* 76:4 (July/August 2006): 72–81.

Pia Ednie-Brown and Alisa Andrasek, 'A Self-Engineering Creature-Culture', in 'Collective Intelligence in Design', special issue, *AD Profile 183* 76:5 (September/October 2006): 18–25.

Harriet Edquist, 'Resurrection City: Ashton Raggatt McDougall's Storey Hall, RMIT', in *Art and Australia* 34 (1996): 178–79.

Michele Emmer, *From Flatland to Hypersurfaces* (Basel, 2003).

Robin Evans, *The Projective Cast: Architecture and its Three Geometries* (Cambridge, Massachusetts, 1995).

Alberto Ferre, et al., *The Yokohama Project: Foreign Office Architects* (Barcelona, 2002).

Gerd Fischer, ed., *Mathematische Modelle*, 2 vols. (Braunschweig/Wiesbaden, 1986).

Foreign Office Architects, 'Spanish Pavilion at Aichi Expo 2005', in Albert Ferre, et al., eds, *Verb Conditioning: The Design of New Atmospheres, Effects and Experiences* (Barcelona, 2007).

Xueyi Fu, et al., 'Beijing Olympic National Swimming Centre: Structural Design', in 'Beijing Olympics 2008', special issue, *Structural Engineer* 85:22 (November 2007): 27–33.

Joseph Giovannini, in *Architecture* 88:3 (March 1999): 96.

Kirsten Hannema, 'Möbius Bridge, Bristol', in 'New European Architecture', special issue, *A10* (November/December 2005).

Michael Hensel, 'Computing Self-Organization: Environmentally Sensitive Growth Modelling', in 'Techniques and Technologies in Morphogenetic

Design', special issue, *AD Profile 180* 76:2 (March/April 2006): 12–17.

Michael Hensel, Achim Menges and Michael Weinstock, 'Emergence: Morphogenetic Design Strategies', special issue, *Architectural Design* 74:3 (May/June 2004).

John H. Holland, *Emergence: From Chaos to Order* (New York, 1999).

Dominik Holzer, et al., 'Linking Parametric Design and Structural Analysis to Foster Transdisciplinary Design Collaboration', Proceedings of the 12th International Conference on Computer-Aided Architectural Design Research in Asia, Nanjing, China, 19–21 April 2007.

Stephen Hyde, et al., *The Language of Shape: The Role of Curvature in Condensed Matter: Physics, Chemistry and Biology* (Amsterdam, 1997).

'I project, Fukuoka, Japan 2002-2005', in 'Toyo Ito: Under Construction', special issue, *A+U* 5:404 (May 2004): 26–43.

Christoph Ingenhoven, *Main Station Stuttgart – Zero Energy Station*, Global Holcim Awards, project booklet.

Rebecca Ivatts, *MP.MQ = MR2: John M. Pickering*, catalogue exhibition, London, Royal Society of British Sculptors, 2002.

Charles Jencks, 'The New Paradigm in Architecture', in *Architectural Record* 191:6 (June 2003): 108–19.

W. M. Jenkins, 'Structural Design Optimization by Evolution', in *The Structural Engineer* (July 2004): 29–

Steven Johnson, *Emergence: The Connected Lives of Ants, Brains, Cities and Software* (New York, 2001).

Jean-Michel Kantor, 'A Tale of Bridges: Topology and Architecture', in *Nexus Network Journal* 7:2 (November 2005): 13–21.

Morris Kline, *Mathematics and the Search for Knowledge* (New York, 1986).

Sanford Kwinter, afterword, in Benjamin Aranda and Chris Lasch, *Pamphlet Architecture 27: Tooling* (New York, 2005), 92.

Henri Lefebvre, *The Production of Space* (Oxford, 1991).

George L. Legendre, *Mathematical Form: John Pickering and the Architecture of the Inversion Principle* (London, 2006).

Marius Leutenegger, *Aesthetic of Disappearance*, vol. 10 (2005/2006), 48–57.

E. H. Lockwood, *A Book of Curves* (Cambridge, England, 1961).

Greg Lynn, *Form* (New York, 2008).

John Macarthur, 'Australian Baroque: Geometry and Meaning at the National Museum of Australia', in *Architecture Australia* 90:2 (March/April 2001): 48–61

Benoît Mandelbrot, *The Fractal Geometry of Nature* (San Francisco, 1983).

———, *Fractals: Form, Chance and Dimension* (San Francisco, 1977).

Martin Manning, et al., 'Beijing Airport Terminal 3', in *Steel Construction* 2:1 (2009): 1–8.

Lionel March, 'Architecture and Mathematics Since 1960', in Kim Williams and José Francisco Rodrigues, eds, *Nexus IV: Architecture and Mathematics* (Turin, 2002).

'Melbourne Rectangular Stadium', in *Australian Stadiums* (austadiums.com), 23 May 2007.

Michael Meredith and Mutsuro Sasaki, *From Control to Design: Parametric/Algorithmic Architecture* (Barcelona, 2008).

Paul Minifie, 'Streaming House', in *Architectural Review Australia* 90 (March 2002): 78–80

'New $190m Soccer, Rugby Stadium for Melbourne', in *Australian Stadiums* (austadiums.com), 6 April 2006.

E. A. O. Nsugbe and Chris J. K. Williams, 'The Generation of Bone-Like Forms Using Analytic Functions of a

Complex Variable', in *Engineering Structures* 23 (2001): 22–28.

...chael J. Ostwald, *Multi-Directional Appropriations of Theory Between Architecture and Sciences of Complexity: An Analysis of Motives and Efficacy*, PhD dissertation, University of Newcastle, New South Wales, 1998.

...kview International and Arup AGU, 'The Auditorium, Work Stage 2 Design Report', vol. 1, *The Foyer & Crystal* (2006).

...gh Pearman, 'A River of Talent', in *The Sunday Times* magazine, 19 June 2005.

...niel Pedoe, *Geometry and the Liberal Arts* (Harmondsworth, England, 1976).

...ger Penrose, *The Road to Reality: A Complete Guide to the Laws of the Universe* (London, 2004).

——, 'The Role of Aesthetics in Pure and Applied Research', in *Bulletin of the Institute of Mathematics and its Applications* (1974).

...dy Peters, 'The Smithsonian Courtyard Enclosure: A Case-Study of Digital Design Processes', in *Expanding Bodies: Art, Cities, Environment*.

...ry Phipps, *Beyond Measure: Conversations Across Art and Science*, catalogue, exhibition, Cambridge, England, Kettle's Yard, 5 April–1 June 2008.

...nri Poincaré, *Science et méthode* (Paris, 1908).

...nity Reed, *Tangled Destinies: National Museum of Australia* (Mulgrave, Victoria, 2002).

...as Risen, 'Kelvin's Conjecture: The Sustainability of Optimization and Integration', 2007 (greenlineblog. com).

...eborg M. Rocker, 'Calculus-Based Form: An Interview with Greg Lynn', in 'Programming Cultures: Art and Architecture in the Age of Software', special issue, *AD Profile 182* 76:4 (July/August 2006): 88–95.

——, 'When Code Matters', in 'Programming Cultures: Art and Architecture in the Age of Software'.

...kos A. Salingaros, 'Architecture, Patterns and Mathematics', in *Nexus Network Journal* 1:1/2 (June 1999): 75–86.

...tsuro Sasaki, 'Morphogenesis of Flux Structure', in *AA Publications* (2007): 41–52.

...er Schroeder, 'Digital Geometry' in Greg Lynn, *Form* (New York, 2008).

...rik Schumacher, 'Deep Plan', in *AA Files* 38 (1999): 23–25.

...stina Shea, 'Explorations in Using an Aperiodic Spatial Tiling as a Design Generator', 1st International Conference on Design Computing and Cognition, MIT, Cambridge, Massachusetts, 19–21 July 2004.

...nes R. Smart, *Modern Geometries* (Pacific Grove, California, 1973).

...chael Speaks, 'Design Intelligence: Part 1: Introduction', in *A+U* 387:12 (December 2002): 10–18.

...s Spuybroek, 'Motor Geometry', in *Architecture and Science* (1997): 164–171

——, *NOX: Machining Architecture* (London, 2004).

...omi Stead, 'Australian Wildlife Health Centre', in *Architecture Australia* 95:2 (March/April 2006): 80–87.

...rcy Thompson, *On Growth and Form* (1917; New York, 1992).

...nnie van Cleef, 'Radical Domesticity: The Möbius House's Reflection of Modern Living', in *Architectural Review* 206:1231 (September 1999): 47.

...eo van Doesburg, 'Towards a Plastic Architecture', in *De Stijl* 12:6/7 (1924).

...on van Schaik and Peter Bickle, 'The Colourful University', in *Architecture Australia* 90:4 (July/August 2001): 46–51.

...chael Webb, 'An Animated Affair', in *Architecture* 92:10 (October 2003): 66–71.

...red North Whitehead, *The Concept of Nature* (Cambridge, England, 1920).

Hugh Whitehead and Brady Peters, 'Geometry Form and Complexity', in David Littlefield, *Space Craft: Developments in Architectural Computing* (London, 2008).

Chris J. K. Williams, 'The Analytical and Numerical Definition of the Geometry of the British Museum Great Court Roof', in Mark Burry, et al., *Mathematics and Design 2001*, 3rd International Conference (Geelong, Victoria, 2001).

Y. M. Xie and G. P. Steven, *Evolutionary Structural Optimization* (London, 1997).

PROJECT CREDITS

Australian Wildlife Health Centre [20]
Minifie Nixon *minifienixon.com*
Project team: Ellen Yap, Sam Rice, Fiona Nixon, Barend Meyer, Paul Minifie, Nicholas Hubicki, Brandon Heng, Matthew Herbert.
Interpretive consultant: Cunningham Martyn Design
Landscape architect: Rush Wright & Associates.
Services consultant: IrwinConsult
Structural consultant: AHW
Tensile engineer: Tattersalls
Specification consultant: Davis Langdon
Building surveyor: Philip Chun & Associates
Quantity surveyor: WT Partnership
Project manager: Root Projects
Builder: Behmer & Wright
Landscape: Healesville Sanctuary Works, Horticultural Departments
Client: Zoos Victoria, Healesville Sanctuary

Beijing International Airport [24]
Foster + Partners *fosterandpartners.com*
Norman Foster, Mouzhan Majidi, Brian Timmoney, Loretta Law, Steven Chiu, Jonathan Parr, Michael Gentz, Luke Fox, Richard Hawkins, Mark Atkinson, John Ball, Cara Bamford, Alan Chan, Young Wei-Yang Chiu, Roberto Davolio, Marcos De Andres, Rodrigo de Castro Pereira, Gunnar Dittrich, Wulf Duerrich, Andrea Etspueler, Tie Fan, Colin Foster, Kristin Fox, Marco Gamini, Gabrielle Ho, Darryn Holder, Da Chun Lin, Jun Luo, Andy McMullen, Justin Nicholls, David Picazo, Sean Roche, Riko Sibbe, Danny Sze, Pearl Tang, William Walshe, Joyce Wang, Irene Wong, Shyue-Jiun Woon, Zheng Yu, Jean Wenyan Zhu
Client: Beijing Capital International Airport Company Ltd
Joint Venture: NACO, Foster + Partners, Arup
Local collaborating architect: (LDI), Beijing Institute of Architectural Design
Airport Consultant: NACO
Structural/mechanical engineers: Arup
Landscape architect: Michel Desvigne
Lighting consultant: Speirs and Major

Inversion Modelling [28]
John Pickering
IJP Corporation *ijpcorporation.com*
Foster + Partners *fosterandpartners.com*

Sagrada Família [34]
Jane Burry, Mark Burry
Jordi Bonet, architect director at the Sagrada Familia church Junta
Australian Research Council, for supporting research leading to this work.

Main Station Stuttgart [40]
Ingenhoven Architects *ingenhovenarchitects.com*
Client: Deutsche Bahn AG, represented by DB Projekt Bau GmbH
Building costs: €250 million
Project management: Drees & Sommer Infra Consult & Management GmbH
Structural engineering: Andrä und Partner, with Happold Ingenieurbüro GmbH
Structural form advice: Frei Otto, with Sonderkonstruktion und Leichtbau
Building services: NEK Ingenieure
Building physics: DS-Plan GmbH
Façade planning: DS-Plan GmbH
Ventilation analysis: Institut für Industrieaerodynamik
Transportation planning: Ingenieurgruppe für Verkehrsplanung und Verfahrenstechnik
Fire protection: Brandschutz Planung Klingsch GmbH
Lighting: Tropp Lighting Design
Landscape architecture: Ingenhoven Architects, with Weber Klein Maas Landschaftsarchitekten

Disney Concert Hall [44]
Gehry Partners *foga.com*
Engineers: John A. Martin & Associates (structural Cosentini Associates, Levine/seegel associates (mechanical), Frederick Russell Brown and Associates (electrical), Psomas and Associates (civil)
Consultants: Nagata Acoustics (acoustics). Charles M. Salter Associates (acoustical isolation), Theatre Projects consultants, fischer dachs Associates (performance spaces), Gordon H. smith (exterior wall), Lerch-Bates (elevator), L'observatoire (lighting), Engineering Harmonics (audio), Finish Hardware Technology (hardware), Bruce Mau Design, Adams Morioka (graphics), Melinda Taylor (garden design), Rosales Organ builders, Glatter-Gotz Orgelbau (organ builders).
Landscape architects: Lawrence Reed Moline
Contractor: L A Mortenson

Abu Dhabi Airport [48]
Kohn Pedersen Fox *kpf.com*

Federation Square [58]
Lab Architecture Studio *labarchitecture.com*
with Bates Smart (Donald L. Bates, Peter Davidson, Robert Bruce, Roger Poole, Jim Milledge)
Landscape architects: Karres en Brands (Bart Brands, Gianni Cito, Marie-Laure Hoedemakers, Rene van de Velde, Thierry Kandjee)
Civil/structural engineers: Hyder Consulting (Pat Strickland, Stu Jones, Ken McLeod)
Structural/façade engineers: Atelier One (Neil Thomas, Dirk Zimmermann, Carolina Bartram, Scobie Alvis, Wayne Sanderson, Anil Hira, Andy Watts, Aran Chadwick)
Structural engineers: Bonacci Group (Stephen Payne, Roger Sykes)
Environmental engineers: Atelier Ten (Patrick Bellew, Tim Elgood)
Services engineers: AHW Consulting Engineers (David Worland, Roger Arnall, Hugh van Essen)
Fire engineers: Arup (David Barber)
Signage and graphics: Tomato (John Warwicker)
Specialist lighting: Lighting Design Partnership (Andre Tammes, Dhruvajyoti Ghose, Frederika Perey)
Acoustic engineers: Marshall Day Acoustics (Peter Fernside, Peter Holmes)

Louvre Abu Dhabi [62]
Ateliers Jean Nouvel *jeannouvel.com*
Client: The Tourism Development and Investment Company
of Abu Dhabi
Services (structural, building services, civil, site traffic,
marine, geotechnical, fire, security, façade, ICT, vertical
transportation and acoustic engineering): Büro Happold

Jyväskylä Music and Arts Centre [68]
Competition design and commissioned design study
Phase 01 [1997]: Kivi Sotamaa, Johan Bettum, Markus
Holmstén, and Kim Baumann Larsen with Lasse Wagner,
Vesa Oiva, Hein van Dam
Phase 02 [2004]: Michael Hensel, Achim Menges and Kivi
Sotamaa, with Hani Fallaha, Shireen Han, Andrew Kudless,
Neri Oxman, Nazaneen Roxanne Shafaie, Cordula Stach,
Nikolaos Stathopoulos, Mark Tynan, Muchuan Xu

Seroussi Pavilion [72]
Biothing *biothing.org*
Principal designer: Alisa Andrasek
Design and computation: Ezio Blasetti, Che Wei Wang
Flower Power custom-written plug-in: Kyle Steinfeld
Design team: Fabian Evers, Lakhena Raingsan, Jin Pyo Jun
Special thanks to Michael Reed, mathematics and rendering
expert

Battersea Power Station [82]
Developer: Parkview International
Architect, theatre: Scéno-Plus
Architect, crystal foyer: Arup AGU
Structural engineer: Arup
Services engineer: Arup
Fire engineer: Arup

The Water Cube [86]
PTW Architects *ptw.com.au*
Ove Arup Australasia
China State Construction Engineering Corporation
Shenzhen Design Institute

Grand Egyptian Museum [92]
Heneghan Peng Architects *hparc.com*
Arup AGU *arup.com*

The Spiral Extension [98]
Daniel Libeskind *daniel-libeskind.com*
Arup AGU *arup.com*

Storey Hall [102]
Ashton Raggatt McDougall *a-r-m.com.au*

Spanish Pavilion [108]
Foreign Office Architects *f-o-a.net*
Competition stage: Farshid Moussavi and Alejandro Zaera-
Polo, with Nerea Calvillo, Kensuke Kishikawa.
Design stage: Farshid Moussavi and Alejandro Zaera-Polo,
with Nerea Calvillo, Izumi Kobayashi, Kenichi Matsuzawa.
Construction stage: Farshid Moussavi and Alejandro Zaera-
Polo, with Izumi Kobayashi, Kenichi Matsuzawa.
Contents: Ingenia Qed, Seville.
Project Manager: Inypsa
Client: SEEI

Centre for Ideas [112]
Minifie Nixon Architects *minifienixon.com*
Rush Wright Associates Landscape Architects *rushwright.com*

British Museum Great Court [122]
Foster + Partners *fosterandpartners.com*
Chris J. K. Williams, Department of Architecture and
Civil Engineering, University of Bath, worked closely with
architects Foster + Partners, structural engineers Büro
Happold, and Waagner Biro, the fabricators who also erected
it on site.
The Digital Architectonics Research Group in the Centre for
Advanced Studies in Architecture of the University of Bath is
involved in a research project sponsored by Informatix, Inc.
to investigate the advantages of using subdivision surface
techniques for generating and optimizing architectural
designs.

Smithsonian Institution [126]
Foster + Partners *fosterandpartners.com*

Qatar Education City Convention Centre [130]
Arato Isozaki & Associates *isozaki.co.jp*
Büro Happold *burohappold.com*
Sasaki Structural Consultants

Melbourne Rectangular Stadium [134]
Cox Architects *cox.com.au*
The stadium is being delivered through a partnering
approach with Major Projects Victoria, Arup, Cox Architects,
Grocon, Sport and Recreation Victoria, and the Melbourne
and Olympic Parks Trust.

Island City Central Park [138]
Toyo Ito & Associates *toyo-ito.com*

The Pinnacle [142]
Kohn Pedersen Fox *kpf.com*

Al Raha Development [148]
Foster + Partners *fosterandpartners.com*

Melbourne Recital Centre [152]
Ashton Raggatt McDougal *a-r-m.com.au*
Arup Acoustics

Möbius House [162]
UN Studio *unstudio.com*
Ben van Berkel, with Aad Krom, Jen Alkema, and Matthias
Blass, Remco Bruggink, Marc Dijkman, Casper le Fevre, Rob
Hootsmans, Tycho Soffree, Giovanni Tedesco, Harm Wassink
Landscape architect: West 8
Structural engineering: ABT

Arnhem Central [166]
UN Studio *unstudio.com*
Ben van Berkel and Tobias Wallisser, with Arjan Dingsté,
Nuno Almeida, Marc Herschel, Rein Werkhoven, Matthew
Johnston, Sander Versluis, Derrick Diporedjo, Misja van
Veen, Ahmed El-Shafei, Daniel Gebreiter, Uli Horner, Freddy
Koelemeijer, Wouter Hilhorst, Maartje van Dehn, Kirstin
Sandner, Elisabeth Beusker, Arnold Walz, Erhan Kulak,
Eugène Kanters, Florian Heinzelmann, Juliane Maier, Julien
Defait, Marc Hoppermann, René Toet, Sadegh Tangestani
Engineering: Arup (Amsterdam); Van der Werf & Lankhort
Fire safety: DGMR

Paramorph II [170]
dECOi: Marc Goulthorpe, Gaspard Giroud, Felix Robbins,
Frank Deschaux, Gabriel Evangellisti
Deakin University, Australia: Mark Burry, Grant Dunlop,
Greg More, Andrew Maher
Engineers: Ove Arup & Partners (David Glover, Ed Clark)

Rapid-prototyping model: University of Hong Kong (Alvise
Simondetti, Chak Chan)
Model, drawings and renderings by Grant Dunlop, Deakin
University

Cape Schanck House [174] **+ Blowhouse** [178]
Paul Morgan Architects *paulmorganarchitects.com*
Project team: Paul Morgan, Sophie Dyring, Karla Martinez,
Yau Ka Man, Timo Carl, Jo Scicluna, Teck Chee Chow
Structural engineer: Doug Turnbull
Civil engineer: Wirrawonga
Quantity surveyor: BSGM
Builder: Drew Head
Carpenters: Shane McGree, John Kunert
Owner/builder: Paul Morgan
Landscape architect: Sally Prideaux

Slavin House [182]
Greg Lynn *glform.com*

Klein Bottle House [186]
McBride Charles Ryan *mcbridecharlesryan.com.au*
Principal architects: Rob McBride, Debbie-Lyn Ryan
Project team: Drew Williamson, Fang Cheah
Clients/builders: Donna and Mark Howlett

Möbius Bridge [192]
Hakes Associates *hakes.co.uk*
Engineers: Büro Happold

Villa Nurbs [194]
Cloud 9 Architects *e-cloud9.com*
Principal architect: Enric Ruiz Geli
Promoter: Familia Gallego Leon
Project architect: Felix Fassbinder, Jordi Fernández Río
Technical architect: Agustí Mallol, Manoli Vila (G3), Dani
Benito Pò, Xavier Badia
Cloud 9 team: Victor Llanos, Miguel Carreiro, Emmanuel
Ruffo, Rosa Duque, André MacedoUra Carvalho, Hye Youn
Yu, Marta YebraMae Durant, Angelina Pinto, Randall
HollWilliam Arbizu, Max Zinnecker, Laia Jutgla Manel Sol,
Megan Kelly-Sweeney, Alessandra Faticanti, Susanne Boda
André Brosel
Asesoramiento Medioambiental: Estudi Ramon Folch
Ceramica: Frederic Amat,Toni Cumella
Glass: Vicky Colombet, Dominique Haim/Galeria Chanim
Cricursa
Design: Emiliana Designestudio
Cocina: ArtificioSheer
Piel Interior: Medio Design
Carpinteria Moratalla
Estructura: Agusti Obiol/Boma S.L. Guillem Baraut
Santos Valladolid
Ingeniería Instalaciones: David Tuset/PGI Group, Guillem
del Oso
Paisagismo: Jerónimo Hagerman Margie Ruddick/WRT

National Museum of Australia [200]
Ashton Raggatt McDougall *a-r-m.com.au*
with Robert Peck von Hartel Trethowan

Metropolitan Opera House [204]
Toyo Ito *toyo-ito.com*
Built by the Taichung City Government, Republic of China
(Taiwan)

De Draai Extension [214]
Karres en Brands *karresenbrands.nl*
Bart Brands, Marco Broekman, Marijke Bruinsma, Kristian

n Schaik, Paul Portheine, Lucy Knox Knight, Lieneke van
ampen, Marc Springer, Jan Martijn Eekhof
oftware: Swiss Federal Institute of Technology Zurich
TZH), CAAD research group: Ludger Hovestadt, Oliver
ritz, Markus Braach, Alex Lehnerer

eshHtwoOexpo Pavilion [218]
ox Architects *nox-art-architecture.com*

creaming House [222]
inifie Nixon Architects *minifienixon.com*

egis Hyposurface [226]
esign conception: Mark Goulthorpe, Oliver Dering, Arnaud
escombes, Mark Burry, Grant Dunlop, Deakin University,
ustralia
rogramming: Peter Wood, University of Wellington, New
ealand; Xavier Robitaille, University of Montreal
echatronics

poorg [230]
ervo *s-e-r-v-o.com*
arcelyn Gow, Ulrika Karlsson, Chris Perry
esign team: Erik Hökby
lectronic and algorithmic design: Pablo Miranda and
smund Gamlesæter
ound design: Leif Jordansson and Martin Q. Larsson
pecial thanks to Jonas Barre, Sue Huang
/ith generous support from Konstnärsnämnden, Sveriges
ildkonstnärsfond, Stiftelsen Framtidens Kultur, BSK
rkitekter, White, Wingårdhs, Royal Institute of Technology,
tmel Norway AS

otel Prestige Forest [234]
loud 9 Architecture *e-cloud9.com*
rincipal architect: Enric Ruiz Geli
lient: PrestigeGroup
ose Moyano, President; Juan Marull, Vice President; Jose
laria Moyano; Ignacio Marull Associate architects: Ruy
htake Arquitetura, São Paulo, Brazil; Acconci Studio, New
ork: Vito Acconci, Dario Unez, Peter Dorsey
loud 9 team: Max Zinnecker, Project Architect; Jose Garcia,
aia Jutglà, Joscha Oberndörfer, Chiara Passa, Titusz Tarnai,
aniel Corsi
tructural engineer: Agusti Obiol, Lluis Moya, Guillem
araut
nstallations engineer: PGI Group, David Tuset, Ismael
arcia, Jordi Llosa, Mar Moreno
lumination (artificial leaves): Guzzini Illuminazione, Josep
lasbernat, Alex Chiva, Fabrizio Tranà, Giancarlo Becacece,
lassimo Gattari, Franco Nibaldi
rototyping stereolitography: Centro CIM
nimation, rendering and compositing: IK Studio, Pere
ifre, Daniel Molina, Jordi Gamell
hysical models: Guillermo Beluzo
lodel lightning system: James Clar
hotography: Lluis Ros, Optical Addiction
olar technology advisor: TFM
ED technology advisor: Mundo Color
tainless-steel mesh advisor: Tenso
extile architecture advisor: Industrias BEC
lunicipal planning authorities: l'Hospitalet Town Council,
ntoni Nogués, Antoni Rodríguez

as Hotel [238]
symptote Architecture *asymptote.net*
lani Rashid, Lise Anne Couture

luscle ReConfigured [242]
yperbody Research Group

Oosterhuis Lénárd *oosterhuis.nl*
Directed by Kas Oosterhuis, principal
Team members: Nimish Biloria, PhD researcher; Chris Fox,
Roi Harari, Jaroslav Hulin, Klaas-Jan de Koning, Johannes
Krohne, Sebastian Lippok, Simsa McNally, Antonio Pisano,
Masterstudents
Dieter Vandoren, Oosterhuis Lénárd

Interactive Wall [242]
Hyperbody Research Group
Oosterhuis Lénárd *oosterhuis.nl*
Project initiator: Dr Wilfried Stoll, Chairman of the
Supervisory Board, Festo AG
Project managers: Kas Oosterhuis, Chris Kievid, Bernard
Sommer, Hyperbody, Delft University of Technology,
Netherlands
Michael Daubner, Andreas Dober, Burkhardt Leitner
Constructiv, Stuttgart, Germany
Markus Fischer, Festo AG & Co KG, Ostfildern, Germany
Project team: Mark-David Hosale, Remko Siemerink, Vera
Laszlo, Dieter Vandoren, Hyperbody, Delft University of
Technology, Netherlands
Robert Glanz, Domenico Farina, Burkhardt Leitner
Constructiv, Stuttgart, Germany
Gerhard Bettinger, Roland Grau, Uwe Neuhoff, Festo AG &
Co KG, Ostfildern, Germany

Digital Water Pavilion [248]
Carlo Ratti Associati *carloratti.com*
Design team: Walter Nicolino, Carlo Ratti, Claudio Bonicco,
Matteo Lai
Interactive Water Wall concept: William J. Mitchell and
Smart Cities Group, MIT Media Laboratory
Research, Zaragoza's Digital Mile: MIT DUSP and Media
Laboratory (William J. Mitchell, Dennis Frenchman
(principal investigators); Michael Joroff, Carlo Ratti (faculty);
Rajesh Kottamasu, Francisca Rojas, Michal Stangel, Susanne
Seitinger, Andres Sevtsuk, Priyanka Shah, Matt Trimble, Jake
Wegmann, Albert Wei (research assistants)
Expo Gateway preliminary design: MIT SENSEable City Lab
(Walter Nicolino, Claudio Bonicco, Justin Lee, Andrea Lo
Papa, Carlo Ratti)
Structural and mechanical engineers: Ove Arup & Partners
(Ignacio Fernandez, Carlos Merino)
Landscape design: Agence Ter (Olivier Philippe, Elisa
Benitez)
Water engineering: Lumiartencia Internacional (Juan
Carretero)
Visuals: Officinestirtori (Riccardo Sirtori, Matteo Lai)
Graphic designers: FM Studio (Milan)
Construction: Siemens (Madrid)

TEXT CREDITS
Text on pages 68–71, 92–97, 108–11, 214–17, 218–21, 230–33,
238–41, 248–51 based on text supplied by the architects.

PHOTO CREDITS
1 Jane Burry; **2–3** Trevor Mein; **14–19** Courtesy Gerd Fisher
(models), Daniel Davis (drawings); **20–23** Jane Burry; **28–33**
© John Pickering, Arthur Pickering, George Legendre/IJP,
Lee Funnell; **34–39** Jane Burry; **40–43** Peter Wels, Holger
Knauf (photos), Frei Otto (chain model); **44–47** Gehry
Partners; **48–51** Kohn Pedersen Fox; **52–57** Courtesy NASA
(satellite photos), Daniel Davis (drawings), Andrew Miller
(attractor); **58–61** Trevor Mein (photos), © Lab Architecture
Studio (model images and drawings); **62–67** Ateliers Jean
Nouvel, Büro Happold Smart Group; **68–71** Collection FRAC

Centre; **72–75** Alisa Andrasek; **76–81** Jan Cilliers, Daniel
Davis, Jane Burry; **82–85** Arup AGU (Francis Archer); **86–91**
Chris Bosse (photos), Arup (drawings); **92–97** Heneghan
Peng Architects, Arup AGU, Richard Davies (model photos),
Archimation (night and day renderings); **98–101** Courtesy
Daniel Libeskind, Arup AGU; **102–107** John Gollings
(photos), Ashton Raggatt McDougall (plans); **108–111** Satoru
Mishima (photos), Foreign Office Architects; **112–115** Peter
Bennetts; **122–125** Foster + Partners; **130–133** Arato Isozaki
& Associates, Büro Happold; **134–137** Cox Architects, Peter
Glenane/Major Projects Victoria 2008, © Arup Melbourne,
© Dominik Holzer; **138–141** Nagano Consultants (aerial
photo), courtesy Mutsuro Sasaki (evolutionary form images);
148–151 Foster + Partners; **152–155** John Gollings (photos),
Ashton Raggatt McDougall; **156–161** Historic Cities Research
Project, Hebrew University of Jerusalem (historic-cities.huji.
ac.il), courtesy Ozgur Tufkecki (map of Königsberg); **162–165**
Christian Richters; **166–169** Christian Richters; **174–177**
Peter Bennetts; **178–181** Peter Bennetts; **182–185** Greg Lynn/
GLform; **186–191** John Gollings (photos), McBride Charles
Ryan; **192–193** Hakes Associates; **194–199** Luis Ros-Koenig;
200–203 John Gollings; **208–213** Courtesy Asymptote
Architecture (Hani Rashid, Lise Anne Couture), courtesy
New York Stock Exchange; **222–225** Paul Minifie; **226–229**
Mark Burry; **230–233** Courtesy MAK Centre (Joshua White);
238–241 Courtesy Asymptote Architecture (Hani Rashid,
Lise Anne Couture); **242–247** Remko Siemerink/Hyperbody
(drawings), Walter Fogel/Angelbachtal (photos); **248–251**
Claudio Bonicco, Max Tomasinelli, Ramak Fazel, Walter
Nicolino.

ACKNOWLEDGMENTS
The authors would like to acknowledge the work of
Andrew Miller for his assiduous background research and
composition of the preliminary layout; Daniel Davis, for
research and creating the original images for the glossary;
and Adam Corcoran for his graphical design. We received
the support of RMIT University School of Architecture and
Design, RMIT Design Research Institute and the RMIT Spatial
Information Architecture Laboratory. At Thames & Hudson,
we would like to thank Lucas Dietrich and Elain McAlpine
for their respective guidance and patient consultation.
Our thanks to all the practices and individuals who have
contributed their time, images and in many cases fascinating
interviews.

Mark Burry is the recipient of an Australian Research
Council Federation Fellowship through which much of this
project has been funded.